Residential Windows

A Guide to New Technologies and Energy Performance

THIRD EDITION

John Carmody
Stephen Selkowitz
Dariush Arasteh
Lisa Heschong

W.W. NORTON & COMPANY
NEW YORK • LONDON

Manufacturing by VonHoffmann
Book design by John Carmody and Kerry Haglund
Production Manager: Leeann Graham

Library of Congress Cataloging-in-Publication Data

Residential windows : a guide to new technologies and energy performance / John Carmody . . .
[et al.] — 3rd edition
p. cm.
Includes bibliographical references and index.
ISBN-13: 978-0-393-73225-2 (pbk.)
ISBN-10: 0-393-73225-8 (pbk.)
1. Windows. 2. Dwellings--Insulation. I. Carmody, John.

TH2275.R474 2007
690'.1823—dc22   2006048066

ISBN-13: 978-0-393-73225-2 (pbk.)
ISBN-10: 0-393-73225-8 (pbk.)

W. W. Norton & Company, Inc., 500 Fifth Avenue, New York, N.Y. 10110
www.wwnorton.com

W. W. Norton & Company Ltd., Castle House, 75/76 Wells Street, London W1T 3QT

0   9   8   7   6   5   4   3   2   1

Contents

Acknowledgments

This book was developed with support from the U.S. Department of Energy's Building Technologies Program, Office of Energy Efficiency and Renewable Energy. In partnership with the building industry, the U.S. Department of Energy supports a range of research, development, and demonstration programs, as well as education and market transformation projects designed to accelerate the introduction and use of new energy-saving window technologies, including many of those described in this book.

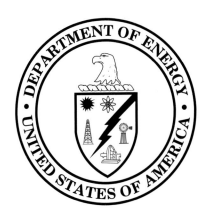

Many people contributed their time and talent toward the completion of this new edition. The book would not have been possible without the continued support of P. Marc LaFrance, Technology Development Manager at the U.S. Department of Energy. Sam Taylor at the U.S. Department of Energy played an important role in developing the original edition of the book.

At the University of Minnesota's Center for Sustainable Building Research, Kerry Haglund created the book design and illustrations and coordinated the entire third edition project. Garrett Mosiman assisted with computer simulations. William Weber and Virajita Singh assisted with earlier versions of the book. This book has benefited greatly from the suggestions and editing of Nancy Green and Kristen Holt-Browning at W.W. Norton.

Much of the technical material in this and previous editions of the book was drawn from window and glazing research completed over the years at Lawrence Berkeley National Laboratory (LBNL). Robin Mitchell, Joe Huang, Brent Griffith, Christian Kohler, Howdy Goudey, Joe Eto, Charlie Huizenga, Robert Sullivan and others at LBNL made contributions.

Significant contributions of new material to this edition were made by Garrett Stone, Brickfield, Burchette, Ritts & Stone (building codes and voluntary programs); Charlie Huizenga, University of California Berkeley (comfort); Jeff Baker, WestLab (condensation); and D. Charlie Curcija and Mahabir Bhandari, Carli, Inc. (condensation). We also appreciate the review and input on this edition from Jim Larsen, Cardinal Glass Industries; Nils Petermann, Alliance to Save Energy; Arlene Stewart, AZS Consulting; Carl Wagus, American Architectural Manufacturers Association (AAMA); James Benney, National Fenestration Ratings Council (NFRC); Jeff Haberer,

Cardinal Glass Industries; and Sam Taylor, U.S. Department of Energy. We thank Joe Lstiburek at Building Science Corporation and Kathy Guidera at the Energy and Environmental Building Association (EEBA) for use of material on window installation.

Many people reviewed and contributed suggestions to this and previous editions of the book. We are grateful to Larry Livermore and Richard Walker, AAMA; Ross McCluney, Florida Solar Energy Center; Roland Temple, PGT Industries; John Hogan, Department of Construction and Land Use, City of Seattle; William duPont, LBNL; John McFee, Window & Door Manufacturers Association (WDMA); Bill Prindle, American Council for an Energy Efficient Economy (ACEEE); Alecia Ward, Midwest Energy Efficiency Alliance; and Ken Nittler, Westlab.

We appreciate the many comments and suggestions we received from many members of the window industry. They include: Michael Koenig, Andersen Corporation; Chris Mathis, MC Squared; James Krahn, Marvin Windows & Doors; Brian Crooks and Michael Curtis, Cardinal Glass Industries; Pat Kenney, PPG; David Duly and Paul Gore, Libby Owens Ford; Marc Sullivan, AFG; and John Meade, Southwall.

We also thank Mary Anderson, JELD-WEN, Inc.; Dennis Anderson, Architectural Testing, Inc.; Tabitha Cromer, Solatube, Inc.; Joseph Johansen, Velux-America, Inc.; Kathy Krafka-Harkema, Pella Corporation; John Sondles, Associated Materials, Inc.; Debbie Liedl, Andersen Corporation; Lori Bell, PGT Industries; Lori Hendershot, Simonton Windows; and Maerenn Ball, Marvin Windows & Doors, for their assistance in obtaining images and photographs.

A Guide to Using This Book

Since the publication of the first and second editions of *Residential Windows*, the development of new window technologies and products has continued at a significant pace. In addition, many programs, tools, and other information have become available to help homeowners, builders, and designers in selecting more energy-efficient windows. Programs such as the Efficient Windows Collaborative (EWC) and ENERGY STAR Windows, both funded by the U.S. Department of Energy, are designed to transform the residential window market. The National Fenestration Rating Council (NFRC) continues to maintain the only fair, credible means of rating and comparing products for energy performance.

In the last few years, high-performance windows that reduce heat loss have become almost standard in much of the northern, heating-dominated climate zones of the United States. High-performance windows that reduce heat gain are gaining acceptance in the southern, cooling-dominated regions of the country as well. Great potential exists to expand the use of high-performance windows in warmer climates to benefit homeowners and to reduce our nation's overall energy consumption and its detrimental environmental effects.

This third edition of *Residential Windows* provides updated and expanded information on window properties and technologies, as well as new sections on topics ranging from window installation to building codes. All of the energy performance data has been revised from the earlier editions based on the latest simulation techniques and industry-accepted assumptions. This book represents one of a family of tools and information products on residential windows developed with funding from the U.S. Department of Energy. The EWC maintains an extensive Web site that provides fact sheets and other information (www.efficientwindows.org).

The purpose of this book is to assist consumers, designers, and builders in understanding the new window products and their energy performance implications. Our hope is that this understanding will lead to greater use of these new products with benefits to homeowners and to society. The broader audience for the book includes anyone who needs to be informed about windows—regulators, standards developers, utilities, and the researchers, manufacturers, and suppliers in the window industry itself.

The book introduces the window technologies, explores the implications of these new technologies on residential design, and then provides a means for selecting appropriate windows. The introductory chapter provides an overview. Chapter 2 presents the basic window properties in four areas: appearance, energy performance, human factors, and technical issues. Chapter 3 describes glazing materials and new technologies in detail. Chapter 4 addresses the complete window assembly, which includes window operation, frame materials, and installation. Chapter 5 reviews traditional window design issues and explores the new design implications of using high-performance windows. Finally, Chapter 6 addresses energy and cost considerations in window selection and provides a step-by-step selection method and tools for use by designers, builders, and homeowners.

Selecting the Right Window

Many readers will want to go beyond comparative guidance provided by the ENERGY STAR® program, the NFRC label, and the EWC web site. New calculation tools such as RESFEN can help you to estimate the energy savings potential of better windows (see Appendix D). If the resulting payback on your investment is short, then it clearly makes sense to purchase the windows. But even if the conclusion is that these windows are not immediate cost savers, there are many other good reasons to proceed with the investment. High-performance windows also have benefits such as increased comfort, reduced condensation problems, heat gain control without losing light and view, reduced fading from ultraviolet light, and in some cases, reduced costs for mechanical equipment in the house.

This book is intended to help you make better, more informed decisions that will be important to your future comfort and to your finances. However, there are so many complex issues that are difficult to balance in selecting the "best" window that you are likely to find there is no absolutely "correct" answer. How much more are you willing to pay for appearance and comfort? The selection of new (or retrofit) windows is a big investment for most homeowners and one that deserves critical and informed attention. Ultimately, decisions must be made based on many trade-offs. This book is intended to help you understand the options and their consequences and make the best decision within the scope of those trade-offs and constraints.

CHAPTER 1

Introduction to Windows in Residential Buildings

Windows are possibly the most complex and interesting elements in residential design. They provide light and fresh air, and offer views that connect the interior spaces with the outdoors. However, windows have also represented a major source of heat loss in winter as well as unwanted heat gain in summer. Today, remarkable new window products and technologies have changed the energy performance of windows in a radical way. With increasing concerns over rising energy prices and the effects of greenhouse gas emissions on climate change, windows will play a key role in the transformation to more energy-efficient, sustainably-designed buildings.

Figure 1-1. New window technologies improve energy efficiency and influence home design.
(Photo: PGT Industries.)

Figure 1-2. Skylights and roof windows can provide daylight but limit undesirable heat gain.
(Photo: Velux-America Inc.)

Until about the end of World War II, housing in the United States was designed with an understanding of site and climate. Although the windows were not particularly energy efficient, traditional house designs evolved that took advantage of the natural elements of sunlight, wind, the earth, and vegetation to help provide light, heating, cooling, and ventilation. A house built in Florida looked quite different from a house built in Maine, reflecting their climate differences. While these buildings were not always comfortable by today's standards, energy use was minimized as much as possible. During this period, many elements of exterior and interior design evolved, in part because of the need to either shade windows from the summer sun or to protect from cold drafts and high heat loss in winter.

Beginning in the 1950s, the availability of very inexpensive energy combined with the use of powerful mechanical heating and cooling systems led to the construction of homes that were not climate sensitive and required a large amount of energy to maintain comfort. Most homes were not designed to take advantage of sunlight and natural ventilation, and windows remained inefficient during this period.

In the 1970s, rapid increases in energy costs occurred, combined with more concern about the environmental impacts of building design and operation. This led to a resurgence of interest in the traditional patterns of designing with climate and

Figure 1-3. More efficient windows provide greater thermal comfort.
(Photo: Andersen Corporation.)

Figure 1-4. Doors and windows can be combined to maximize views.
(Photo: JELD-WEN, Inc.)

site. During this period, design approaches in colder regions included reshaping building layout and orienting windows to capture the maximum amount of sunlight in every room, various schemes to store and distribute solar heat, and movable insulation over windows to keep heat from escaping at night. These approaches reflected the fact that windows were necessary for light and to capture solar heat, but they came with the drawback of significant heat loss.

These passive solar and self-sufficient house designs never became mainstream practice. However, the concern over energy and environment since 1970 has led to significant improvements in house performance based on the use of more efficient building envelopes and mechanical systems. During this period, windows have undergone a technological revolution. They are no longer the weak link in energy-efficient home design.

It is now possible to have expansive views and daylight without sacrificing comfort or energy efficiency. This remarkable change has had two important effects. First, any house can be made considerably more energy efficient by using high-performance windows. Second, and possibly more important, technologically advanced windows perform so much better and differently than their predecessors of just twenty years ago that many of the assumptions of both traditional and more recent energy-efficient design must be reexamined. In addition, comfort can be more easily achieved with smaller heating and cooling systems.

Figure 1-5. With high-performance glazings, the benefits of large window areas can be obtained without the energy penalty associated with older, less efficient windows.
(Photo: Associated Materials, Inc.)

11

The remainder of this chapter includes a short history of windows followed by a brief overview of current and emerging window technologies. Examples of the energy savings are discussed, as are the broader global and economic impacts of using higher performance windows. The next section of the chapter describes important influences on the market transformation to high performance windows—these include the sustainable building movement as well as building codes and voluntary programs. Finally, the window selection process is summarized with highlights of available programs and tools to assist homeowners, builders and designers.

A SHORT HISTORY OF WINDOWS

Figure 1-6. Limitations in the size of glass resulted in early architectural innovations to provide larger views.
(Photo: John Carmody)

In a way, windows are a luxury. Primitive homes were often built without windows. A door, of course, is essential to let people and contents in and out. But windows are a refinement, an amenity, to make the place more livable. As such, they have been under continual development throughout the ages.

A smoke hole might be considered the earliest form of a window. It let the smoke from cooking and heating fires escape out the wall or roof, greatly enhancing indoor air quality. Inadvertently, the hole also provided a shaft of daylight that brightened the general gloom of the interior, and, of course, allowed most of the heat to escape.

A single shuttered opening came next. It was like another door—a hole in the wall with an opaque cover that could be opened to let in light and air, along with intruders, rain, insects, and dust. It could be closed for security, darkness, and protection from the elements.

A Room with a View

The addition of translucent materials, such as oiled paper or an animal skin, framed into the window hole offered more control options. The shutter itself might be made of translucent material, thereby creating an operable window. Not until the advent of transparent window glass, which was first used in Roman times, could windows provide daylight, wind control, and view, all at the same time.

The largest known piece of Roman glass was three feet by four feet (0.9 by 1.2 m), installed in a public bath in Pompeii. By the Middle Ages, Venice had become established as the premier center of glass making, for both decorative glassware and clear window glass. Small panes of flat glass could be produced by first blowing a bubble or cylinder of glass, cutting it open while still hot, and then rolling it out flat. This technology was brought to the New World and used to produce most of the glass for colonial American windows. These small panes of glass, pieced together into multiple frames, have become one of our enduring domestic images.

The French Glass Revolution

A new technique to cast plate glass was developed in France in the 1600s. The finer quality and larger sizes of glass that became available with this process greatly popularized the use of glass, both for grand mirrors, such as those at the Hall of Mirrors at Versailles Palace, and for large windows, as epitomized by the "French door."

Many innovations in the production of glass were seen in the nineteenth century, making larger, stronger, and higher-quality glass ever more available to the general public. While the size and number of windows in buildings increased dramatically, there was still essentially one type of glass available: clear, single-pane glass.

Figure 1-7. Elaborate architectural elements have developed in order to control light, air flow, sound, and comfort near windows.
(Photo: John S. Reynolds, AIA)

The clear, single-pane glass stopped the wind and allowed light to enter, but all of the other subtleties in window control were provided by additional devices such as overhangs, trellises, awnings, shutters, storm windows, security grates, insect screens, venetian blinds or roll-down shades, light curtains, or heavy drapes. A window became an elaborate and decorative architectural system for controlling all the physical and emotive forces that converged at that hole in the wall. All of these controls have been incorporated into the general aesthetics of windows.

Modern Developments

In the 1950s the technique of producing float glass was developed (molten glass "floats" over a tank of molten tin), which provides extremely flat surfaces, uniform thicknesses, and few if any visual distortions. This float glass is used in virtually all residential windows today. This was a key breakthrough that has become important decades later because the high-quality surface of float glass is required for the application of thin coatings that are commonly used in windows today.

Before 1965, single-glazed windows with storm windows and screens were prevalent in the United States. The most important trend in windows between 1965 and 1980 was a significant change to insulating glazing (two panes of glass sealed together with an air space in between). Although double-glazed units were developed before 1965, the seals were not maintained consistently, resulting in some product failure. In the late 1970s, in response to the energy crisis of that time, triple-glazed units were developed as well. The change to insulating glazing was accelerating by 1980—the market reflected this trend with window sales of 50 percent single glazing, 45 percent double glazing, and 5 percent triple glazing. Today, nearly 90 percent of all residential windows sold are insulated glazing (two or more layers). The market for conventional triple-glazed windows has diminished because of a number of other technological breakthroughs such as low-E coatings that have created energy-efficient windows without adding another layer of glazing. However, the drive for higher performance has resulted in a renewed interest in a triple-glazed window often using a lighter plastic film as the middle layer. Driven by codes, incentive programs, and better information, 56 percent of all residential windows sold in 2005 have some type of low-E coating.

TECHNOLOGICAL IMPROVEMENTS TODAY

A progression of innovations has integrated more elements of control into the window assembly or the glass itself. Some technological innovations that are appearing in today's fenestration products are described briefly below (see Chapters 3 and 4 for more detail on these technologies).

- **Glazing unit structure**

    Multiple layers of glass or plastic films improve thermal resistance and reduce the heat loss attributed to convection between window layers. Additional layers also provide more surfaces for low-E or solar control coatings.

- **Low-emittance coatings**

    Low-emittance or low-E coatings are highly transparent and virtually invisible, but have a high reflectance (low emittance) to long-wavelength infrared radiation. This reduces long-wavelength radiative heat transfer between glazing layers by a factor of 5 to 10, thereby reducing total heat transfer between two glazing layers. Low-emittance coatings may be applied directly to glass surfaces, or to thin sheets of plastic (films) which are suspended in the air cavity between the interior and exterior glazing layers.

- **Solar control glazings and coatings**

    To reduce cooling loads, new types of tinted glass and new coatings can be specified that reduce the impact of the sun's heat without sacrificing view. Spectrally selective glazings and coatings absorb and reflect the infrared portion of sunlight while transmitting visible daylight, thus reducing solar heat gain coefficients and the resulting cooling loads. These solar control coatings can also have low-emittance characteristics.

- **Low-conductance gas fills**

    With the use of a low-emittance coating, heat transfer across a gap is dominated by conduction and natural convection. While air is a relatively good insulator, there are other gases (such as argon, carbon dioxide, krypton, and xenon) with lower thermal conductivities. Using one of these nontoxic gases in an insulating glass unit can reduce heat transfer between the glazing layers.

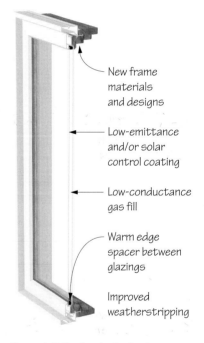

New frame materials and designs

Low-emittance and/or solar control coating

Low-conductance gas fill

Warm edge spacer between glazings

Improved weatherstripping

Figure 1-8. Technological advances have significantly improved window energy performance in recent years.

- **Warm edge spacers**

  Heat transfer through the metal spacers that are used to separate glazing layers can increase heat loss and cause condensation to form at the edge of the window. "Warm edge" spacers use new materials and better designs to reduce this effect.

- **Thermally improved sash and frame**

  Traditional sash and frame designs often contribute to heat loss and can represent a large fraction of the total loss when high-performance glass is used. New materials and improved designs can reduce this loss.

- **Improved weatherstripping**

  Better weatherstrips are now available to reduce air leakage, and most are of more durable materials that will provide improved performance over a longer time period.

Emerging Technologies

It is clear that there has been great progress in improving window energy efficiency in recent years, but even greater potential lies ahead. In the 1970s, special coatings and gas fills seemed a long way off. Now they are standard products. Research and development time for advanced window technologies has been shortening, and their introduction into the commercial market has been accelerating.

It is difficult to predict which of the many research directions now being pursued will find a secure place in the market. Researchers continue to experiment with a variety of very highly insulating windows including vacuum glazing, aerogel foams, and multilayer glazings.

Researchers are also developing "smart windows" that will be designed to respond to our needs: programmed to automatically modulate the flow of light or solar heat across the window. Various microscopically thin coatings can be designed to change their properties in response to heat, light, or electronic signals. The concept of a "smart window" is sometimes explained using the metaphor of a biological cell wall, which actively filters energy and material flows between the inside and outside environments, and changes its filtration rate according to the needs of the cell's metabolism. Smart windows could adjust energy flows to meet the thermal needs of the house, as well as the need for light, view, or privacy. One type of smart

---

BENEFITS OF HIGH-PERFORMANCE WINDOWS

Cooling and Heating Season Energy Savings

Low-E coatings and other technologies can significantly reduce winter heat loss and summer heat gain.

Improved Daylight and View

New glazings with low solar gain low-E coatings have a minimal loss of visible light (compared to many tints and films).

Improved Comfort

In both summer and winter occupant comfort is increased; window temperatures are more moderate and there are fewer cold drafts.

Reduced Condensation

Frame and glazing materials that resist heat conduction do not become cold, resulting in less condensation.

Reduced Fading

Coatings on glass or plastic films within the window assembly can significantly reduce the ultraviolet (UV) and other solar radiation that causes fading of fabrics and furnishings.

Lower Costs for Mechanical Equipment

Using windows that significantly reduce solar heat gain means that cooling equipment costs may be reduced.

window, electrochromic glazing, is now on the market and available in residential windows and skylights. See Chapter 3 for more information on emerging technologies.

Net Zero Energy Window

A goal for state of the art homes today is the "Net Zero Energy Home"—a home that does not require energy from the grid. Such a home will need components with excellent energy performance. With continuing improvements in frame and spacer design, overall window U-factors as low as 0.10 are possible. Such windows would have a remarkable energy performance that could contribute to the Zero Energy Home. The loss of heat is so low that the diffuse sunlight gained through a north-facing window on a cold, cloudy winter day is greater than the heat losses over the full day. At this threshold of performance, a window can take on a new role in buildings as a net zero energy window or even a net energy provider rather than a net energy loser. Thus, very high-performance windows can have a lower seasonal heating loss than even a highly insulated wall in a cold climate. South-facing windows have always had this potential; however, highly efficient multilayer window technologies mean that a window facing in any direction can be a passive solar collector.

Lawrence Berkeley National Laboratories with support from the U.S. Department of Energy has developed a highly-insulating, dynamic window prototype. Based on the desire to develop a prototype at affordable cost and one that could build on existing manufacturing capacity, a three layer window was utilized with commercially available low-E technology and krypton gas fill. A rigid center plastic layer is added as a low-cost convection barrier, and a wood/fiberglass combination frame is used. The dynamic solar control is provided using electrochromic glazing as the outer layer. This prototype is a Zero Energy Window in many U.S. climates and better than half way to the ultimate goal of being a Zero Energy Window in all U.S. climates.

THE IMPACT OF HIGH PERFORMANCE WINDOWS

As Figure 1-10 illustrates, for a heating-dominated climate, if windows are inefficient (A and B), increasing the glazing area increases energy costs significantly. As the windows become more efficient with low-E coatings (window C), increasing the glazing area has a diminishing effect on energy costs. With

Figure 1-9. Technologies, such as electrochromics, are now available in the residential windows market. The skylight on the left is switched to the "on" position—reducing glare and reducing solar heat gain. The skylight on the right is switched to the "off" position. (Photo: VELUX-America, Inc. and Sage Electrochromics, Inc.)

the most efficient triple-glazed low-E unit (window D), there is no significant heating energy increase even though total glazing area is tripled.

Figure 1-11 illustrates the benefits of high performance glazing in a cooling-dominated climate. With no exterior shading, conventional clear windows (A and C) have high cooling energy costs. Even the tinted window B provides little improvement. The low-solar-gain low-E window (D), however, provides significant savings even in an unshaded condition. When shading strategies are used, the energy use is reduced for all window types but window D continues to outperform the other options.

Window A
Double Glazing
Clear
Aluminum Frame w/break
U-Factor=0.63
SHGC=0.62
VT=0.63

Window B
Double Glazing
Clear
Wood/Vinyl Frame
U-Factor=0.49
SHGC=0.56
VT=0.59

Window C
Double Glazing
Low-E (high solar gain)
Wood/Vinyl Frame
U-Factor=0.37
SHGC=0.53
VT=0.54

Window D
Triple Glazing
Low-E (mod. solar gain)
Insulated Vinyl Frame
U-Factor=0.18
SHGC=0.40
VT=0.50

See Chapter 2 for descriptions of U-factor and SHGC. See Chapters 3 and 4 for glazing and frame descriptions. See Appendix A for window descriptions.

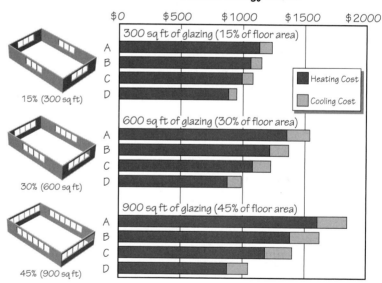

Figure 1-10. Impact of window glazing area on annual energy use for a 2000-square-foot house with six window types in Minneapolis, Minnesota.

Note: The annual energy performance figures shown here were generated using RESFEN for a typical (new construction) 2000 sq ft house. The windows are equally distributed on all four sides of the house and include typical shading (interior shades, overhangs, trees, and neighboring buildings). U-factor, SHGC, and VT are for the total window including frame. The costs shown here are annual costs for space heating and space cooling only and thus will be less than total utility bills. Costs for lights, appliances, hot water, cooking, and other uses are not included in these figures. The mechanical system uses a gas furnace for heating and air conditioning for cooling. The gas and electric prices used in these figures are provided by the Energy Information Administration (EIA) (www.eia.doe.gov). RESFEN is a computer program for calculating the annual cooling and heating energy use and costs due to window selection and is available from Lawrence Berkeley National Laboratory (windows.lbl.gov/software/resfen). See Appendix A for pricing and modeling assumptions.

Global and Economic Impacts

Politicians now openly discuss our "addiction to oil" which might more properly be called an addiction to energy. Others look ahead to the issue of global warming and climate change, now widely acknowledged to be a result of human activities. The American Institute of Architects has issued a call to reduce energy use in new buildings by 2010 and to make buildings "carbon neutral" by 2030—implying even lower energy use which is then supplemented with renewable energy. These goals are challenging but achievable and the design and selection of high performance windows is a critical step in reaching these goals. Selecting energy-efficient windows

Figure 1-11. Impact of shading on annual energy use for a 2000-square-foot house with six window types in Phoenix, Arizona.

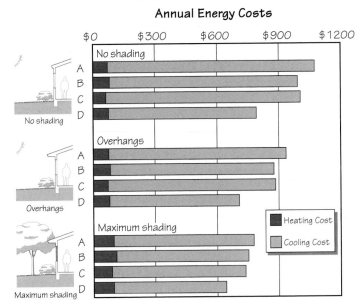

Annual Energy Costs

Window A
Double Glazing
Clear
Aluminum Frame w/break
U-Factor=0.63
SHGC=0.62
VT=0.63

Window B
Double Glazing
Bronze/Gray Tint
Aluminum Frame w/break
U-Factor=0.63
SHGC=0.52
VT=0.48

Window C
Double Glazing
Clear
Wood/Vinyl Frame
U-Factor=0.49
SHGC=0.56
VT=0.59

Window D
Double Glazing
Low-E (low solar gain)
Wood/Vinyl Frame
U-Factor=0.34
SHGC=0.30
VT=0.51

Note: The annual energy performance figures shown here were generated using RESFEN for a typical (new construction) 2000 sq ft house with 300 sq ft of window area. The windows are equally distributed on all four sides of the house. U-factor, SHGC, and VT are for the total window including frame. The costs shown here are annual costs for space heating and space cooling only and thus will be less than total utility bills. Costs for lights, appliances, hot water, cooking, and other uses are not included in these figures. The mechanical system uses a gas furnace for heating and air conditioning for cooling. The gas and electric prices used in these figures are provided by the Energy Information Administration (EIA) (www.eia.doe.gov). RESFEN is a computer program for calculating the annual cooling and heating energy use and costs due to window selection and is available from Lawrence Berkeley National Laboratory (windows.lbl.gov/software/resfen). See Appendix A for pricing and modeling assumptions.

See Chapter 2 for descriptions of U-factor and SHGC. See Chapters 3 and 4 for glazing and frame descriptions. See Appendix A for window descriptions.

is a "win-win" proposition—it not only reduces bills for the homeowner but the collective actions of all homeowners have important benefits at a national scale.

Windows impact our national energy requirements due to heating and cooling needs. Reducing oil needs for heating in the northeast can help the country move toward energy independence by reducing our dependence on foreign oil imports. Lowering gas usage for heating reduces pressure on tight supplies and lowers market costs, and may also slow the trend toward construction of coastal terminals for imported liquefied national gas (LNG) which creates yet another dependence on imported energy. Finally, the electric grid in the U.S. is under pressure to maintain adequate supply in the face of growing demand. The single largest source of electricity is from burning coal, which is the dirtiest fuel in terms of carbon emissions. Windows that are selected to reduce cooling energy use and peak electric demand will slow the need for new power plants and reduce carbon emissions.

Energy efficiency is not always viewed as a strategy that can have major impacts on national policy. But consider these two examples that illustrate the connections between energy demand and energy supply.

Better windows reduce our need for heating energy in winter, some of which comes from oil. Consider the following two alternatives to create the equivalent of 36 million barrels of oil:

1. An offshore oil platform contains ten operating wells each producing 10,000 barrels of oil per day. These are costly capital-intensive operations with the risk of coastal oil spills and have a nominal life of ten years before the fields are pumped dry. Over its ten-year useful lifetime this platform will provide approximately 36 million barrels of oil.

2. A low-E coating plant provides coated glass to a window manufacturer. The coating plant can produce 20 million square feet of coated glass per year and has a nominal life of ten years. The windows produced with the low-E glass save energy in the home, compared to uncoated glass. The cumulative energy savings from these low-E windows over a twenty-year operating period is also the equivalent of 36 million barrels of oil! The cost of building and operating the coating plant as well as its environmental impact is less than the oil platform.

Consider a second example where windows are selected to reduce cooling loads in buildings. Studies have shown that selection of windows with spectrally selective low-E coatings can not only reduce cooling energy use and cost to the homeowner but can reduce the size of the cooling system needed by about 25 percent or one ton. On the hottest days of the year this will result typically in a one kiloWatt reduction in chiller power and fan power for an average air conditioning unit. In parts of the country where utilities are building new power plants to keep up with growing demand, the cost of adding one kiloWatt of new capacity can range from $350 to over $1000 depending upon the type of power plant that is added (size, base load versus peaker, etc). In some cases the transmission infrastructure also has to be increased, adding to the cost. So installing windows that substantially reduce cooling loads reduce the investments needed by the utility industry on the order of $350—1000 per house. In some areas in the country there are innovative incentive programs that pay the homeowner to make these investments, as it may be cheaper than adding the new plant capacity.

So investments in high performance windows have numerous positive societal paybacks in addition to the savings that they return directly to the bill payers.

THE SUSTAINABLE BUILDING MOVEMENT

An increasingly important trend in the building industry is the emergence of the sustainable or green building movement. Sustainable design addresses goals such as energy efficiency, water conservation, healthy indoor environments, and reduced impact on the natural eneviroment through material selection and other design decisions. Awareness of global warming and climate change has become a particularly strong driving force in this movement.

Windows have an important role to play in making buildings more sustainable and the green building movement may also influence the evolution of the window industry. Clearly, high performance windows can help reduce energy use and greenhouse gas emissions. Daylight and views provided by windows are important in creating a quality indoor environment. The goal of reducing the life cycle environmental effects of all building materials and products may lead to product design and manufacturing changes resulting in lower embodied environmental impacts. Windows may also be designed to be more easily reused or recycled when a building is renovated.

Figure 1-12. Sustainable design is influencing the use, design, and manufacturing of windows.
(Photo: Andersen Corporation.)

21

In the residential sector, there are many green building guidelines, rating systems and standards. Two prominent national examples are LEED for Homes™ from the U.S. Green Building Council and NAHB Green Building Guidelines from the National Association of Home Builders (NAHB) promoted by the Green Building Initiative. There are also many regional and local green building programs throughout the U.S. Usually these programs are voluntary with point systems resulting in different levels of achievement, although in some cases guidelines will be required in a particular jurisdiction or for certain projects. There may be no prescriptive requirement specifically addressing windows but some guidelines may reference the ENERGY STAR program criteria. In cases where guidelines or rating systems reward whole building energy performance, efficient windows can be one of the leading strategies to achieve higher levels. One of the key concepts of successful sustainable design involves looking at a building not as individual components but as a whole system. A classic example of this integrated approach to design is the use of high-performance windows that result in lower heating and cooling loads as well as a less costly mechanical system.

BUILDING ENERGY CODES AND VOLUNTARY PROGRAMS

Decisions to select a particular window, which are typically made by a homeowner or builder, are often strongly influenced by mandatory building energy codes or voluntary government and utility energy-efficiency programs. In states and localities that have adopted building energy codes, these codes typically set a minimum level of window thermal or home energy performance to which the builder, remodeling or replacement window contractor, or homeowner must adhere. As a result, the responsible decision-maker (builder, contractor or homeowner) should start the window selection process by first consulting building code requirements, since these requirements generally set the legal minimum level of energy efficiency that must be achieved. Voluntary programs, offered by both utilities and government agencies, provide homeowners and builders with complementary information about efficiency performance, direct or indirect financial incentives, or marketing support, all of which are intended to drive the market towards the selection of more efficient windows.

State and Local Adoption of Building Energy Codes

Building codes traditionally include window-related safety and structural requirements, such as tempered or laminated glass, as well as requirements for light transmission, ventilation, wind loading, and emergency egress. In addition, building codes today typically have an energy efficiency/conservation code subset intended to guarantee that a minimum level of cost-effective, energy-efficient technologies are part of the design package. These energy code requirements typically establish minimum threshold specifications or characteristics for buildings and their component products, whether they are windows, wall insulation, or other building components. Up-to-date codes that are clear and easy to enforce can be especially effective at ensuring energy efficiency and maximizing occupant comfort.

Building energy codes are adopted at a state or local level. With a few notable exceptions, most jurisdictions do not develop their own energy codes from scratch. Instead, they rely on adopting uniform model energy codes developed by national code writing entities, occasionally tailoring or amending these codes to suit the particular needs of their jurisdiction. The first uniform energy codes were developed under the name Model Energy Code (MEC); today, the successor to the MEC and the currently nationally accepted uniform code is referred to as the International Energy Conservation Code or IECC, which was first published in 1998 by the International Code Council (ICC).

Remarkable progress has been made in the past few years in adopting and updating state and local energy codes, with a majority of states and numerous localities adopting or upgrading to a code based on some version of the IECC. However, despite the availability of the IECC and the benefits provided by adopting the IECC as written, states or localities with similar climates and similar construction practices have sometimes adopted very different codes due to state or local political issues. For example, a few states have no energy codes (often localities adopt such codes when states cannot or do not); some have older codes that pre-date the IECC; some have adopted earlier versions of the model codes and not upgraded; some have adopted substantial amendments (typically either eliminating or strengthening one or more model code requirements); and a few have developed their own codes.

A large portion of the progress that has been achieved toward adopting the most advanced, up-to-date, uniform energy

Figure 1-13. Window selection can be influenced by building energy codes or voluntary energy-efficiency programs. (Photo: Andersen Corporation)

codes is the result of national educational and promotional efforts undertaken both by government and private entities. At the time of this writing, the baseline national standard for states is the 2000 version of the IECC. However, DOE has initiated its review of the 2003 and 2006 versions of the IECC, and it is anticipated that the baseline will be soon updated to the 2006 version of the IECC. There are a number of other national efforts aimed at greater adoption of the model codes. These include the Building Codes Assistance Project (www.bcap-energy.org) and the Responsible Energy Codes Alliance (www.reca-codes.org).

As of August 2006, according to BCAP, 38 states have adopted mandatory residential energy codes, and 34 states have adopted residential energy codes (mandatory or voluntary) deemed to be equal to or more stringent than the IECC 2000. Current state-by-state adoption of energy codes is shown in Figure 1-14.

Meeting and complying with national model energy codes is also a first required step for obtaining an energy-efficient mortgage (where lenders give homeowners a greater credit limit and possibly a lower interest rate because their monthly energy bills will be lower as a result of installing energy-efficient products and features), as well as for obtaining federal energy efficiency tax credits.

Figure 1-14. States adopting or referencing the International Energy Conservation Code (as of January 2007). The Building Codes Assistance Project (BCAP) Web site has current information regarding the status of state codes, maps and overviews.
Source: Building Codes Assistance Project, www.bcap-energy.org

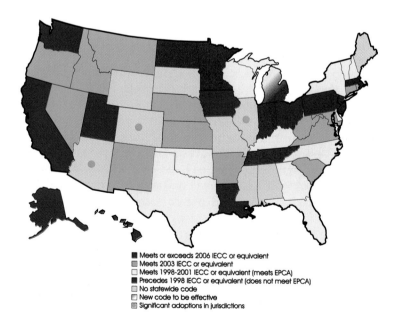

■ Meets or exceeds 2006 IECC or equivalent
▨ Meets 2003 IECC or equivalent
☐ Meets 1998-2001 IECC or equivalent (meets EPCA)
■ Precedes 1998 IECC or equivalent (does not meet EPCA)
☐ No statewide code
☐ New code to be effective
▨ Significant adoptions in jurisdictions

2006 IECC: A Simpler Approach to Building Energy Codes

The 2006 IECC represents the next stage in the evolution of model energy codes in general and window requirements specifically. This version is based on the important concept that simplified, easy-to-understand requirements will lead to more/better code adoption, compliance and enforcement. The 2006 IECC is far shorter and less complex than previous versions. Its genesis was a code proposal developed by DOE over a number of years and first adopted by the ICC in 2004. Because the changes were so substantial, the ICC published an interim 2004 Supplement version of the IECC. The 2006 version reflects refinements adopted in the following cycle.

The 2006 IECC establishes only 8 climate zones nationwide and assigns each county to a single zone (Figure 1-15). It establishes a single prescriptive compliance path for all building envelope components, including specific U-factor maximums for fenestration (with separate requirements for skylights) and SHGC maximums for all glazed fenestration. Diverging sharply from previous versions of the IECC and MEC, the prescriptive path in the 2006 IECC does not vary with window area as percentage of wall area, recognizing that past limits on window area are no longer necessary with energy efficient windows. These same requirements apply to all windows, doors and skylights in new homes, additions and remodeling, and for replacement purposes. These requirements are displayed in Figure 1-16. It should be noted that many of these requirements are similar to those required for the ENERGY STAR windows program. Air infiltration requirements for windows are displayed in Figure 1-17.

All of the versions of the model codes (MEC and IECC) generally provide various compliance options, which allow a builder to satisfy the baseline requirements of the code in several ways. First, there are climate dependent prescriptive packages of component requirements, which dictate insulation levels, window properties, mechanical system efficiencies, etc. These approaches are basically recipes that assure compliance if followed exactly. As noted above, prior to the 2004 and 2006 IECCs, these requirements have also varied depending on how much glazing is used. Second, all of the MEC/IECC codes also allow for a trade-off approach whereby the builder trades off area-weighted U-values of various building envelope components to meet overall U-value targets. Some states have approved the use of REScheck, software prepared under contract to DOE, to facilitate these types of trade-offs. A third option available

Figure 1-15. Eight climate zones referenced in the 2006 IECC.

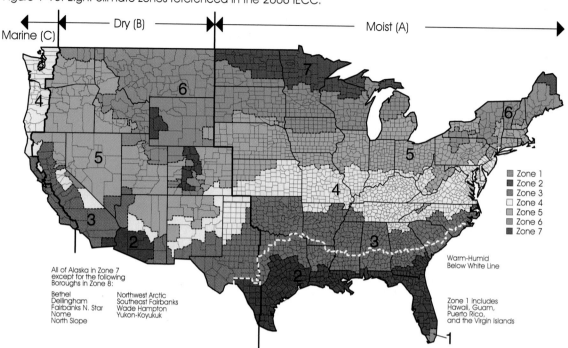

Figure 1-16. Fenestration U-factor and SHGC maximums from the 2006 IECC for all fenestration products installed in new residential dwellings and for replacement and remodeling of existing homes.

Climate Zone	Fenestration U-Factor	Skylight U-factor	Fenestration SHGC*
1	1.20	0.75	0.40
2	0.75	0.75	0.40
3	0.65	0.65	0.40
4 except Marine	0.40	0.60	NR
5–8 and Marine 4	0.35	0.60	NR

*There are no SHGC requirements in "Marine" zones.
Source: Table 402.1.1 of the 2006 IECC. The 2006 IRC, 2004 IECC and 2004 IRC contain the same requirements (although the configuration of the climate zones were changed slightly in the 2006 versions).

Figure 1-17. Allowable air infiltration rates for windows, sliding doors, and swinging doors.

Windows (cfm/sq. ft.)	Sliding Doors (cfm/sq. ft.)	Swinging Doors (cfm/sq. ft.)
0.3	0.3	0.5

When tested according to NFRC 400 or AAMA/WDMA/CSA 101/I.S.2/A440 by an accredited, independent laboratory and listed and labeled by the manufacturer. Site-built windows and skylights are an exception to this requirement.
Source: 2006 IECC section 402.4.2.

under all of the MEC/IECC codes is to determine the energy use of a "standard reference design" house of the same floor area as the proposed house; the builder can then substitute features in the standard house with those for the proposed house, as long as it can be shown that the proposed house will use less overall energy (or have a lower energy cost) than the standard house. This third approach typically utilizes a sophisticated building energy simulation program to provide this more customized compliance analysis. With potentially rising energy prices in the future, using trade-offs to allow for lower performing windows is not recommended.

The 2006 IECC permits all of these approaches. However, with the move to the single, simple prescriptive path, it is expected that the primary compliance path under these codes in most jurisdictions will be to follow this simple prescriptive recipe. The 2006 IECC also contains one noteworthy addition when trade-off approaches are used. The 2006 IECC establishes mandatory maximum fenestration U-factors and SHGCs that cannot be traded away under any of the compliance paths (for windows and doors: 0.50 SHGC in the southern US; 0.48 U-factor in the central US; 0.40 U-factor in the northern US; see section 402.6 of the 2006 IECC; see also section 402.5.1 of the 2004 IECC). These trade-off limits are in recognition of the importance of installing reasonably energy efficient windows in every home for comfort, peak demand, and condensation considerations. The end result of this approach is, for the most part, to mandate low-e windows, doors and skylights nationwide, wherever the 2006 IECC is adopted.

Voluntary Building Energy-Efficiency Programs

Voluntary programs work in tandem with building codes by encouraging builders and homeowners to adopt even more energy-efficient building practices and technologies before they become incorporated into new codes. Increased industry familiarity and acceptance of new practices and technologies paves the way for regular updates to the codes.

Government agencies and utilities are the most common sponsors of voluntary programs. Often, government and utility programs are developed and implemented in a coordinated manner. For example, the federal government has sponsored uniform window-rating procedures (see the description of the National Fenestration Rating Council in Appendix B). These ratings then form the basis for eligibility requirements for governmental and utility–sponsored programs to encourage efficient products.

Utility-sponsored or demand side management programs (DSM) stimulate the adoption of energy-efficient technologies in a variety of ways including providing customers or builders with information, technical assistance, and direct (e.g., cash rebates and discounted rates) and indirect (e.g., lower cost financing) financial incentives. Direct financial incentives or rebates, including lower rates for energy efficient homes, have been a dominant strategy employed by utility programs.

Market transformation programs, undertaken by both government and utilities, do not refer to a distinct type of voluntary program. However, they do refer to a change in the objectives for these programs. For example, utility rebate programs were by and large focused on influencing individual decisions to purchase energy efficient products. In contrast, market transformation programs focus on permanently shifting the entire market from its present state to one in which a currently underutilized (yet cost-effective) energy-efficient technology emerges as the standard or base product for the industry. Hence, while many of the same program strategies might be used in a market transformation program (e.g., information, technical assistance, direct/indirect financial incentives), the strategies are consciously integrated toward effecting lasting changes in the markets they target.

At a national level, the National Fenestration Rating Council (by providing a uniform and accurate metric for evaluating window energy efficiency), the Efficient Windows Collaborative (EWC), and the ENERGY STAR Windows program have all focused on elements necessary to transform the market for residential windows.

A final voluntary program offered only by governments to encourage efficient technologies is a tax credit, either at the state or federal level. Tax credits can have a major impact in promoting the increased sale of efficient products because these products are typically higher in first cost compared to standard, less efficient products.

For more details on qualification for federal tax credits, review of IRS guidance issued early in 2006 and other publications is recommended (see www.irs.gov). There is also extensive information on the website of the Tax Incentives Assistance Project (www.energytaxincentives.org). States may also adopt tax credits for energy efficient products. States have considered and/or implemented sales tax holidays and exemptions for such products as well as state income tax credits.

WINDOW SELECTION

While individuals make window purchasing decisions based on many unique priorities and circumstances, there are some common considerations that most buyers need to address to make an effective choice. These may include appearance, visible light transmittance, thermal comfort, condensation resistance, and numerous other technical properties. These selection considerations are discussed in more detail in Chapter 2. When selecting any window, three important priorities are energy performance, durability, and proper installation. The step-by-step guide below assists in selecting energy-efficient windows based on ENERGY STAR and other methods. The insulated glazing unit should be certified to ensure long term energy efficient performance of a window. Proper installation is also essential so that a window performs for its expected lifetime (see Chapter 4).

Window selection also involves cost. Usually, decisions about windows are the result of relatively short term thinking. Buyers either seek the lowest first cost or if a more efficient window is chosen, they seek a short term payback based on today's energy prices. No one knows what future energy prices will be and government predictions showing relatively little increase in the next twenty years seem conservative. Based on current events and global trends, it would be prudent to have a longer term perspective when buying a window that will be in place for 30 years or more. One can imagine that political instability, war, and increasing frequency of natural disasters combined with carbon taxes or regulations designed to reduce greenhouse gas emissions will drive up energy prices. Investing in the highest performance windows one can afford is a way to protect against these future possibilities.

A STEP-BY-STEP GUIDE TO SELECTING ENERGY-EFFICIENT WINDOWS

The Efficient Windows Collaborative Web site provides extensive information on selecting windows and skylights, including fact sheets and computer simulations for typical houses using a variety of windows in over 90 U.S. cities (www.efficientwindows.org). Beginning with the simplest and least time-consuming and moving to the more complex, here are four basic steps in efficient window selection:

Figure 1-18. The Efficient Windows Collaborative (EWC) provides extensive information on selecting windows including fact sheets and computer simulations for typical houses using a variety of windows in over 90 U.S. cities (www.efficientwindows.org).

29

Figure 1-19. Look for the ENERGY STAR
Label (www.energystar.gov).

1. Look for the **ENERGY STAR** Label

The Department of Energy (DOE) and the Environmental
Protection Agency (EPA) have developed an **ENERGY
STAR** designation for products meeting certain energy
performance criteria. Since energy-efficient performance
of windows, doors, and skylights varies by climate, product
recommendations are given for four U.S. climate zones.
ENERGY STAR labels are found on windows, doors, and
skylights. For making comparisons among **ENERGY STAR**
products, use the NFRC label or directory. See Chapter 2
for descriptions of U-factor and SHGC. See Chapters 3 and
4 for U-factors and SHGC of typical glazings and frames.

Figure 1-20. ENERGY STAR zones and requirements for windows, doors and skylights.

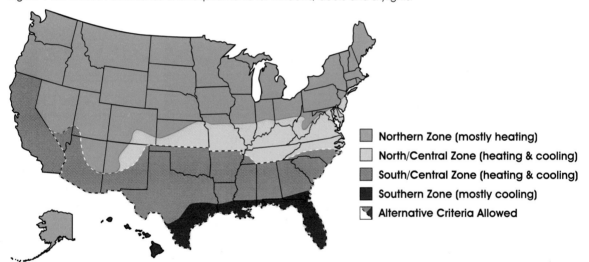

- Northern Zone (mostly heating)
- North/Central Zone (heating & cooling)
- South/Central Zone (heating & cooling)
- Southern Zone (mostly cooling)
- Alternative Criteria Allowed

Windows & Doors

Climate Zone	U-Factor[1]	SHGC[2]	
Northern	≤ 0.35	Any	
North/Central	≤ 0.40	≤ 0.55	
South/Central	≤ 0.40	≤ 0.40	Prescriptive
	≤ 0.41	≤ 0.36	Equivalent Performance
	≤ 0.42	≤ 0.31	(excluding CA)
	≤ 0.43	≤ 0.24	Products meeting these criteria also qualify in the Southern zone
Southern	≤ 0.65	≤ 0.40	Prescriptive
	≤ 0.66	≤ 0.39	Equivalent Performance
	≤ 0.67	≤ 0.39	
	≤ 0.68	≤ 0.38	
	≤ 0.69	≤ 0.37	
	≤ 0.70	≤ 0.37	
	≤ 0.71	≤ 0.36	
	≤ 0.72	≤ 0.35	
	≤ 0.73	≤ 0.35	
	≤ 0.74	≤ 0.34	
	≤ 0.75	≤ 0.33	

Skylights

Climate Zone	U-Factor[3]	U-Factor[4]	SHGC[2]
Northern	≤ 0.60	≤ 0.45	Any
North/Central	≤ 0.60	≤ 0.45	≤ 0.40
South/Central	≤ 0.60	≤ 0.45	≤ 0.40
Southern	≤ 0.75	≤ 0.75	≤ 0.40

[1] U-factor in Btu/h-ft^2-°F
[2] Solar Heat Gain Coefficient in fraction of incident solar radiation
[3] Qualification criteria based on 2001 NFRC simulation and certification procedures that rate skylights at a 20-degree angle
[4] NFRC certification using the 1997 NFRC procedures for residential windows (RES97) that rated skylights at a 90-degree angle.

2. Look for the NFRC Label

The National Fenestration Rating Council (NFRC) is a non-profit, public/private organization created by the window, door, and skylight industry. It is composed of manufacturers, suppliers, builders, architects and designers, specifiers, code officials, utilities, and government agencies. The NFRC has developed a window energy rating system based on whole product performance. The NFRC label provides the only reliable way to determine the window energy properties and to compare products. The NFRC label appears on all products certified to the NFRC standards and on all window, door, and skylight products which are part of the ENERGY STAR program. At this time, NFRC labels on window units give ratings for U-factor, solar heat gain coefficient (SHGC), visible transmittance (VT), and condensation resistance (CR). These properties are defined in Chapter 2 and recommended window properties for U.S. regions are given in Chapter 6. Note that comparing the NFRC rating numbers alone may not always directly indicate the more energy-efficient product since the properties each influence heating and cooling costs differently in different locations.

3. Compare Annual Energy Costs for a Typical House in Your Region

Some of the basic thermal and optical properties (U-factor, solar heat gain coefficient, and visible transmittance) can be identified if the window is properly labeled and compliance with energy codes determined. However, consumers still do not know how these basic properties influence annual heating and cooling energy use. This can be determined by looking at the impact of window choice on a typical house or by using computer tools on your specific house. The annual energy use from computer simulations for a typical house in your region can be compared for different window options. The Efficient Window Collaborative's web site (www.efficientwindows.org) and other tools can help determine the most energy-efficient window selection for your specific needs. Examples appear in Chapter 6 for a range of U.S. climates.

National Fenestration
Rating Council

Figure 1-21. Look for the NFRC label (www.nfrc.org).

4. Estimate and Compare Annual Energy Costs for Your House

Using a computer program such as RESFEN to compare window options is the only method of obtaining reasonable estimates of the heating and cooling costs for your climate, house design, and utility rates. Users define a specific "scenario" by specifying house type (single-story or two-story), geographic location, orientation, electricity and gas cost, and building configuration details (such as wall, floor, and HVAC system type). Users also specify size, shading, and thermal properties of the windows they wish to investigate. The thermal properties that RESFEN requires are: U-factor, solar heat gain coefficient, and air leakage rate. The relative energy and cost impacts of different window options can be compared. See Chapter 6 and Appendix A for more information on RESFEN.

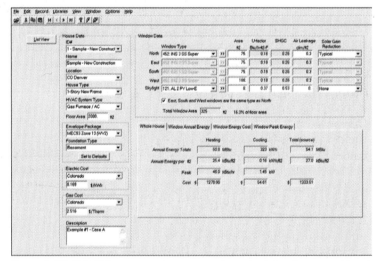

Figure 1-22. RESFEN is a computer program for calculating the annual heating and cooling energy use and costs due to fenestration systems. RESFEN also calculates their contribution to peak heating and cooling loads. It is available at no charge from windows.lbl.gov/software.

CHAPTER 2

Window Properties

Selecting a window or skylight involves many considerations such as appearance, energy performance, human factors issues, technical performance, and cost. This chapter provides an overview of many of these properties. Detailed energy performance and cost information for windows in several U.S. climates appears in Chapter 6.

Seeking the desired appearance of a window in terms of both the exterior facade and the interior design is often the starting point. These aesthetic characteristics are identified in the first section of the chapter.

The second section of the chapter addresses energy performance characteristics of window units. There is a brief introduction to the basic mechanisms of heat transfer and how they apply to windows. This is followed by a description of the key energy-related characteristics of windows—insulating value, ability to control heat gain from solar radiation, and ability to control air leakage.

The third section of the chapter addresses window properties related to human factors such as visible light transmittance (daylight and view), glare control, thermal comfort, ventilation, and sound control. Of these issues, thermal comfort plays an important role in affecting energy use patterns.

The last section addresses a number of technical window properties that affect long term performance. These include condensation resistance, fading resistance, durability, maintenance, structural capability, and water resistance. The durability of the insulated glazing unit, coatings and gas fills is a particularly important issue to ensure long term energy efficient performance of a window.

Figure 2-1. Human factor issues such as daylight, view, glare control, thermal comfort, ventilation, and sound control should be considered when selecting windows.
(Photo: Velux-America Inc.)

APPEARANCE

The way a window or skylight looks can sometimes override all other technical and cost considerations. After all, a primary basis for selecting a window is to help achieve a certain exterior and interior design concept. The appearance of the window frame—its style, materials, and use of mullions—is perhaps one of the most important considerations in selecting any window. In most cases, the desired size and shape of a window can be found in numerous product lines. In a few cases, the need for an unusual shape, such as an arched window, may limit the buyer to certain manufacturers.

The color and finish of the interior frame materials (wood, vinyl, or metal) is a major selection criterion for many designers and homeowners: vinyl and metal exterior frame material or cladding are available in a variety of colors and finishes

Figure 2-2. The style and overall appearance of windows are primary selection considerations.
(Photo: Andersen Corporation.)

but may not be paintable by the homeowner. Fiberglass and wood, of course, allow for choice of paint color after installation. Choosing window size and shape and frame type are subjective decisions—they depend on the house design and the personal preferences of the designer or homeowner.

The appearance of the glazing—its visual clarity—is another issue. Most new good-quality glass has minimal optical distortion. Differences in temperature and pressure can cause sealed insulated glass units to bow slightly inward or outward. Tempered or heat-strengthened glass can show more distortion than standard window glass, particularly at the edges. Another visual characteristic of glass is haze, the degree to which the glass itself diffuses light and softens the view of objects beyond. With modern glass technology, most consumers need not consider visual clarity a problem unless a window obviously appears distorted or hazy. In some cases, however, diffusing glass with a variety of patterns may be selected to provide privacy. In very old homes when historic preservation is an issue, consult a specialist on glass appearance and replacement.

Glass color is a matter of importance to some homeowners. Not only does tinted glass diminish the amount of light, but the light that passes through heavily tinted glass can appear colored—either gray, bronze, green, or blue-green—and it can change both the appearance of objects indoors seen under the colored light and objects viewed through the glass. With new glazing products such as spectrally selective low-E coatings, solar heat gain can be reduced without the appearance of tinted glass. However, some low-E coatings impart a subtle color shift, especially when viewed at an angle.

These are aesthetic characteristics worth considering. The best way to assess these effects is to observe sample glazings under different light conditions and, if possible, visit a house that uses the glazing option being considered.

ENERGY PERFORMANCE

Heat flows through a window assembly in three ways: conduction, convection, and radiation. Conduction is heat traveling through a solid material, the way a frying pan warms up. Convection is the transfer of heat by the movement of gases or liquids, like warm air rising from a candle flame. Radiation is the movement of heat energy through space without relying on conduction through the air or by movement of the air, the way you feel the heat of a fire.

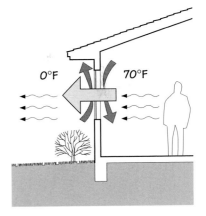

Figure 2-3. This drawing illustrates heat loss through the window in winter by conduction combined with radiation and air movement (convection) on the surfaces of the glazing. The U-factor of a window is a combination of these conductive, convective, and radiative heat transfer mechanisms.

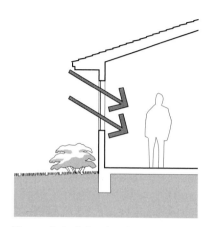

Figure 2-4. Solar heat gain passes through glazing to some extent, depending on the glazing type. This gain can be beneficial in winter but undesirable in summer.

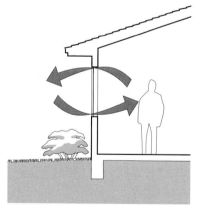

Figure 2-5. Infiltration through cracks in the window assembly is another mechanism for energy transfer.

When these basic mechanisms of heat transfer are applied to the performance of windows, they interact in complex ways. Thus, conduction, convection, and radiation are not typically discussed and measured separately. Instead, three energy performance characteristics of windows are used to portray how energy is transferred and are the basis for how energy performance is quantified. They are:

- Insulating value. When there is a temperature difference between inside and outside, heat is lost or gained through the window frame and glazing by the combined effects of conduction, convection, and radiation. This is indicated in terms of the U-factor of a window assembly.

- Heat gain from solar radiation. Regardless of outside temperature, heat can be gained through windows by direct or indirect solar radiation. The ability to control this heat gain through windows is measured in terms of the solar heat gain coefficient (SHGC) or shading coefficient (SC) of the window.

- Infiltration. Heat loss and gain also occur by air leakage through cracks in the window assembly. This effect is measured in terms of the amount of air (cubic feet or cubic meters per minute) that passes through a unit area of window (square foot or square meter) under given pressure conditions. In reality, infiltration varies slightly with wind-driven and temperature-driven pressure changes. Air leakage also contributes to summer cooling loads in some climates by raising the interior humidity level.

Each of these energy performance characteristics is described below, along with a brief discussion of approaches to improve energy efficiency in each area. Methods of determining the insulating value, solar heat gain values, and air leakage values of windows are also presented.

Insulating Value

Heat flow from the warmer to the colder side of a window and frame is a complex interaction of all three heat transfer mechanisms described above—conduction, convection, and radiation. Figure 2-6 shows the manner in which these heat transfer mechanisms interact. The ability of the window assembly to resist this heat transfer is referred to as its insulating value. Heat flows from warmer to cooler bodies, thus from inside to outside in winter, and reverses direction in summer during periods when the outside temperature is greater than indoors.

Compared to a well-insulated wall, heat transfer through a typical older window is generally much higher. A single-glazed window has roughly the same insulating qualities as a sheet of metal—most of the insulating value comes from the air layer on each surface of the glass. Such a window can be considered a thermal hole in a wall and typically has a heat loss rate ten to twenty times that of an insulated wall. A window with such a poor insulating value allows heat to flow out of a space almost unimpeded. If the temperature inside is 70°F and outside 0°F (20°C and -18°C), the glass surface of a single-glazed window would be about 17°F (-8°C)—cold enough to form frost on the inside of the glass.

Convection affects the heat transfer in three places in the assembly: the inside glazing surface, the outside glazing surface, and inside any air spaces between glazings. A cold interior glazing surface chills the air adjacent to it. This denser cold air then falls to the floor, starting a convection current. People typically perceive this cold air flow as a "draft" caused by leaky windows, and are tempted to plug any holes they can find, rather than to remedy the situation correctly with a better window that provides a warmer glass surface.

On the exterior, a component of the insulating value of a window is the air film against the glazing surface. As wind blows (convection), this air film is removed or replaced with colder air, which contributes to a higher rate of heat loss. Finally, when there is an air space between layers of glazing, convection currents facilitate heat transfer through this air layer. By adjusting the space between the panes of glass, as well as choosing a gas fill that insulates better than air, double-glazed windows can be designed to minimize this effect.

All objects emit invisible thermal radiation, with warmer objects emitting more than colder ones. Hold your hand in front of an oven window and you will feel the radiant energy emitted by that warm surface. Your hand also radiates heat to the oven window, but since the window is warmer than your hand, the net balance of radiant flow is toward your hand and it is warmed. Now imagine holding your hand close to a single-glazed window in winter. The window surface is much colder than your hand. Each surface emits radiant energy, but since your hand is warmer, it emits more toward the window than it gains and you feel a cooling effect. Thus, a cold glazing surface in a room chills everything else around it.

Through radiant exchange, the objects in the room, and especially the people (who are often the warmest objects), radiate their heat to the colder window. People often feel the

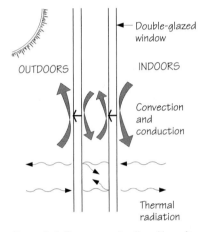

Figure 2-6. Components of heat transfer through a window that are related to insulating value.

chill from this radiant heat loss, especially on the exposed skin of their hands and faces, but they attribute the chill to cool room air rather than to a cold window surface. Because of this misconception, few people realize that pulling a curtain across the window as a barrier to the radiant heat loss could be more effective in improving their immediate comfort than turning up the thermostat.

The thermal performance of a roof window or skylight changes according to the angle at which it is mounted. This is because the rate of convective exchange on the inner and outer surfaces as well as within the air space is affected by the slope. Also, skylights and roof windows that point toward the cold night sky have more radiant heat losses at night than windows that view warmer objects such as the ground, adjacent buildings, and vegetation.

Determining Insulating Value

The U-factor (also referred to as U-value) is the standard way to quantify insulating value. It indicates the rate of heat flow through the window. The U-factor is the total heat transfer coefficient of the window system (in Btu/hr-sq ft-°F or W/sq m-°C), which includes conductive, convective, and radiative heat transfer. It therefore represents the heat flow per hour (in Btus per hour or watts) through each square foot (or square meter) of window for a 1°F (1°C) temperature difference between the indoor and outdoor air temperature. The R-value is the reciprocal of the total U-factor (R=1/U). As opposed to an R-value, the smaller the U-factor of a material, the lower the rate of heat flow.

In addition to the thermal properties of the materials in the window assembly, the U-factor depends on the weather conditions, such as the temperature differential between indoors and out, and wind speed. Window manufacturers typically list a U-factor for winter that is determined under relatively harsh conditions: 15 mph (25 km/hr) wind, 70°F (20°C) indoors, 0°F (-18°C) outdoors. These conditions have been standardized with a set temperature and wind speed so that product ratings can be used for comparison purposes.

The U-factor of a total window assembly is a combination of the insulating values of the glazing itself, the edge effects that occur in the insulated glazing unit, and the window frame and sash.

The U-factor of the glazing portion of the window unit is affected primarily by the total number of glazing layers, the dimension separating the various layers of glazing, the

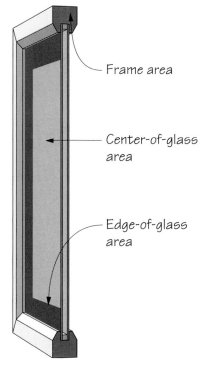

Frame area

Center-of-glass area

Edge-of-glass area

Figure 2-7. Principle zones for determining heat loss through a window assembly.

type of gas that fills the separation, and the characteristics of coatings on the various surfaces. The U-factor for the glazing alone is referred to as the center-of-glass U-factor (Figure 2-7). Center-of-glass U-factors for typical glazings are shown in Figure 2-8.

Figure 2-8. Comparison of U-factors for different glazing types.

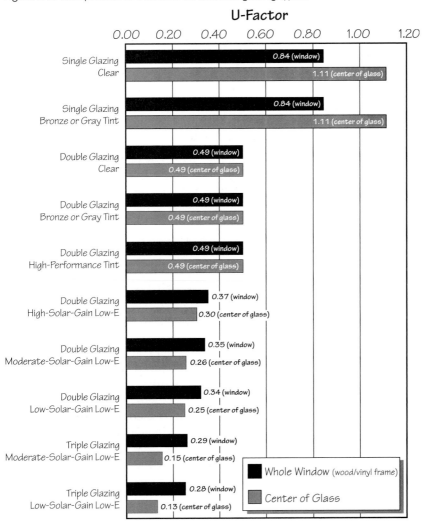

Note: All whole window values assume the glazing is in a wood or vinyl frame. Detailed descriptions of glazing and frame materials appear in Chapters 3 and 4.

A center-of-glass U-factor calculation assumes that heat flows perpendicular to the plane of the window. However, windows are complex three-dimensional assemblies, in which materials and cross sections change in a relatively short space.

For example, metal spacers at the edge of an insulating glass unit have much higher heat flow than the center of the insulating glass, which causes increased heat loss along the outer edge of the glass. The relative impact of these "edge effects" becomes more important as the insulating value of the rest of the assembly increases.

The heat loss through a window frame can be quite significant: in a typical four-foot by three-foot (1.2 by 0.9 m) double-hung wood frame window, the frame and sash can occupy approximately 30 percent of the window area.

In a frame with a cross section made of one uniform, solid material, the U-factor is based on the conduction of heat through the material. However, hollow frames and composite frames with various reinforcing or cladding materials are more complex. Here, conduction through materials must be combined with convection of the air next to the glazing and radiant exchange between the various surfaces.

Furthermore, window frames rarely have the same cross section around a window. For example, a horizontal slider may have eight different frame cross sections, each with its own rate of heat flow. Because of these complications, determining the U-factor through a window frame is very complex and is best calculated by specialized heat transfer computer programs.

Overall U-factor

Since the U-factors are different for the glass, edge-of-glass zone, and frame, it can be misleading to compare U-factors if they are not carefully described. In order to address this problem, the concept of a total window U-factor is utilized by the National Fenestration Rating Council (NFRC). A specific set of engineering assumptions and procedures must be followed to calculate the overall U-factor of a window unit using the NFRC method. Figure 2-8 indicates the center-of-glass U-factor and the overall U-factor for several types of window units. When the glazing U-factor is worse than a wood or vinyl frame (as in single glazing), the whole window has a better U-factor than the glass alone. When improved glazings are superior to the frame in insulating value, the overall U-factor is lower than the U-factor for the glass alone. Figure 2-9 illustrates the impact of frame type on U-factor.

The U-factor of a window unit is typically described for the unit in a vertical position. A change in mounting angle can affect its U-factor. A roof window in a vertical position might have a U-factor of 0.50; the same unit installed on a sloped roof at 20 degrees from horizontal would have a U-factor of 0.56 (12 percent higher under winter conditions).

Figure 2-9. Comparison of U-factors for windows with different frame types.

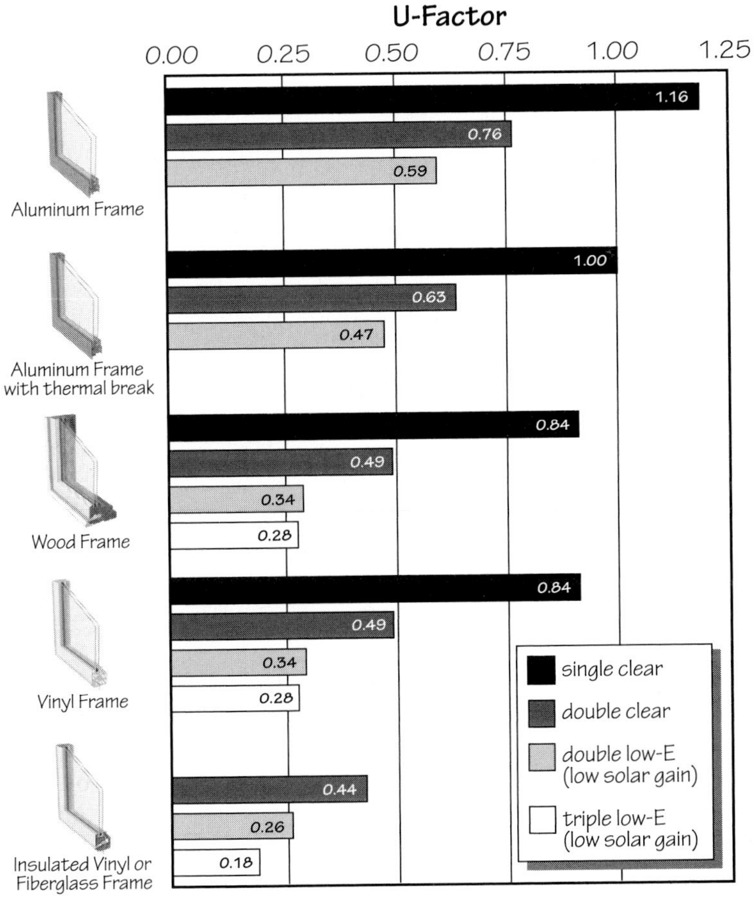

U-Factor

Note: All values are for whole window including frame. Detailed descriptions of glazing and frame materials appear in Chapters 3 and 4.

Energy Effects of U-factor

Figure 2-10 illustrates the effect of changing the window U-factor on annual energy cost in a typical house in two climates. Even though the total window area is a small percentage of the total building envelope, the impact of changing the U-factor can be a significant factor in the overall building performance. In general, reducing the U-factor has a more significant impact on reducing heating costs than cooling costs. In a cooling-dominated climate such as Phoenix, the impact of improving the U-factor is relatively small. In a heating-dominated climate such as Minneapolis, however, the total annual energy costs are lowered substantially. As shown in Figure 2-10 for Minneapolis, cooling costs actually increase slightly as the U-factor decreases. This occurs because there are times when losing heat to the

Figure 2-10. Effect of window U-factor on annual energy costs.

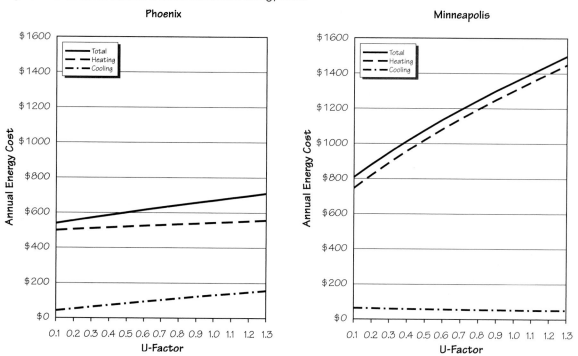

Note: The annual energy performance figures shown here were generated using RESFEN for a typical 2000 sq ft house with 300 sq ft of window area (15% of floor area). The windows are equally distributed on all four sides of the house and include typical shading (interior shades, overhangs, trees, and neighboring buildings). The heating system is a gas furnace with air-conditioning for cooling. U-factor, SHGC, and VT are for the total window including frame. The SHGC in all cases is 0.5 and the air leakage in all cases is 0.5 cfm/sf. The gas and electric prices used in these figures are provided by the Energy Information Administration (EIA) (www.eia.doe.gov). RESFEN is a computer program for calculating the annual cooling and heating energy use and costs due to window selection and is available from Lawrence Berkeley National Laboratory (windows.lbl.gov/software/resfen). See Appendix A for pricing and modeling assumptions.

outside in summer helps cool the house and a lower U-factor inhibits this effect. The slightly increased cooling cost is more than offset by the greatly reduced heating cost.

Solar Radiation Control

The second major energy-performance characteristic of windows is the ability to control solar heat gain through the glazing. Solar heat gain through windows tends to be the single most significant factor in determining the air-conditioning load of a residential building. The intensity of heat gain from solar radiation can greatly surpass heat gain from other sources, such as outdoor air temperature or humidity.

The origin of solar heat gain is the direct and diffuse radiation coming from the sun and the sky or reflected from the ground and other surfaces. Some radiation is directly transmitted through the glazing to the space, and some may be absorbed in the glazing and then indirectly admitted to the space. Other thermal (nonsolar) heat transfer effects are included in the U-factor of the window. Sunlight is composed of electromagnetic radiation of many wavelengths, ranging from short-wave invisible ultraviolet, to the visible spectrum, to the longer, invisible near-infrared waves. About half of the sun's energy is visible light; the remainder is largely infrared with a small amount of ultraviolet. This characteristic of sunlight makes it possible to selectively admit or reject different portions of the solar spectrum. While reducing solar radiation through windows is a benefit in some climates and during some seasons, maximizing solar heat gain can be a significant energy benefit under winter conditions. These often conflicting directives can make selection of the "best" window a challenging task.

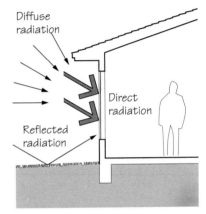

Figure 2-11. Solar heat gain includes direct, reflected, and diffuse radiation.

Determining Solar Heat Gain

There are two means of indicating the amount of solar radiation that passes through a window. These are solar heat gain coefficient (SHGC) and shading coefficient (SC). In both cases, the solar heat gain is the combination of directly transmitted radiation and the inward-flowing portion of absorbed radiation (Figure 2-11). However, SHGC and SC have a different basis for comparison or reference.

Shading Coefficient

In the past, the shading coefficient (SC) was the primary term used to characterize the solar control properties of glass in windows. Although it is being replaced by the solar heat gain coefficient, you will still find it referenced in books or product literature. The SC was originally developed as a single number that could be used to compare glazing solar control under a wide range of conditions. Its simplicity, however, is offset by a lack of accuracy in a number of circumstances.

The shading coefficient (SC) is only defined for the glazing portion of the window and does not include frame effects. It represents the ratio of solar heat gain through the system relative to that through 1/8-inch (3 mm) clear glass at normal incidence. The SC has also been used to characterize performance over a wide range of sun positions; however, there is some potential loss in accuracy when applied to sun positions at high angles to the glass. The shading coefficient is expressed as a dimensionless number from 0 to 1. A high shading coefficient means high solar gain, while a low shading coefficient means low solar gain.

The SC value is strongly influenced by the type of glass selected. The shading coefficient can also include the effects of any integral part of the window system that reduces the flow of solar heat, such as multiple glazing layers, reflective coatings, or blinds between layers of glass. The SHGC is influenced by all the same factors as the SC, but since it can be applied to the entire window assembly, the SHGC is also affected by shading from the frame as well as the ratio of glazing and frame. For any glazing, the SHGC is always lower than the SC. If you find an older information source with SC values only, you can make an approximate conversion to SHGC for the glazing by multiplying the SC value by 0.87. Total window SHGC is used throughout this book and is found on the NFRC labels.

Solar Heat Gain Coefficient

The window industry is now moving away from use of the shading coefficient to the solar heat gain coefficient (SHGC), which is defined as that fraction of incident solar radiation that actually enters a building through the window assembly as heat gain. The SHGC generally refers to total window system performance and is a more accurate indication of solar gain under a wider range of conditions. The solar heat gain coefficient is expressed as a dimensionless number from 0 to 1. A high coefficient signifies high heat gain, while a low coef-

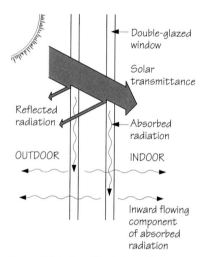

Figure 2-12. Simplified view of the components of solar heat gain. Heat gain includes the transmitted solar energy and the inward flowing component of absorbed radiation.

ficient means low heat gain. Typical SHGC values for the whole window unit and center of glass are shown in Figure 2-13.

Energy Effects of SHGC

Figure 2-14 illustrates the effect of changing the solar heat gain coefficient on energy costs in a typical house in two climates. In general, reducing the SHGC of the glazing reduces the cooling costs but increases the heating costs since pas-

Figure 2-13. Solar heat gain characteristics of typical windows.

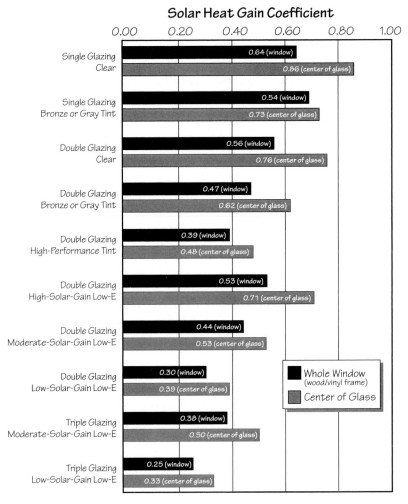

Note: All whole window values assume the glazing is in a wood or vinyl frame. Detailed descriptions of glazing and frame materials appear in Chapters 3 and 4.

sive solar gain is diminished during the heating season. In a predominantly cooling climate such as Phoenix, Arizona, reducing the SHGC results in a noticeable decrease in the total annual energy costs. In a heating-dominated climate such as Minneapolis, however, reducing the SHGC results in a modest increase in total annual energy costs, since the benefits in the cooling season are more than offset by the lost solar gain in the heating season.

Air Leakage (Infiltration)

Air leakage (infiltration) can be defined as ventilation that is not controlled and usually not wanted. It is the leakage of air through cracks in the building envelope. Air leakage leads to increased heating or cooling loads when the outdoor air entering the building needs to be heated or cooled. Windows

Figure 2-14. Effect of solar heat gain coefficient (SHGC) on annual energy costs.

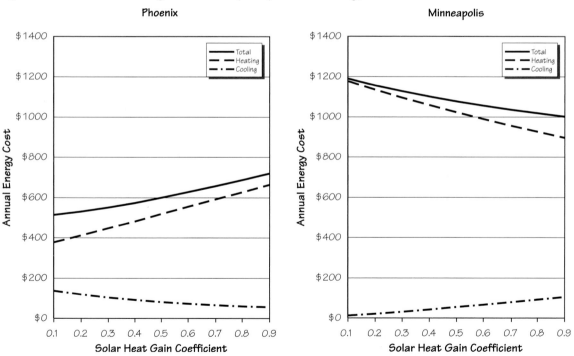

Note: The annual energy performance figures shown here were generated using RESFEN for a typical 2000 sq ft house with 300 sq ft of window area (15% of floor area). The windows are equally distributed on all four sides of the house and include typical shading (interior shades, overhangs, trees, and neighboring buildings). The heating system is a gas furnace with air-conditioning for cooling. The heating system is a gas furnace with air-conditioning for cooling. U-factor, SHGC, and VT are for the total window including frame. The U-factor in all cases is 0.5 and the air leakage in all cases is 0.5 cfm/sf. The gas and electric prices used in these figures are provided by the Energy Information Administration (EIA) (www.eia.doe.gov). RESFEN is a computer program for calculating the annual cooling and heating energy use and costs due to window selection and is available from Lawrence Berkeley National Laboratory (windows.lbl.gov/software/resfen). See Appendix A for pricing and modeling assumptions.

and doors are typically responsible for a significant amount of the air leakage in homes. In extreme conditions, depending on the window type and quality, air leakage can be responsible for as much heat loss or gain as the rest of the window. Tight sealing and weatherstripping of windows, sash, and frames is of paramount importance in controlling air leakage.

The use of good-quality fixed windows helps to reduce air leakage because these windows are easier to seal and keep tight. Operable windows are necessary for ventilation, but they are also more susceptible to air leakage. Operable window units with low air-leakage rates are characterized by good design and high-quality construction and weatherstripping. They also feature mechanical closures that positively clamp the window shut against the wind. For this reason, compression-seal windows such as awning, hopper, and casement designs are generally more effectively weatherstripped than are sliding-seal windows. Sliding windows rely on wiper-type weatherstripping, which is more subject to wear over time and can be bypassed when the window flexes under wind pressure.

The level of air leakage depends upon local climate conditions, particularly wind conditions and microclimates surrounding the house. Wind effects increase rapidly as you move away from the protection of trees, shrubs, or other buildings. Air leakage can be a significant issue in heating costs, especially where winter temperature differentials between inside and outside are quite high and during windy weather conditions. Air leakage generally plays a much lesser role relative to cooling cost, because the difference between indoor and outdoor temperatures tends to be lower and accompanied by milder winds. In very humid locations, however, air leakage can introduce a large latent cooling load.

Figure 2-16 illustrates the effect of changes in window air leakage on annual energy use in a typical house in two climates (Phoenix and Minneapolis). In general, air leakage has a greater effect on heating costs. Thus, the savings from tighter windows are more significant in a heating-dominated climate such as Minneapolis. Most industry groups and building code officials recommend air leakage values of 0.30 cfm/sq ft or lower. Even though window air leakage is not as significant as insulating value or control of solar radiation, it still can have a noticeable negative effect if windows are not tight.

Cracks and air spaces left between the window unit and the building wall can also account for considerable infiltration. Insulating and sealing these areas during construction or renovation can be very effective in controlling air leakage. A

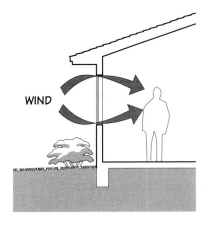

Figure 2-15. The pressure difference created by wind is a major influence on air leakage through cracks in the window assembly. Wind exposure is determined by house location and site design.

proper installation ensures that the main air barrier of the wall construction, such as house wrap material, is effectively sealed to the window, door, or skylight assembly so that continuity of the two air barriers is maintained (see Chapter 4).

The amount of air that leaks through all of the cracks in and around a window sash and frame is a function of crack length, tightness of the seals and joints, and the pressure differential between the inside and outside. American window manufacturers currently report air leakage test values as cfm/sq ft (cubic feet per minute per square foot of window area). In the past, air leakage may have been reported as cfm/lf (cubic feet per minute per lineal foot of sash crack) but this form of reporting is no longer supported.

Figure 2-16. Effect of window air leakage on annual energy performance. Most manufacturers produce windows rated at 0.30 cfm/sq ft or below. Higher leakage rates represent older window designs or windows without weatherstripping.

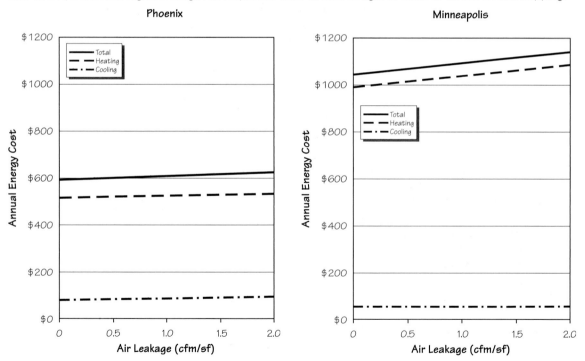

Note: The annual energy performance figures shown here were generated using RESFEN for a typical 2000 sq ft house with 300 sq ft of window area (15% of floor area). The windows are equally distributed on all four sides of the house and include typical shading (interior shades, overhangs, trees, and neighboring buildings). The heating system is a gas furnace with air-conditioning for cooling. U-factor, SHGC, and VT are for the total window including frame. The U-factor in all cases is 0.5 and the SHGC in all cases is 0.5. The gas and electric prices used in these figures are provided by the Energy Information Administration (EIA) (www.eia.doe.gov). RESFEN is a computer program for calculating the annual cooling and heating energy use and costs due to window selection and is available from Lawrence Berkeley National Laboratory (windows.lbl.gov/software/resfen). See Appendix A for pricing and modeling assumptions.

HUMAN FACTORS

Visible Transmittance

Visible transmittance is the amount of light in the visible portion of the spectrum that passes through a glazing material. This property does not directly affect heating and cooling loads in a building, but it is an important factor in evaluating energy-efficient windows. Transmittance is influenced by the glazing type, the number of layers, and any coatings that might be applied to the glazings. These effects are discussed in more detail in Chapter 3 in conjunction with a review of various glazing and coating technologies. Visible transmittance of glazings ranges from above 90 percent for water-white clear glass to less than 10 percent for highly reflective coatings on tinted glass. Typical visible transmittance values for the whole window unit and center of glass are shown in Figure 2-19.

Visible transmittance is an important factor in providing daylight, views, and privacy, as well as in controlling glare and fading of interior furnishings. These are often contradictory effects: a high light transmittance is desired for view out at night, but this may create glare at times during the day. These

Figure 2-17. Visible transmittance measures the visible light that passes through glazing.

Figure 2-18. The desire for daylight is one major influence on the design and selection of windows.
(Photo: Pella Corporation.)

49

opposing needs are often met by providing glazing that has high visible transmittance and then adding window attachments such as shades or blinds to modulate the transmittance to meet changing needs.

NFRC now reports visible transmittance as a rating on its label. Note that NFRC's rating is a whole window rating that combines the effect of both glazing and window frame. There are many cases where the transmittance of glazing alone will be required, so it is important to make sure that the appropriate properties are being compared.

Figure 2-19. Visible transmittance characteristics of typical windows.

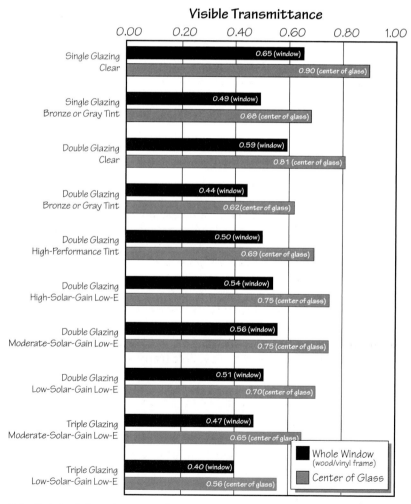

Note: All whole window values assume the glazing is in a wood or vinyl frame. Detailed descriptions of glazing and frame materials appear in Chapters 3 and 4.

Figure 2-20. Solar heat gain coefficient and visible transmittance properties for different glazings.

Glazing	Type	Whole Window		Center of Glass		
		SHGC	VT	SHGC	VT	LSG
single	clear	0.64	0.65	0.86	0.90	1.05
single	bronze or gray tint	0.54	0.49	0.73	0.68	0.93
double	clear	0.56	0.59	0.76	0.81	1.07
double	bronze or gray tint	0.47	0.44	0.62	0.62	1.00
double	high-performance tint	0.39	0.50	0.48	0.69	1.60
double	high-solar-gain low-E	0.53	0.54	0.71	0.75	1.06
double	moderate-solar-gain low-E	0.44	0.56	0.53	0.79	1.49
double	low-solar-gain low-E*	0.30	0.51	0.39	0.70	1.80
triple	moderate-solar-gain low-E	0.38	0.47	0.50	0.65	1.30
triple	low-solar-gain low-E*	0.25	0.40	0.33	0.56	1.70

* also known as "spectrally selective"
SHGC = solar heat gain coefficient, VT = visible transmittance, LSG = light-to-solar-gain ratio (VT/SHGC)

Note: Whole window values are based on glazing with a wood or vinyl frame. The data presented here are averages of similar (but not identical) products from several manufacturers. Specific products will have performance properties slightly higher or lower. Users are encouraged to check with specific manufacturers for product specific NFRC performance properties.

In the past, windows that reduced solar gain (with tints and coatings) also reduced visible transmittance. However, new high-performance tinted glass and low-solar-gain low-E coatings have made it possible to reduce solar heat gain with little reduction in visible transmittance. Because the concept of separating solar gain control and light control is so important, the light-to-solar-gain ratio (LSG) has been developed. Values for typical glazings are listed in Figure 2-20.

The LSG ratio is defined as a ratio between visible transmittance (VT) and solar heat gain coefficient (SHGC). For example, a double-glazed unit with clear glass has a visible transmittance (VT) of 0.81 and a solar heat gain coefficient (SHGC) of 0.76, so the LSG is VT/SHGC = 1.07. Bronze-tinted glass in a double-glazed unit has a visible transmittance of 0.62 and a solar heat gain coefficient of 0.62, which results in an LSG ratio of 1.00. This illustrates that while the bronze tint lowers the SHGC, it lowers the VT even more compared to clear glass. The double-glazed unit with a high performance tint has a relatively high VT of 0.69 but a lower SHGC of 0.48, resulting in an LSG of 1.44—significantly better than the bronze tint. A double-glazed unit with a low solar gain low-E coating reduces the SHGC significantly to 0.39 but retains a relatively high VT of 0.70, producing an LSG ratio of 1.79—far superior to those for clear or tinted glass.

Glare Control

Although daylight is generally desirable, too much direct light, especially through smaller openings, can result in uncomfortable glare. Glare problems result when the light source is much brighter than the surrounding room surfaces. Providing good visual comfort should be a priority in rooms that are used for demanding visual tasks, such as home offices. If a window that reduces visible transmittance is chosen, then the potential for glare will be reduced as well. However, the goal is often to provide as much daylight as possible while controlling glare problems. This can be handled in the architectural design of the space as well as by the use of overhangs, diffusing curtains, or shades. Some techniques for managing daylight and controlling glare are described in Chapter 5. Note that the NFRC transmittance value (VT) accounts for the effect of the frame as well as the glazing in blocking light.

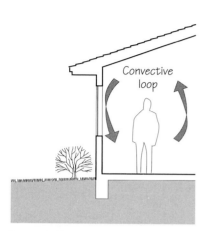

Figure 2-22. Drafts occur as air next to the window is cooled and drops to the floor. It is then replaced by warmer air from the ceiling creating a convective loop.

Thermal Comfort

A prospective window buyer may be persuaded to purchase energy-efficient products based on the energy they save, but the comfort provided by high-efficiency windows is an even more persuasive selling point. Although energy-efficient windows can make up for their cost premium by savings on energy bills, the increased thermal comfort they offer in winter and summer is a benefit that begins immediately. Furthermore, the thermal comfort of a space directly affects the quality of the space and its usefulness. Monitoring studies on houses with efficient windows invariably elicit comments such as, "I could sit next to the windows on a cold night without having to wear a heavy sweater!"

Thermal comfort is determined by air temperature, humidity, air movement, mean radiant temperature, and the presence of direct solar radiation. Surface temperatures in a room, which determine the mean radiant temperature, can have a big effect on thermal comfort. Even when room air is maintained at a comfortable temperature, occupants may experience significant discomfort as a result of radiant heat exchange with window surfaces. Window surface temperatures fluctuate much more significantly than those from other surfaces in a room. As a result, windows have the potential to "make or break" the thermal comfort of a space. Generally in winter, the more efficient a window is, the less the window surface temperature will deviate from the conditioned room air temperature and the less discomfort an occupant will feel.

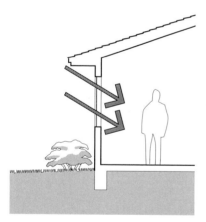

Figure 2-23. In summer, strong direct sunlight strikes people and interior surfaces, creating overheating and discomfort.

Sources of Discomfort from Windows

Windows affect human comfort in several ways. On a cold winter night, exterior temperatures will drive window interior glass surface temperatures down below the room air temperature; how low the glass temperature drops depends on the insulating quality of the window. If people are exposed to the effects of a cold surface, they experience significant radiant heat loss to that cold surface and they feel uncomfortable, even in the presence of comfortable room air temperatures. The closer they are to a window, the more they will feel its influence. The fact that this heat loss occurs on one side of the body more than the other is called radiant asymmetry, and this leads to further discomfort. A familiar example of radiant asymmetry is the experience of sitting around a campfire on a winter night. The side of the body facing the fire is hot, while the side facing away is cold. With the case of a cold window, a person may be cold in warm clothes in a 70°F room air temperature if part of the body is losing heat to a cold window.

Drafts near windows are the second major source of winter discomfort. Many people falsely attribute drafts to leaky windows when in fact they are the result of cold air patterns initiated by cold window surfaces. Air next to the window is cooled and drops to the floor. It is then replaced by warmer air from the ceiling, which in turn is cooled. This sets up an air movement pattern that feels drafty and accelerates heat loss. Cold temperature induced drafts occur at the same time as radiant discomfort. This emphasizes the need for insulating windows that maximize interior glass surface temperatures under cold environmental conditions.

Drafts can also be caused by leaky windows. These leaks can be a result of poor installation and/or ineffective weatherstripping. Such drafts are directly correlated to air infiltration levels. Radiant heat loss, convective currents from cold window surfaces, and drafts from air infiltration leaks all cause people to turn up thermostats. However, as explained above, this action has little effect on increasing comfort levels.

Directly transmitted solar radiation has fairly obvious impacts on thermal comfort as well. During cold periods, solar radiation (within limits) can be a pleasant sensation. During warm weather, however, it is invariably a significant detractor to comfort. People often close blinds to prevent sunlight from entering even though this means they can no longer enjoy the view from the window. Just as people turn up the heat in response to cold windows in winter, they may

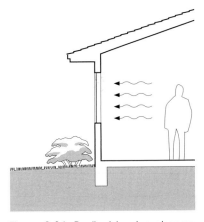

Figure 2-24. Radiant heat exchange (loss) can occur at the window surface.

use air-conditioning to counter the effects of warm window surfaces and sunlight in summer. If air conditioners are not sized or installed properly, some areas of a room may become comfortable while others will not, causing significant waste of energy.

Solar radiation will increase the surface temperature of the glass. How much the surface temperature increases depends on the absorptance of the glass and the environmental conditions. Typical clear glass windows do not absorb enough solar radiation to make a significant difference in their temperature. With tinted glass, surface temperature increases can be significant. While poorly insulated tinted glass can actually feel quite comfortable on a cold sunny day, this practice is not recommended—the comfort consequences at night and on hot summer days can be disastrous. During the summer, the interior surface temperatures of tinted glass and clear glass with tinted film can get hot. Some tinted glass surfaces get as hot as 140°F. These surfaces radiate heat to building occupants and can also create convection drafts of warm air that can cause discomfort.

Quantifying Discomfort

Quantifying human comfort is a difficult task and the subject of much current research. Typically, thermal comfort experiments are conducted on a large number of human subjects

Figure 2-25. Comparison of inside glass surface temperature for different glazing types at 20°F and 0°F outside temperatures and 70°F interior air temperature.

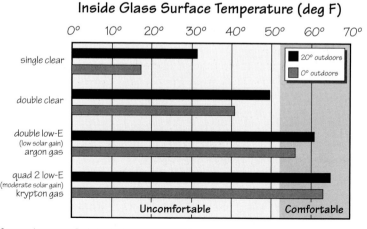

Source: Lawrence Berkeley National Laboratory.

who report their comfort levels under widely varying conditions in a lab set up to represent a room or office. Crude guidelines exist for the most basic causes of discomfort under static conditions.

For example, ASHRAE Standard 55 (the North American comfort standard) suggests that surface temperatures under 50°F or over 90°F will lead to radiant discomfort. Other factors to consider are how many hours per year the user will experience this discomfort, how well the individual tolerates discomfort, clothing levels, distance from the window, and the ability of the HVAC system to meet peak conditions.

Figure 2-25 indicates the glass surface temperatures for several typical window products at outside temperatures of 20°F and 0°F. When it's cold outside, the window's interior surface temperature drops. How far it drops depends on the window's insulating value. The surface temperature of single glazing, for example, is only 10–15°F higher than outdoor temperatures. The interior surface temperature of clear double glazing is much warmer but still significantly lower than room air temperature. The double-glazed window with a low-emissivity (low-E) coating and argon gas fill has an interior surface temperature that is warmer still. The window with three to four glazing layers, multiple low-E coatings, and gas fills has interior glass surface temperatures very close to the indoor air temperature. The two high-performance windows in Figure 2-25 provide glass temperatures in the comfort range, while clear single and double-glazed windows do not. Frames, which can make up 10–30 percent of the area of a typical window, also have noticeable effects; surface temperatures of insulating frames will be much warmer than those of highly conductive frames.

The comparison in Figure 2-25 represents a very conservative approach since it does not consider asymmetrical radiant discomfort or any accompanying drafts. In reality, many people will feel uncomfortable from these other factors in the lower end of the comfortable area. From this comparison, we can project that in most northern climates, low-emissivity coated double-glazed windows are good insurance against winter discomfort.

Another way to quantify discomfort is through the percentage of people who report discomfort. Figures 2-26 and 2-27 show the probability of discomfort for standard ASHRAE Winter (cold night) and Summer (hot sunny day) conditions. In both cases, efficient windows significantly reduce the probability of discomfort. Note that when using these

Figure 2-26. Probability of discomfort near window in winter.

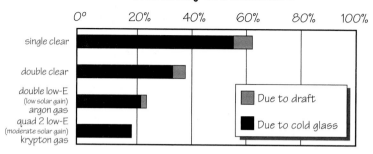

Source: Lawrence Berkeley National Laboratory.

Figure 2-27. Probability of discomfort near window in summer.

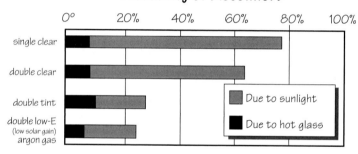

Source: Lawrence Berkeley National Laboratory.

comfort rating procedures, it is never possible for everyone to be comfortable—at best 10 percent of a group of people will always consider themselves uncomfortable.

Comparing Windows Based on Thermal Comfort

The importance of any measure of thermal comfort must be put into perspective. The climate will determine to what extent either winter or summer comfort will be a priority. In addition, thermal comfort will matter more in situations where window areas are larger and when people will be seated close to the windows.

To enable comparisons between windows, the Center for the Built Environment at University of California Berkekley has proposed a method for determining a Winter and Summer Thermal Comfort Index shown in Figure 2-28 (Huizenga et al. 2006). The Winter Comfort Index represents the minimum exterior temperature that will provide indoor comfort for a given window. As shown in Figure 2-29, the index is nearly 60°F for single glazing (U=1.02). This means that the window has the potential to be uncomfortable at outdoor temperatures below this level. The index for double glazing (U=0.48) is reduced to 44.2°F and clear triple glazing (U=0.30) is reduced to 28.2°F. Double glazing with either high- or low-solar-gain low-E coatings further reduce the Winter Comfort Index to 20.8°F and 16.7°F. Triple glazed low-E options perform the best with Winter Comfort Indices of -18.4 to -21.5°F meaning that they remain comfortable as long as it is above these subzero temperatures.

The Summer Comfort Index developed by the Center for the Built Environment can be determined two ways, The first approach only includes diffuse solar radiation, assuming a person in direct sunlight would either move or adjust the shades in the room. The second approach includes direct as well as diffuse solar radiation. The diffuse rating is shown and discussed here. As shown in Figure 2-30, the Summer Comfort Index is around 1.00 for clear glazings whether they are single-, double- or triple-glazed units (SHGC=0.60-0.80). Bronze-tinted single-glazing (SHGC=0.62) actually has a worse Summer Comfort Index (1.06) than the clear glazings because of its increased heat absorption and surface temperature. Different types of low-E coatings perform very differently in terms of summer comfort. Double-glazing with a high solar-gain low-E coating (SHGC=0.59) has a Summer Comfort Index of 1.00 while a double-glazed unit with a low-solar-gain low-E coat-

Figure 2-28. Winter and Summer Comfort Index for typical windows.

GLAZING	U-factor	SHGC	VT	Winter Comfort Index Minimum Exterior Temp. (°F)	Summer Comfort Index Diffuse	Summer Comfort Index Direct
single, clear	1.02	0.82	0.883	59.5	0.99	0.89
single, bronze	1.02	0.62	0.53	59.5	1.06	0.80
double, clear	0.48	0.70	0.79	44.2	1.01	0.83
double, high gain low-E	0.32	0.59	0.75	20.8	1.00	0.76
double, low gain low-E	0.30	0.36	0.67	16.7	0.53	0.43
triple, clear	0.30	0.62	0.70	28.2	1.06	0.80
triple, high gain low-E	0.16	0.45	0.65	-18.4	0.82	0.60
triple, low gain low-E	0.16	0.31	0.58	-21.5	0.51	0.39

Source: Center for the Built Environment, 2006 (Huizenga et al.).

Figure 2-29. Winter Comfort Index for typical windows.

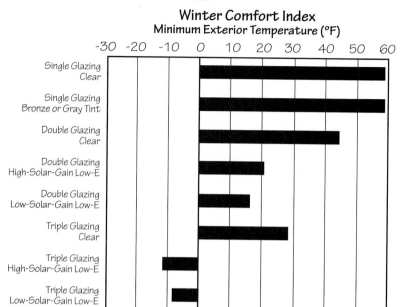

Source: Center for the Built Environment, 2006 (Huizenga et al.).

Figure 2-30. Summer Comfort Index for typical windows.

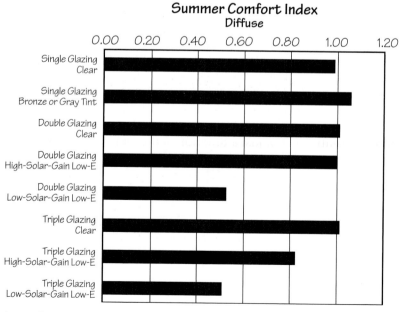

Source: Center for the Built Environment, 2006 (Huizenga et al.).

ing (SHGC=0.36) has a much lower Summer Comfort Index of 0.53. In triple-glazed units, the high-solar-gain low-E unit (SHGC=0.45) improves to a Summer Comfort Index of 0.82 but is still well above the 0.51 index for low-solar-gain low-E (SHGC=0.31).

It is better to install efficient windows than to rely on heating, ventilation, and air-conditioning (HVAC) systems to solve thermal comfort problems. Not only do HVAC systems often create nonuniform interior conditions, only partially relieving thermal discomfort, but power outages on peak days can lead to extremely uncomfortable conditions.

A window with poor energy-performance characteristics will also be an uncomfortable window. A window with good energy-performance characteristics will generally provide greater thermal comfort than a poorer energy performer. Paying more for better-performing windows is often viewed only in relationship to fuel cost savings; however, thermal comfort is a clear benefit and should be considered an additional value worth paying for when selecting windows. There is little point in spending money to improve or add a room that is unusable at times because of thermal comfort problems.

Ventilation

Another consideration related to windows and skylights is ventilation. The ventilation capability of a window unit is based on the opening size and the frame operating type. Hinged windows (casements, awnings, and hoppers) can be opened so that the full window area provides ventilation. Roof windows are another example of a hinged unit. Sliding windows (double hung and horizontal sliders) only can be opened to provide ventilation through about half of the total window area. A sliding sash does not have this problem but offers reduced ventilation. The ability of a window to provide good ventilation is not just a function of the window unit, but is more strongly influenced by the placement of the windows in relationship to breezes and the other windows, as well as the house layout. Chapter 5 addresses ventilation strategies in window and skylight placement. Ventilation is a concern in selecting windows and skylights mainly in terms of the opening size and frame operating type. Issues of window placement are part of the design, not the selection, process.

Figure 2-31. Providing ventilation is a basic window function that influences design and selection.
(Photo: JELD-WEN, Inc.)

Sound Control

The acoustical properties of windows are tied very closely to technologies for infiltration control and to some degree to technologies for heat loss control. A side benefit to houses with tight, insulated windows is that they are dramatically quieter than older homes with leaky, single-pane windows. This reduction in noise transmission from outside to inside can be a major benefit for homes in noisy locations or to occupants who value privacy and quiet.

The most significant step which can be taken to reduce sound transmission is to minimize air infiltration. Using tight-fitting products will make a significant difference over moderate or poorly sealed products. Care should be taken to ensure that the windows are properly installed to minimize infiltration between the wall and the window frame. Windows that latch shut against a compression seal (like casement windows) are much tighter than operator types that slide against one another (like double-hung windows or horizontal sliders).

Beyond minimizing air infiltration and using double glazing to decrease direct transmission, there are a number of steps that can be taken to further reduce direct sound transmission; they are listed below. These techniques often are custom features that add to the cost of the product.

- wide air/gas gaps between glazings (5/8-inch or greater instead of the usual 1/2-inch or less)

- replacing air with argon, krypton, or SF_6 between the glazings

- a 1/4-inch-thick exterior light with an inner light of a different thickness (often laminated with 1/8-inch or 3/16-inch-thick glass)

- triple glazing with varying glass thicknesses including glass greater than 1/8-inch thick

Sound transmission ratings are helpful in evaluating acoustics issues but may or may not be exactly pertinent to determining sound transmission through windows (AAMA, 1997). ASTM Standard E 413, developed in 1970 as a method for determining a Sound Transmission Class (STC) for products, dramatically simplified the process of comparing the acoustic performance of different products. Although the numerical values in this standard "correlate in a general way with subjective impressions of sound transmission for speech, radio, television and similar sources of noise in offices and buildings," they are not appropriate for other sources such as machinery, industrial processes, and transportation (motor vehicles, aircraft, trains, etc.). Specifically, the STC system is not accurate for incident sound that is dominated by low-frequency energy (125 Hz and below), which is characteristic of "railways, airport and highway noise" (AAMA TIR A1-02).

ASTM Standard E 1332 was developed in the late 1980s for comparing product performance for lower-frequency sound sources—80 to 4,000 Hz, with particular attention to the 80 to 100 Hz range that is typically the objectionable portion of the sound emanating from aircraft, trains, and traffic. This standard determines the Outdoor-Indoor Transmission Class (OITC) of a product. Many existing products rated for STC exhibit better performance against mid- and high-frequency incident sound; an OITC rating for the same products may be 5 to 10 points lower if low-frequency sound is a dominant concern in the product's performance. Given the differences in STC and OITC ratings, architects or specifiers would be wise to require products with an OITC rating for installations that are near transportation noise sources.

TECHNICAL PROPERTIES

Condensation Resistance

Condensation has been a persistent and often misunderstood problem associated with windows. In cold climates, single-glazed windows characteristically suffer from water condensation and the formation of frost on the inside surface of the glass in winter. The surface temperature of the glass drops below either the dew point or frost point of the inside room air. Frost patterns on the windows were often one of the first signs of approaching winter.

Excessive condensation can contribute to the growth of mold or mildew, damage painted surfaces, and eventually rot wood trim. Since the interior humidity level is a contributing factor, reducing interior humidity is an important component of controlling condensation. This is done by first removing humidity at its source—with vent fans in kitchens and bathrooms and limited use of humidifiers. Then, the remaining humid air can be diluted with drier outside air. In tight, newer houses an air-to-air heat exchanger is often required for ventilation and accomplishes humidity removal as well. Finally, dehumidification can be used if necessary.

Condensation can also be a problem on the interior surfaces of window frames. Metal frames, in particular, conduct heat very quickly, and will "sweat" or frost up in cold weather. Solving this condensation problem was a major motivation for the development of thermal breaks for aluminum windows (see Chapter 4).

Infiltration effects can also combine with condensation to create problems. If a path exists for warm, moisture-laden air to move through or around the window frames, the moisture will condense wherever it hits its dewpoint temperature, often inside the building wall. This condensation can contribute to the growth of mold in frame or wall cavities, causing health problems for some people, and it encourages the rotting or rusting of window frames. Frames must be properly sealed within the wall opening to prevent this potential problem.

Condensation can cause problems in skylights and roof windows as well as typical windows. "Leaky" skylights are frequently misdiagnosed. What are perceived to be drops of water from a leak are more often drops of water condensing on the cold skylight surfaces. A skylight is usually the first place condensation will occur indicating too much moisture in the interior air. Insulating the skylight well and providing adequate air movement assists in reducing condensation. Also, the use of more highly insulating glazing with a well designed frame can help solve this problem. In many systems, a small "gutter" is formed into the interior frame of the skylight where condensate can collect harmlessly until it evaporates back into the room air.

Impact of Glazing Type and Spacers on Condensation

Figure 2-32 indicates condensation potential for four glazing types at various outdoor temperature and indoor relative humidity conditions. Condensation can occur at any point that fall on or above the curves. As the U-factor of glass improves, there is a much smaller range of conditions where condensation will occur. Figure 2-32 must be used with caution since it shows condensation potential for the center of glass area only (the area at least 2.5 inches from the frame/glass edge). Usually condensation will first occur at the lower edge of the window where glass temperatures are lower than in the center.

As Figure 2-32 shows, double-glazed windows create a warmer interior glass surface than single-glazing, reducing frost and condensation. The addition of low-E coatings and argon gas fill further reduce condensation potential. The triple-glazed window with low-E coatings and insulating frames has such a warm interior surface that condensation on any interior surfaces may be eliminated if humidity levels are maintained at reasonable levels.

Figure 2-33 shows interior patterns of condensation potential on three window types: (1) clear double glazing with a standard aluminum spacer, (2) double glazing with a low-E coating and a low-conductivity foam spacer, and (3) triple glazing with two low-E coatings and a low-conductivity foam spacer. Each window type is shown three times, representing different outdoor temperature conditions (-20°F [-29°C], 0°F [-18°C], and 20°F [-7°C]). Within each figure are areas indicating where condensation will occur at three different levels of indoor relative humidity (30, 50, and 70 percent). Figure 6-11 illustrates that the temperature at the glass edge or the frame is lower than at the center of glass. Condensation forms at the coldest locations, such as the lower corners or edges of an insulated window even when the center of glass is

Example 1: At 20°F (-7°C) outside temperature, condensation will form on the inner surface of double glazing any time the indoor relative humidity is 52% or higher. It will form at an indoor relative humidity of 70 percent or higher if a double-pane window with low-E and argon is used.

Example 2: In a cold climate where winter night temperatures drop to -10°F (-23°C), we want to maintain 65% humidity without condensation. A double-glazed window with low-E and argon will show condensation at 57% relative humidity, so the triple glazing with two low-E coatings and argon is needed to prevent condensation.

Figure 2-32. Condensation for typical glazing types.

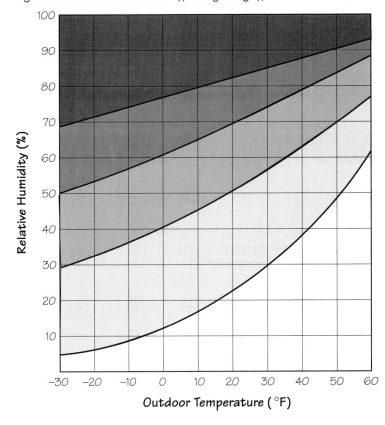

Condensation for typical glazing types occur at points in the following shaded areas on the graph.

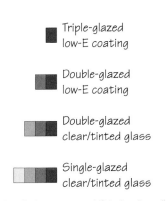

■ Triple-glazed low-E coating

■ Double-glazed low-E coating

Double-glazed clear/tinted glass

Single-glazed clear/tinted glass

Note: all air spaces are 1/2 inch; all coatings are e = 0.10.

Figure 2-33. Area on a glazing unit where condensation will form for different glazing types at three temperatures and three levels of indoor relative humidity.

Double insulating glass unit with clear glass and aluminum spacer

Outdoor temperature: -20°F

Outdoor temperature: 0°F

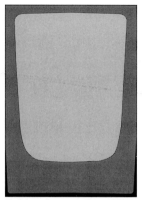
Outdoor temperature: 20°F

Double insulating glass unit with low-E coating and foam spacer

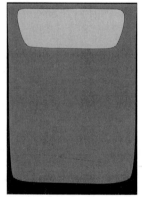
Outdoor temperature: -20°F

Outdoor temperature: 0°F

Outdoor temperature: 20°F

Condensation occurs at or above the following indoor conditions:

Triple insulating glass unit with two low-E coatings and foam spacer

Outdoor temperature: -20°F

Outdoor temperature: 0°F

Outdoor temperature: 20°F

above the limit for condensation. Generally, as the insulating value of the glazing is improved, the area where condensation can occur is diminished. As expected, condensation potential increases as the outdoor temperature is lowered and the indoor relative humidity increases.

Condensation Rating

Both the National Fenestration Rating Council (NFRC) and the American Architectural Manufacturers Association (AAMA) have developed systems for rating the condensation resistance (CR) of fenestration products.

AAMA 1503, developed in the 1970s, gives a dimensionless rating, the Condensation Resistance Factor (CRF), ranging from 0 to 100; the higher the number, the better a product resists forming condensation. Adopted in 2002, NFRC 500 determines Condensation Resistance (CR) based on computer simulation. The rating value is based on interior surface temperatures at 30 percent, 50 percent, and 70 percent indoor relative humidity for a given outside air temperature of 0 degrees Fahrenheit under 15 mph wind conditions.

Computer simulation can be used to model the expected performance of fenestration in buildings and optimize designs for condensation resistance. WINDOW 5 and THERM 5, developed by the Lawrence Berkeley National Laboratory for the United States Department of Energy, can simulate U-factors for fenestration products as outlined in NFRC 100. The surface temperatures calculated by the software can also be input to the equations in NFRC 500 to determine the potential CR rating of a proposed design.

The CR rating now appears on the NFRC label. Figure 2-34 shows the CR for a range of double-glazed windows. The CR is a function of the frame, spacer and glazing type—a higher CR is better. The worst performance occurs with non-thermally broken aluminum frames where the CR falls in a range of 10 to 23 regardless of glazing type. The CR for aluminum frames with thermal breaks is higher—in the range of 30 to 42. The greater insulating value of wood and vinyl frames results in even better consdensation performance resistance. Because the wood or vinyl frame is no longer the dominant factor, the glazing type affects the CR to a greater degree. With clear glass, the CR range is 35-48 while with low-E glazings, the range is 40 to 60. The wide range in CR reflects differences in types of low-E coatings and spacers. Even better performance can be achieved with wood or vinyl framed triple-glazed low-E window units where a CR of 65 to 70 is possible.

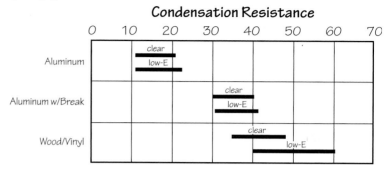

Figure 2-34. Condensation Resistance Ratings (CR) for various frame and glazing types.

Outdoor Condensation

Under some climate conditions, condensation may occur on the exterior glass surface of a window. This is more likely to occur on higher-performance windows with low-E coatings or films, and low-conductance gas fills that create very low U-factors. By preventing heat from escaping from the interior, the exterior surfaces of the window approach outside air temperatures. These exterior temperatures may be below the exterior dew point causing condensation on the glass surfaces. This is most likely to happen when there is a clear night sky, still air, and high relative humidity, in addition to the right temperature conditions. Like other dew formed at night, exterior window condensation will disappear as surfaces are warmed by the sun. It is the excellent thermal performance of well-insulated glazing that creates the condition where the outer glass surface can be cold enough to cause condensation to form.

Condensation Between Glazings

A more annoying problem can arise with double-pane windows: condensation between the panes. Moisture can migrate into the space between the panes of glass and condense on the colder surface of the exterior pane. This condensation is annoying not only because it clouds the view and stains the interior glass surfaces, but because it may mean that the glazing unit must be replaced (if it is a sealed insulating glass unit). In a nonsealed unit, simpler remedies may correct the situation.

Factory-sealed insulated glass utilizes a permanent seal to prevent the introduction of moisture. The void may be filled with air or dry gases, such as argon. A desiccant material in the edge spacer between the panes is used to absorb any residual moisture in the unit when it is fabricated or any small amount that might migrate into the unit over many years. These windows will fog up when moisture leaking into the air space through the seals overwhelms the ability of the desiccant to absorb it. This could happen early in the window's life (the first few years) if there is a manufacturing defect, or many decades later because of diffusion through the sealant. Quality control in manufacture, sealant selection, window design, and even installation all can influence the rate of failure. Once a sealed window unit fails, it is not generally possible to fix it, and the sealed unit must be replaced. Moisture in the unit is also likely to reduce the effectiveness of low-E coatings and suggests that gas fills may be leaking out. Most manufacturers offer a warranty against sealed-glass failure which varies from a limited period to the lifetime of the window.

When condensation occurs between glazings in a nonsealed unit, there are several possible remedies. Most manufacturers who offer nonsealed double glazing include a small tube connecting the air space to the outside air, which tends to be dry during winter months. Check to be sure that the inner glazing seals tightly to the sash, and clear the air tube if it has become obstructed. In some cases, reducing interior room humidity levels may help alleviate the problem.

Fading Resistance

Many organic materials, such as carpet, fabrics, paper, artwork, paints, and wood may fade upon exposure to sunlight. The potential for damage largely depends on: (1) the nature of the materials and dyes in the materials; (2) the type of radiation (UV, daylight) to which they are subjected; (3) the intensity of radiation; and (4) the duration of exposure. Window selection can influence the type and intensity of transmitted radiation. The most harmful radiation in sunlight are the ultraviolet (UV) rays, which are the most energetic and thus most likely to break chemical bonds, leading to fading and degradation. However, the blue end of the visible spectrum can also contribute to fading. Window companies often use different criteria for reporting the ability of a window to stop transmission of damaging wavelengths of radiation. Some report UV alone while others report damage weighted transmission. A method for determining the damage-weighted transmission has been developed that is a more accurate reflection of the true fading effects through glazing than just a measure of the UV transmission alone (Krochmann 1978). Figure 2-35 illustrates the damage-weighted transmission through several types of glazing with and without plastic laminates. Damage-weighted transmission represents the average effect on a group of materials. Fading effects on a particular material (such as artwork) can vary from the average. Although the damage-weighted method is one of the best available indicators, there is not yet an agreed-upon rating procedure in the U.S. for fading from sunlight.

The amount of harmful UV and visible radiation depends on a variety of climatic factors, such as water vapor levels and pollution in the atmosphere. Glass blocks all UV radiation below 300 nm, but transmits UV from 300–380 nm. Coatings on glass can reduce the UV transmitted by up to 75 percent. UV absorbers can be incorporated into thin plastic films in multilayer windows or as an interlayer in laminated glass. In both cases, the UV transmission can be reduced to less than 1 percent. However, it is important to note that the remaining

Figure 2-35. Comparison of damage-weighted transmission for different glazing types.

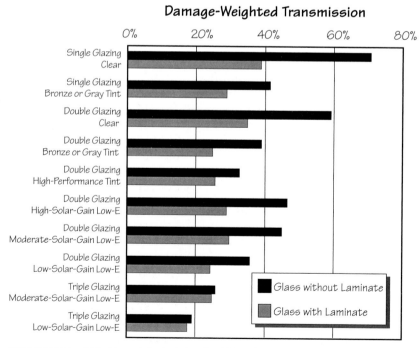

Note: Damage-weighted transmission includes ultraviolet and visible light (Krochmann 1978). All values are for glazing unit only without frame. Detailed descriptions of glazing appear in Chapter 3.
Source: Lawrence Berkeley National Laboratory.

visible light that is transmitted can still cause serious fading in some materials. Using low-E coated glass or windows incorporating plastic layers rather than clear uncoated glass will reduce fading for many modern interior furnishings. However, none of these strategies will provide complete protection from fading. Place valuable artifacts that are highly susceptible to fading in hallways or other spaces without exposure to substantial window area, or in rooms that have appropriate drapes and shades to substantially reduce daylight transmittance. Museum conservators limit light levels to less than 150 lux, or only 1/700 the level of bright sunlight, to protect artwork.

Durability

The durability of a window or skylight directly affects its energy performance. If, for example, insulating glass seals or low-emissivity coatings fail, a product's thermal performance will be seriously compromised. Durability denotes a product's ability to perform as designed over a period of time. Important elements of a fenestration product's durability include the ability to resist condensation and air and water infiltration while maintaining thermal and structural performance as well as aesthetic features.

The durability of a proposed fenestration design can best be assessed in accelerated weathering tests as well as field studies. These tests, typically conducted over extended time periods, determine whether a window system can meet the demands of weather and temperature differences that it will likely encounter during its lifetime. Window systems rather than individual components are typically tested. Suppliers and manufacturers also examine the durability of materials, components, and assemblies with positive and negative pressure cycling tests, temperature cycling, and motion testing.

Impact of Durability Issues on Energy Performance

A durable window system will meet its energy performance criteria—U-factor, solar heat gain coefficient, and air infiltration parameters—over time. Failure of components such as sealants and gaskets will degrade thermal performance and may lead to loss of insulating gas in units with gas infill, in addition to permitting air and water to penetrate the glazing system and the building. The National Fenestration Rating Council is in the process of developing long-term durability test procedures aimed at determining the effects of individual physical weathering and durability impacts on specific product

U-factors, solar heat gain coefficients, air-infiltration rates, and condensation resistance.

The durability of insulating glass units is critical to maintaining the energy performance of window and door assemblies. Minimum performance levels have been established in the United States and Canada requiring that insulating glass units conform to ASTM E 2190 or CAN/CGSB 12.8. Proof of compliance may be by a test report from an independent accredited laboratory or by certification of the IGU by IGMA, IGCC, ALI or another certifying agency acceptable to the specifier. These certification programs require compliance with the performance standards and the establishment of a reliable quality control program at the manufacturing plant. The IGMA technical manual, TM-4000-02 "Insulating Glass Manufacturing Quality Procedure Manual", and IGU certification represents a significant increase in quality assurance requirements for the manufacture of insulating glass.

The IGMA quality assurance provisions, or equivalent, should be the minimum level of quality assurance acceptable for IGU production. However, there are a number of quality assurance provisions that are referenced in ISO EN 1279—which should be considered by the manufacturer. Standards related to durability and durability testing are listed in the references. Most of these standards relate to the durability of individual components (such as IGU sealants) or impacts from specific conditions (such as seismic and wind).

There is no simple rating or absolute guarantee of the durability of a window. Just as in making any other important choices, the designer or homeowner must study the design and workmanship of the window, and then rely on the recommendations from others who have used similar products and the manufacturer's reputation. The advice of experienced architects and builders can be helpful to the homeowner. As with other products, warranties can be an indicator of the reliability of the window and its manufacturer. Durability may vary with location; for example, some materials are degraded by salt near the ocean.

Figure 2-37. Design and workmanship of an energy-efficient window is important when durability is an important factor. (Photo: Pella Corporation.)

Maintenance

Older windows with wood exposed on the exterior require periodic painting and replacement of the glazing compound that holds the glass in place. Newer windows made with vinyl or metal frames or cladding over the wood frame require very little exterior maintenance. If the exterior frame material is wood, then the cost and effort of periodic painting should be considered in selecting a window. However, many new wood windows have a very durable exterior finish, applied in the factory, which is far better than traditional paint finishes.

Structural Capability and Water Resistance

Windows available on the market must meet numerous standards and building regulations, so basic structural characteristics are not of direct concern to the homeowner selecting a window. In special cases, such as a building in a hurricane-prone area, building codes may require glazing of a certain strength and type to resist breakage during storm conditions. Laminated glass is often used in these cases (see Chapter 3).

Preventing water transmission and minimizing unwanted air movement are prime requirements of windows and other fenestration products. Uncontrolled water can destroy window and door framing members, destroy or deteriorate interior furnishings, promote the growth of mold and mildew, and deteriorate the elements of walls and wall cavities found below window- and doorsills. Manufactured window units are designed to prevent water intrusion and if it does occur, divert it to the exterior. Water that appears to be the result of leaking windows and doors is often a result of penetration at another location. The vast majority of field calls for water leakage are actually due to poor installation. Installation is discussed in Chapter 4.

If the consumer is selecting windows without the input of a contractor or architect, the local building code should be reviewed to determine requirements for wind load resistance and water penetration resistance. Organizations such as AAMA and WDMA provide these standards (see Appendix D) as do local building departments.

CHAPTER 3

Window Glazing Materials

The remarkable advances in the performance of windows in recent years are based mainly on technological developments in glass coatings and insulated glazing assemblies. The first section of the chapter defines key properties of glazing that affect energy performance: transmittance, reflectance, absorptance, and emittance. The next sections describe standard and advanced glazing materials that are currently on the market. Then the ongoing developments of specialty and experimental glazings are discussed. Finally, we look at the use of thermograms (surface temperature maps) to illustrate relative window performance.

The overall energy performance of a window assembly is dependent not only on the glazing and frame materials themselves, but on a number of architectural and interior design decisions. These include exterior features such as overhangs, awnings, screens, and other shading devices. On the interior,

Figure 3-1. Vacuum chambers are used in the production of low-emittance glass.
(Photo: Cardinal Glass Industries.)

drapes, blinds, shades, and movable insulation all contribute to the overall performance. It is interesting to note that as more advanced glazing products are used, the energy-related impact and importance of these traditional control strategies may be diminished, since the glazing itself is providing significant solar control and thermal resistance.

PROPERTIES OF GLAZING MATERIALS RELATED TO RADIANT ENERGY TRANSFER

Three things happen to solar radiation as it passes through a glazing material. Some is transmitted, some is reflected, and the rest is absorbed. These three components determine many of the other energy performance properties of a glazing material, such as the solar heat gain coefficient and shading coefficient discussed in Chapter 2. Manipulating the proportion of transmittance, reflectance, and absorptance for different wavelengths of solar radiation has been the source of much recent innovation in window energy performance.

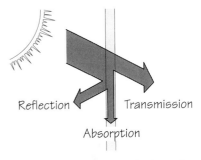

Figure 3-2. The passage of solar radiation through a glazing material.

Before the technical innovations available today existed, the primary characteristic of glass was its ability to transmit visible light. However, as attention focused on improving the total energy performance of glass, it became clear that transparency to visible light is only part of the picture.

Visible light is a small portion of the electromagnetic spectrum (Figure 3-3). Beyond the blues and purples lie ultraviolet radiation and other higher-energy short wavelengths, from X rays to gamma rays. Beyond red light are the near-infrared, given off by very hot objects, the far-infrared, given off by warm room-temperature objects, and the longer microwaves and radio waves.

Glazing types vary in their transparency to different parts of the spectrum. On the simplest level, a glass that appears to be tinted green as you look through it toward the outside will transmit more sunlight from the green portion of the visible spectrum, and absorb/reflect more of the other colors. Similarly, a bronze-tinted glass will absorb/reflect the blues and greens and transmit the warmer colors. Neutral gray tints absorb/reflect most colors equally.

This same principle applies outside the visible spectrum. Most glass is partially transparent to at least some ultraviolet radiation, while plastics are commonly more opaque to ultraviolet. Glass is opaque to far-infrared radiation but generally transparent to near-infrared. Strategic utilization of these variations has made for some very useful glazing products.

The four basic properties of glazing that affect radiant energy transfer are transmittance, reflectance, absorptance, and emittance. Each is described below, and their application in developing new products is presented later in the chapter.

Transmittance

Transmittance refers to the percentage of radiation that can pass through glazing. Transmittance can be defined for different types of light or energy, e.g., "visible transmittance," "UV transmittance," or "total solar energy transmittance." Each describes a different characteristic of the glazing.

Transmission of visible light determines the effectiveness of a type of glass in providing daylight and a clear view through

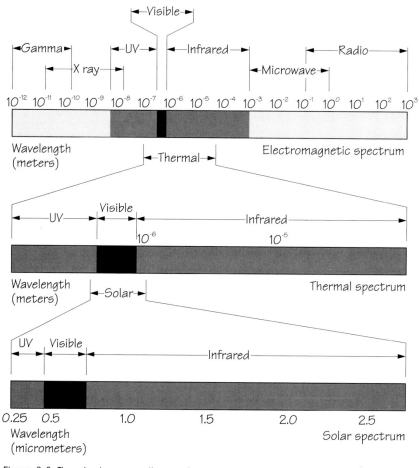

Figure 3-3. The electromagnetic spectrum.
Note the wavelength scale changes between the three charts.

the window. For example, tinted glass has a lower visible transmittance than clear glass. While the human eye is sensitive to light at wavelengths from about 0.4 to 0.7 micrometers, its peak sensitivity is at 0.55, with lower sensitivity at the red and blue ends of the spectrum. This is referred to as the photopic sensitivity of the eye.

More than half of the sun's energy is invisible to the eye and reaches us as either ultraviolet (UV) or, predominantly, as near-infrared (Figure 3-4). Thus, "total solar energy transmittance" describes how the glazing responds to a much broader part of the spectrum and is more useful in characterizing the quantity of solar energy transmitted by the glazing.

Ultraviolet radiation fades furniture, drapes, and carpets. Therefore, a reduction in the ultraviolet transmittance is typically considered a benefit. We see this in advertisements for sunglasses, but the same principles apply to windows. As noted above, most glass types are at least partially transparent to ultraviolet, while plastics tend to be more opaque to UV. Since visible light plays some role in fading as well, eliminating UV transmittance alone does not provide complete fade protection.

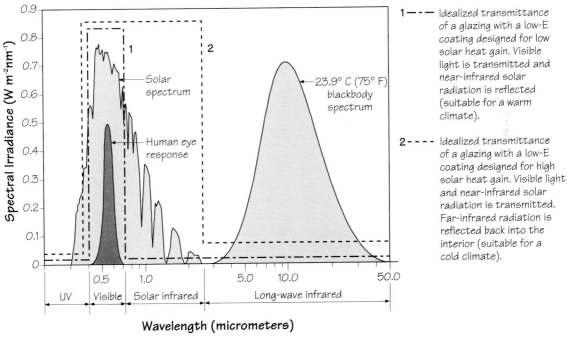

Figure 3-4. Ideal spectral transmittance for glazings in different climates. (Source: McCluney, 1996.)

Optical Properties Database

A database of solar optical properties is maintained jointly by Lawrence Berkeley National Laboratory and the National Fenestration Rating Council.

This database contains transmittance, reflectance, absorptance, and emittance for all commercially available glazings in standard thicknesses. The database is at:

windows.lbl.gov/materials/igdb

With the recent advances in glazing technology, manufacturers can control how glazing materials behave in these different areas of the spectrum. The basic properties of the substrate material (glass or plastic) can be altered, and coatings can be added to the surfaces of the substrates. For example, a window optimized for daylighting and for reducing heat gains should transmit an adequate amount of light in the visible portion of the spectrum, while excluding unnecessary heat gain from the near-infrared part of the electromagnetic spectrum. One sometimes hears of coatings that transmit "cool sunlight" meaning that the near infrared energy is rejected and only the visible light is transmitted. But since visible light is still a form of radiant energy, a glazing with high light transmittance will still contribute to cooling loads since it will be transmitting about 50 percent of total solar energy available.

On the other hand, a window optimized for collecting solar heat gain in winter should transmit the maximum amount of visible light as well as the heat from the near-infrared wavelengths in the solar spectrum, while blocking the lower-energy radiant heat in the far-infrared range that is an important heat loss component. These are the strategies of various types of low-emittance coatings, described later in the chapter.

Reflectance

Just as some light reflects off of the surface of water, some light will always be reflected at every glass surface. A specular reflection from a smooth glass surface is a mirror-like reflection similar to when you see an image of yourself in a store window. The natural reflectivity of glass is dependent on the quality of the glass surface, the presence of coatings, and the angle of incidence of the light. Today, virtually all glass manufactured in the United States is float glass and has a very similar quality with respect to reflectance. At normal incidence (sunlight striking perpendicular to the glass) standard glass reflects about 8 percent of sunlight (4 percent as the light strikes the first surface of the glass and another 4 percent as it exits the glass into the air.). The sharper the angle at which the light strikes, however, the more the light is reflected rather than transmitted or absorbed (Figure 3-5). Even for clear glass, the reflectance increases from 8 to 50 percent or more at incident angles greater than about 80 degrees. (The incident angle is formed with respect to a line perpendicular to the glass surface.)

Since coatings change surface reflectance, they can often be detected by careful examination of a reflected bright image, even if the coating is a transparent low-E coating. Hold a match several inches from a window at night and observe the reflections of the match in the glass. You will see two closely spaced images for each layer of glass, since the match reflects off the front and back surface of each layer of glass. A wider spacing between the two sets of pairs of images occurs with a wider air space between the glass panes. A subtle color shift in one of the reflected images normally indicates the presence of a low-E coating.

The reflectivity of various glass types becomes especially apparent during low light conditions. The surface on the brighter side acts like a mirror because the amount of light passing through the window from the darker side is less than the amount of light being reflected from the lighter side. This effect can be noticed from the outside during the day and from the inside during the night. For special applications when these surface reflections are undesirable (i.e., viewing merchandise through a store window on a bright day), special coatings can virtually eliminate this reflective effect.

The reflectivity of glass can be increased by applying various metallic coatings to the surface. Early processes used a liquid alloy of mercury and tin to create mirrors. A silvering process developed in 1865 improved the performance of mirrors. Today,

Figure 3-5. Sunlight transmitted and reflected by 1/8-inch (3 mm) clear glass as a function of the incident angle.

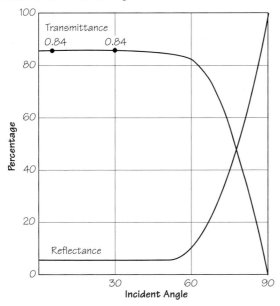

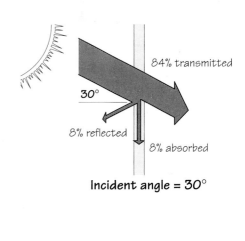

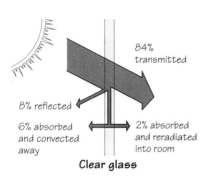

84%
transmitted

8% reflected

6% absorbed
and convected
away

2% absorbed
and reradiated
into room

Clear glass

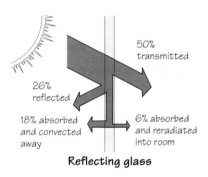

50%
transmitted

26%
reflected

18% absorbed
and convected
away

6% absorbed
and reradiated
into room

Reflecting glass

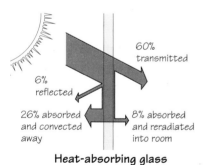

60%
transmitted

6%
reflected

26% absorbed
and convected
away

8% absorbed
and reradiated
into room

Heat-absorbing glass

Figure 3-6. Solar energy transmission through three types of glass.

mirror-like surfaces can be created by using vacuum-deposited aluminum or silver, or with a durable pyrolytic coating applied directly to the glass as it is manufactured. Thick coatings can be fully reflective and virtually opaque; a thinner coating is partially reflective and partially transmitting. "One-way glass" has such a partial metallic coating, which acts like a full mirror when viewed from the side with brighter light conditions and yet appears transparent when viewed from the side with dimmer light. This simple technology for the production of partial mirrors also led to the creation of more sophisticated reflective coatings for window glass.

Most common coatings reflect in all regions of the spectrum. However, in the past twenty years, researchers have learned a great deal about the design of coatings that can be applied to glass and plastic to reflect only selected wavelengths of radiant energy and this has now been incorporated into a wide range of products. Varying the reflectance of far-infrared and near- infrared energy has formed the basis for high-solar-gain low-E coatings for cold climates, and for low-solar-gain low-E coatings for hot climates (see later sections of this chapter).

Absorptance

Energy that is not transmitted through the glass or reflected off of its surfaces is absorbed. Once glass has absorbed any radiant energy, the energy is transformed into heat, raising the temperature of the glass. The absorbed energy ultimately finds it way through the glazing into the room, or back outdoors, depending upon the glazing system properties and the environmental conditions.

Typical 1/8-inch (3 mm) clear glass absorbs only about 8 percent of sunlight at a normal angle of incidence (also at 30° angle of incidence as shown in Figure 3-5). The absorptance of glass can be increased by using glass additives that absorb solar energy or it can be reduced by carefully extracting chemicals normally found in the materials used to make glass. If the additives absorb visible light, the glass appears darker. If they absorb ultraviolet radiation or near-infrared, there will be little or no change in visual appearance. Clear glass absorbs very little visible light, while dark tinted glass absorbs a considerable amount (Figure 3-6). The absorbed energy is converted into heat, warming the glass. Thus, when these "heat-absorbing" glasses are in the sun, they feel much hotter to the touch than clear glass. They are generally gray, bronze, or blue-green and are used primarily to lower the solar heat gain coefficient and to control glare. Since they block some of the sun's energy, they reduce the cooling load placed on the building and its air-conditioning equipment. Absorption is not the most efficient way to reduce cooling loads, as discussed later.

All glass and most plastics, however, are generally very absorptive of far-infrared energy. This property led to the use of clear glass for greenhouses, where it allowed the transmission of intense solar energy but blocked the retransmission of the low-temperature heat energy generated inside the greenhouse and radiated back to the glass.

Emittance

When heat or light energy is absorbed by glass, it is either convected away by moving air or reradiated by the glass surface. This ability of a material to radiate energy is called its emissivity. Windows, along with all other household objects, typically emit, or radiate, heat in the form of long-wave far-infrared energy. This emission of radiant heat is one of the important heat transfer pathways for a window. Thus, reducing the window's emission of heat can greatly improve its insulating properties.

Standard clear glass has an emittance of 0.84 over the long wavelength portion of the spectrum, meaning that it emits 84 percent of the energy possible for an object at its temperature. It also means that for long-wave radiation striking the surface of the glass, 84 percent is absorbed and only 16 percent is reflected. By comparison, low-E glass coatings have an emittance as low as 0.04. This glazing would emit only 4 percent of the energy possible at its temperature, and thus reflect 96 percent of the incident long-wave infrared radiation. These concepts are further discussed in the section on low-E coatings.

BASIC GLAZING MATERIALS

Two basic materials are used for window glazing: glass, which is by far the most common, and plastics, which have many specialized applications.

Glass

Traditionally, windows have been made of clear glass. The earliest clear glass, produced largely from available sand and formed into sheets with glassblowing techniques, tended to have a greenish color, entrained bubbles, and an uneven surface. As technology has advanced, the glass color has become "whiter," there are no longer visible impurities, and the surfaces have become more parallel and polished.

Most residential-grade clear glass today is produced with the float technique, described in Chapter 1, in which the glass is "floated" over a bed of molten tin. This provides extremely flat surfaces, uniform thicknesses, and few if any visual distortions. The glass has a slight greenish cast, due to iron impurities, but this is generally not noticeable except from the edge. An even higher-quality glass with reduced iron content eliminates the greenness and also provides a higher solar energy transmittance. This "low-iron" glass is commonly called "water-white glass."

Obscure glasses still transmit most of the light but break up the view in order to provide privacy, as in bathroom windows. This effect is generally achieved either with decorative embossed patterns or with a frosted surface that scatters the light rays.

With the use of additives during the float glass process, glazing can be produced in a wide variety of colors, as we know from stained glass. Glass colors are typically given trade names, but the most frequently used colors can be generally described as clear, bronze, gray, and blue-green. After clear glass, the gray glasses are most commonly used in residential construction, as they have the least effect on the perceived color of the light. Tinted glass is discussed later in the chapter.

The mechanical properties of glass can be altered, as can its basic composition and surface properties. Heat-strengthening and tempering make glass more resistant to breakage. Heat-strengthened glass is about twice as strong as standard glass. Tempered glass is produced by reheating and then quickly cooling the glass. Tempered glass is about four times as strong as annealed glass. When broken, it breaks into small fragments, rather than into long, possibly dangerous shards. Laminated glass is a sandwich of two outer layers of glass with a plastic inner layer that holds the glass pieces together in the event of breakage. Fully tempered and/or laminated glass is required by building codes in many door, skylight, and window applications.

Advanced technologies that have significantly improved the thermal performance of glass are discussed below, in the section on Improved Glazing Products.

Figure 3-7. Tempered glass is required in sliding glass doors.
(Photo: Simonton Windows.)

Plastics

Several plastic materials have been adapted for use as glazing materials. Their primary uses are windows with special requirements and skylights.

The following list of plastic glazing materials does not cover every commercially available product, but it indicates the major types of plastic glazing materials and compares their general properties:

- Clear acrylic is widely available and relatively inexpensive. It is available in various tints and colors. It has excellent visible transmittance and longevity. However, it is softer than glass, which makes it vulnerable to scratching.

- Frosted acrylic is like clear acrylic, except that it diffuses light and obscures the view. It comes in varying degrees of light transmittance. Many bubble skylights are made of frosted acrylic.

- Clear polycarbonate is like acrylic sheet, but it is harder and tougher, offering greater resistance to scratching and breakage. It is more expensive than acrylic.

- Fiber-reinforced plastic is a tough, translucent, flexible sheet material with good light-diffusing properties. Short

---

Comparison of Glass and Plastic Materials

- Glass is extremely durable and essentially maintenance-free. The surface and/or transparency of plastic may degrade with time and exposure to moisture and sunlight.

- Glass has lower thermal expansion than plastic and can readily tolerate higher or lower environmental temperatures.

- Glass is impermeable to gases and moisture and can thus be used with hermetically sealed, gas-filled insulating units. Plastics are not normally fabricated in sealed units.

- Glass and plastic can be fabricated with tints and light-diffusing properties. Rigid plastics are not normally coated, although plastic films (used inside of sealed units or applied to glass) are widely coated with low-temperature processes. Glass can be coated easily by a variety of high- and low-temperature processes.

- Plastics are less brittle than glass and do not shatter when broken. Tempered glass reduces injury potential when glass breaks. Plastics are tougher and can resist vandals. Conventional glass can be laminated with plastics to produce a wide range of burglar- and bullet-resistant glazings.

- Plastics are lighter weight than an equal thickness of glass, which reduces structural requirements for frames.

- Plastics can be formulated to screen out virtually all ultraviolet radiation (UV); glass is not UV-absorbing, although additives, coatings, and plastic laminates can provide some UV control.

- Glass is nonflammable but may break in a fire. Fire-rated glass is available. Plastics are typically flammable, may also melt in the heat of a fire, and may give off toxic fumes when they burn.

lengths of fiberglass are embedded in a polymer matrix to form flat or ribbed sheets. Stiff, insulating, translucent panels are created by bonding double layers to a metal frame and adding fiberglass insulation. It is also formed into corrugated sheets as a translucent roofing material. Surface erosion may shorten its useful life.

- Extruded multicell sheet, usually made with acrylic or polycarbonate plastic, is a transparent or tinted plastic extruded into a double- or triple-wall sheet with divider webs for stiffness, insulating value, and light diffusion.

- Polyester is a thin plastic film used to carry specialized coatings and/or to divide the air space between two layers of glass into multiple air spaces. Highly transparent, it is protected from abuse and weathering by the two exterior glass layers. It can also be used in tinted or coated forms as film that is glued to the inner surface of existing windows for retrofitting applications.

GLAZING TECHNOLOGY USED IN RESIDENTIAL CONSTRUCTION

There are three fundamental approaches to improving the energy performance of glazing products:

1. Alter the glazing material itself by changing its chemical composition or physical characteristics. An example of this is tinted glazing.

2. Apply a coating to the glazing material surface. Reflective coatings and films were developed to reduce heat gain and glare, and more recently, low-emittance coatings have been developed to improve both heating and cooling season performance.

3. Assemble various layers of glazing and control the properties of the spaces between the layers. These strategies include the use of two or more panes or films, low-conductance gas fills between the layers, and thermally improved edge spacers. Laminated glazing is another form of assembling layers to achieve certain properties.

Two or more of these approaches may be combined as discussed below. Thermal improvements to the window sash and frame are discussed in Chapter 4.

Clear Single Glazing

Figures 3-8 and 3-9 illustrate the performance of a typical single-glazed unit with clear glass. Relative to all other glazing options, clear single glazing allows the highest transfer of energy (i.e., heat loss or heat gain depending on local climate conditions) while permitting the highest daylight transmission.

Tinted Glazing

Both plastic and glass materials are available in a large number of tints. The tints absorb a portion of the light and solar heat. Tinting changes the color of the window and can increase visual privacy. The primary uses for tinting are to reduce glare from the bright outdoors and reduce the amount of solar energy transmitted through the glass.

Tinted glazings retain their transparency from the inside, although the brightness of the outward view is reduced and the color is changed. The most common colors are neutral gray, bronze, and blue-green, which do not greatly alter the perceived color of the view and tend to blend well with other architectural colors. Many other specialty colors are available for particular aesthetic purposes.

Tinted glass is made by altering the chemical formulation of the glass with special additives. Its color changes with the thickness of the glass and the addition of coatings applied after manufacture. Every change in color or combination of different glass types affects transmittance, solar heat gain coefficient, reflectivity, and other properties. Glass manufacturers list these properties for every color, thickness, and assembly of glass type they produce.

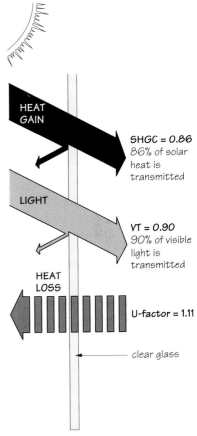

SHGC = 0.86
86% of solar heat is transmitted

VT = 0.90
90% of visible light is transmitted

U-factor = 1.11

clear glass

HEAT GAIN

LIGHT

HEAT LOSS

Figure 3-9. Center-of-glass properties for clear single glazing.

Note: These values are for the center of glass only. They should only be used to compare the effect of different glazing types, not to compare total window products. Frame choice can drastically affect performance.

Figure 3-8. Whole window properties for different frames using clear single glazing.

Frame Type	U-factor	SHGC	VT
aluminum	1.16	0.76	0.75
aluminum with thermal break	1.00	0.70	0.70
wood or wood-clad	0.84	0.64	0.65
vinyl or wood/vinyl hybrid	0.84	0.64	0.65
insulated vinyl or fiberglass	–	–	–

Note: The data presented here are averages of similar (but not identical) products from several manufacturers. Specific products will have performance properties slightly higher or lower. Users are encouraged to check with specific manufacturers for product specific NFRC performance properties. All glass is 1/8-inch (3 mm) thick. Skylight U-factors will be higher because of slope and exposure.

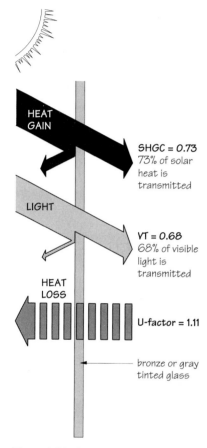

Figure 3-10. Center-of-glass properties for single glazing with bronze or gray tint.

Note: These values are for the center of glass only. They should only be used to compare the effect of different glazing types, not to compare total window products. Frame choice can drastically affect performance.

Tinted glazings are specially formulated to maximize their absorption across some or all of the solar spectrum and are often referred to as "heat-absorbing." All of the absorbed solar energy is initially transformed into heat within the glass, thus raising the glass temperature. Depending upon climatic conditions, up to 50 percent of the heat absorbed in a single layer of tinted glass may then be transferred via radiation and convection to the inside. Thus, there may be only a modest reduction in overall solar heat gain compared to other glazings. Heat-absorbing glass provides more effective sun control when used as the outer layer of a double-pane window, as discussed later in the chapter.

Tinted glazings can be distinguished by their differing impacts on light and total solar heat transmission. Traditional tints diminish light as well as heat gain, and newer spectrally selective tints reduce heat gain but allow more light to be transmitted to the interior. The traditional tinted glazing often forces a trade-off between visible light and solar gain. For these bronze and gray tints, there is a greater reduction in visible transmittance than there is in solar heat gain coefficient. This can reduce glare by reducing the apparent brightness of the glass surface, but it also reduces the amount of daylight entering the room. For windows where daylighting is desirable, it may be more satisfactory to use a spectrally selective tint or coating along with other means of controlling solar gain. Tinted glazings can provide a measure of visual privacy during the day when they reduce visibility from the outdoors. However, at night the effect is reversed and it is more difficult to see outdoors from the inside.

Figures 3-10 and 3-11 illustrate the performance of a typical single-glazed unit with bronze (or gray) tinted glass. The

Figure 3-11. Whole window properties for different frames using single glazing with bronze or gray tint.

Frame Type	U-factor	SHGC	VT
aluminum	1.16	0.65	0.56
aluminum with thermal break	1.00	0.59	0.53
wood or wood-clad	0.84	0.54	0.49
vinyl or wood/vinyl hybrid	0.84	0.54	0.49
insulated vinyl or fiberglass	–	–	–

Note: The data presented here are averages of similar (but not identical) products from several manufacturers. Specific products will have performance properties slightly higher or lower. Users are encouraged to check with specific manufacturers for product specific NFRC performance properties. All glass is 1/8-inch (3 mm) thick. Skylight U-factors will be higher because of slope and exposure.

primary purpose of bronze or gray tinted glass is to reduce solar heat gain, but it also reduces visible light as compared to clear single glazing. The tint has no effect on the U-factor.

To address the problem of reducing daylight with traditional tinted glazing, glass manufacturers have developed high-performance tinted glass that is sometimes referred to as "spectrally selective." This glass preferentially transmits the daylight portion of the solar spectrum but absorbs the near-infrared part of sunlight. This is accomplished with additives during the float glass process. Like other tinted glass, it is durable and can be used in both monolithic and multiple-glazed window applications. These glazings have a light blue or light green tint and have visible transmittance values higher than conventional bronze- or gray-tinted glass, but have lower solar heat gain coefficients. Typical spectral transmittance plots are shown in Figure 3-12. Because they are absorptive, as with

---

Characteristics of Tinted Glazing

- Reduces solar heat gain.

- Lowers visible transmittance, which reduces glare but diminishes available daylight.

- Alters glass color but views in daytime are not significantly diminished.

- Predominantly used in commercial buildings.

Figure 3-12. Spectral transmittance curves for common tinted and low-emittance glazings.

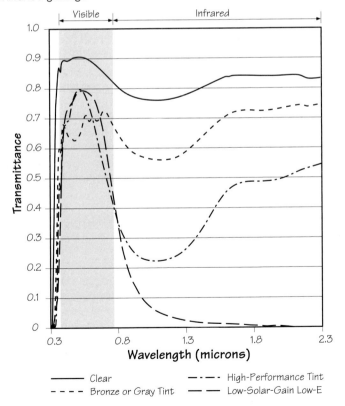

Source: Lawrence Berkeley National Laboratory

Characteristics of Reflective Coatings and Films

• Reduces solar heat gain.

• Lower visible transmittance, which reduces glare but diminishes available daylight.

• May produce exterior mirroring effects.

• Predominantly used in commercial buildings.

conventional tints, they are best used as the outside glazing in a double-glazed unit. They can also be combined with low-E coatings to enhance their performance further. High performance tinted glazings provide a substantial improvement over conventional clear, bronze, and gray glass, and a modest improvement over the existing green and blue-green colored tinted glasses that already have some selectivity.

Tinted glazing is much more common in commercial windows than in residential windows. Residential solar gains are more typically controlled using blinds, drapes, or other decorative window treatments. However, tinted glazings can be used in combination with the more traditional residential sun controls, where increased solar gain control or privacy is needed. In retrofit situations, when windows are not being replaced, tinted plastic film may be applied to the inside surface of the glazing. The applied films are effective at reducing solar gains and glare but are not as durable as tinted glass.

Tinted glazing is in place for the life of the window; this has both advantages and disadvantages. On the positive side, the tinted glazing requires no maintenance or operation from the inhabitants. On the other hand, it cannot respond to changing conditions. It cuts out solar heat and light not only in the summer but also in the winter, when they might be desired.

Reflective Coatings and Films

As the SHGC is lowered in single-pane tinted glazings, the daylight transmission (VT) drops even faster, and there are practical limits on how low the SHGC can be made using tints. If larger reductions are desired, a reflective coating can be used to lower the solar heat gain coefficient by increasing the surface reflectivity of the material. These coatings usually consist of thin metallic layers. The reflective coatings come in various metallic colors (silver, gold, bronze), and they can be applied to clear or tinted glazing. The solar heat gain coefficient of the substrate can be reduced a little or a lot, depending on the thickness and reflectivity of the coating, and its location in the glazing system. Some reflective coatings are durable and can be applied to exposed surfaces; others must be protected in sealed insulating glass units.

Similar to tinted films in retrofit situations, reflective coatings may be applied to the inner glass surface of an existing window by means of an adhesive-bonded, metallic-coated plastic film. The applied films are effective at reducing solar gains but are not as durable as some types of coated glass.

As with tinted glazing, the visible transmittances of reflective glazings are usually reduced substantially more than the solar heat gain coefficient. Reflective glazings are usually used in commercial buildings for large windows, for hot climates, or for windows where substantial solar heat gains and/or glare are present. In residences, they are usually reserved for special cases. For example, a picture window looking west over a large body of water experiences substantial solar gains and reflected glare during summer afternoons and may require a reflective glazing. Since reflective glazing is seldom used in residences, no performance data are given.

Special thought should always be given to the effect of the reflective glazing on the outside. Acting like a mirror, the reflective glass intensifies the sun's effects, and could momentarily blind pedestrians or drivers, burn plants, or overheat a patio. It is also important to remember that reflective glass acts like a mirror on the side facing the light. Thus, a reflective window that acts like a mirror to the outside during the day will look like a mirror on the inside during the night.

Double Glazing

As noted in Chapter 1, storm windows added onto the outside of window frames during the stormy winter season were the first double-glazed windows. The intent was to reduce infiltration from winter winds by providing a seal all around the operating sash. Improving the insulating value of the glazing was an important secondary effect.

Figures 3-13 and 3-14 illustrate the performance of a typical double-glazed unit with two layers of clear glass. The inner and outer layers of glass are both clear, and they are separated by

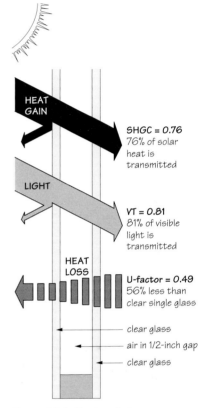

Figure 3-14. Center-of-glass properties for clear double glazing.

Note: These values are for the center of glass only. They should only be used to compare the effect of different glazing types, not to compare total window products. Frame choice can drastically affect performance.

Figure 3-13. Whole window properties for different frames using clear double glazing.

Frame Type	U-factor	SHGC	VT
aluminum	0.76	0.68	0.68
aluminum with thermal break	0.63	0.62	0.63
wood or wood-clad	0.49	0.56	0.59
vinyl or wood/vinyl hybrid	0.49	0.56	0.59
insulated vinyl or fiberglass	0.44	0.60	0.63

Note: The data presented here are averages of similar (but not identical) products from several manufacturers. Specific products will have performance properties slightly higher or lower. Users are encouraged to check with specific manufacturers for product specific NFRC performance properties. All glass is 1/8-inch (3 mm) thick. Skylight U-factors will be higher because of slope and exposure.

87

Characteristics of Double Glazing

- Thermal resistance is increased, which reduces winter heat loss and summer heat gain.

- Visible transmittance is only slightly diminished.

- Best thermal performance occurs with about 1/2-inch (12 mm) space between panes when filled with air.

an air gap. Double glazing, compared to single glazing, cuts heat loss approximately in half due to the insulating air space between the glass layers. In addition to reducing the heat flow, a double-glazed unit with clear glass will allow transmission of high levels of visible light and solar heat gain.

When manufacturers began to experiment with factory-sealed, double-pane glass to be installed for year-round use, they encountered a number of technical concerns, such as how to allow for differential thermal movement between the two panes, how to prevent moisture from entering between the panes and condensing on an inaccessible surface, and how to allow for changes in atmospheric pressure as the assembly was moved from factory to installation site. These issues have been successfully addressed over the years with a variety of manufacturing techniques and material selections.

When double-glass units first came on the market, the two glass layers were often fused around the perimeter to make a permanently sealed air space. In recent years, however, spacers and polymer sealants have largely replaced glass-to-glass seals, and have proven sufficiently durable for residential applications. The layers of glass are separated by and adhere to a spacer, and the sealant, which forms a gas and moisture barrier, is applied around the entire perimeter. Normally, the spacer contains a desiccant material to absorb any residual moisture that may remain in the air space after manufacture. Sealed insulating glass units are now a mature, well-proven technology. Designs utilizing high-quality sealants and manufactured with good quality control should last for decades without seal failure.

In addition to sealed insulating glass (IG) units, some manufacturers offer double-glazed units with nonsealed removable glazing panels. A blind or shade may be located between the glazings, or the inner glazing may be added in winter and removed in summer. In these double-glazed designs, the inner glazing fits snugly to the sash, and the unsealed air space is normally vented to the exterior with a small tube to prevent condensation from forming in the air space. Three or more glazing layers can provide even more insulating value.

Double Glazing with a Bronze or Gray Tint

Double-pane units can be assembled using different glass types for the inner and outer layers. Typically, the inner layer is standard clear glass, while the outer layer is tinted. Compared to a clear double IG unit, the solar heat gain coefficient is primarily reduced because the tinted glass reduces transmitted radiation. In addition, this design further reduces solar heat gain because the inner clear glass as well as any gas fill and any low-E coating keep much of the heat absorbed by the outer glass from entering the building interior.

Figures 3-15 and 3-16 illustrate the performance of a typical double-glazed unit with bronze- or gray-tinted glass. The outer layer of glass is bronze or gray and the inner layer is clear. These two layers are separated by a 1/2-inch air gap. Bronze- and gray-tinted glass products are similar in energy performance. Compared to clear double glazing, the tint has no effect on the U-factor but reduces solar gain, which may be a benefit in the summer and a liability in the winter depending on local climate conditions. The bronze or gray tint also reduces visible light transmission compared to double-glazed units with clear panes.

Double Glazing with a High-Performance Tint

Figures 3-17 and 3-18 illustrate the performance of a typical double-glazed unit with high-performance tinted glass (also referred to as spectrally selective tinted glass). This tinted glass reduces solar heat gain to below that of bronze or gray tinted but has a visible transmittance closer to clear glass. High-performance tinted glass products are typically light

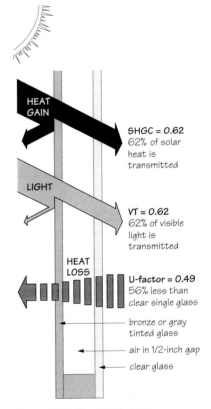

SHGC = 0.62
62% of solar heat is transmitted

VT = 0.62
62% of visible light is transmitted

U-factor = 0.49
56% less than clear single glass

— bronze or gray tinted glass
— air in 1/2-inch gap
— clear glass

Figure 3-16. Center-of-glass properties for double glazing with a bronze or gray tint.

Note: These values are for the center of glass only. They should only be used to compare the effect of different glazing types, not to compare total window products. Frame choice can drastically affect performance.

Figure 3-15. Whole window properties for different frames using double glazing with a bronze or gray tint on the outer pane.

Frame Type	U-factor	SHGC	VT
aluminum	0.76	0.56	0.51
aluminum with thermal break	0.63	0.52	0.48
wood or wood-clad	0.49	0.47	0.44
vinyl or wood/vinyl hybrid	0.49	0.47	0.44
insulated vinyl or fiberglass	0.44	0.49	0.48

Note: The data presented here are averages of similar (but not identical) products from several manufacturers. Specific products will have performance properties slightly higher or lower. Users are encouraged to check with specific manufacturers for product specific NFRC performance properties. All glass is 1/8-inch (3 mm) thick. Skylight U-factors will be higher because of slope and exposure.

green or light blue. Similar to the bronze/gray tints, high-performance tints have no effect on the U-factor compared to clear double glazing.

Low-Emittance Coatings

The principal mechanism of heat transfer in multilayer glazing is thermal radiation from a warm pane of glass to a cooler pane. Coating a glass surface with a low-emittance material and facing that coating into the gap between the glass layers blocks a significant amount of this radiant heat transfer, thus lowering the total heat flow through the window. The improvement in insulating value due to the low-E coating is roughly equivalent to adding another pane of glass to a multipane unit.

The solar spectral reflectances of low-E coatings can be manipulated to include specific parts of the visible and infrared spectrum. This is the origin of the term "spectrally selective glazings," which can allow specific portions of the energy spectrum to be "selected," so that desirable wavelengths of energy are transmitted and others specifically reflected. A glazing material can then be designed to optimize energy flows for solar heating, daylighting, and cooling (Figure 3-19).

With conventional clear glazing, a significant amount of solar radiation passes through the window, and then heat from objects within the house is reradiated back to the glass and then from the glass outside (Figure 3-20). However, a glazing design for maximizing energy efficiency in the winter would ideally allow all of the solar spectrum to pass through, but would block the reradiation of heat from the inside of the house (Figure 3-21). The first low-E coatings were designed

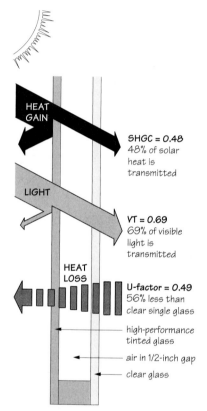

Figure 3-18. Center-of-glass properties for double glazing with a high-performance tint.

Note: These values are for the center of glass only. They should only be used to compare the effect of different glazing types, not to compare total window products. Frame choice can drastically affect performance.

Figure 3-17. Whole window properties for different frames using double glazing with a high-performance tint on the outer pane.

Frame Type	U-factor	SHGC	VT
aluminum	0.76	0.47	0.57
aluminum with thermal break	0.63	0.43	0.54
wood or wood-clad	0.49	0.39	0.50
vinyl or wood/vinyl hybrid	0.49	0.39	0.50
insulated vinyl or fiberglass	0.44	0.41	0.54

Note: The data presented here are averages of similar (but not identical) products from several manufacturers. Specific products will have performance properties slightly higher or lower. Users are encouraged to check with specific manufacturers for product specific NFRC performance properties. All glass is 1/8-inch (3 mm) thick. Skylight U-factors will be higher because of slope and exposure.

Figure 3-19. Spectral transmittance curves for glazings with low-emittance coatings.

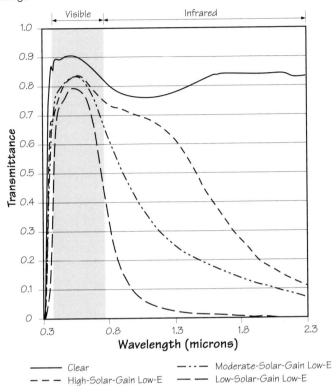

Source: Lawrence Berkeley National Laboratory.

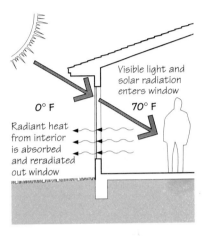

Figure 3-20. Clear glass allows solar heat gain and but does not reduce winter heat loss.

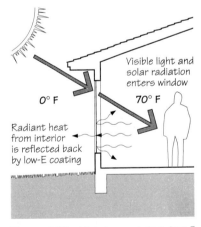

Figure 3-21. High-transmission low-E glass provides solar heat gain and reduces winter heat loss.

to have a high solar heat gain coefficient and a high visible transmittance to transmit the maximum amount of sunlight into the interior while reducing the U-factor significantly.

A glazing designed to minimize summer heat gains but allow for some daylighting would allow most visible light through, but would block all other portions of the solar spectrum, including ultraviolet light and near-infrared, as well as long-wave heat radiated from outside objects, such as paving and adjacent buildings. These second-generation low-E coatings were designed to reflect the solar near-infrared, thus reducing the total solar heat gain coefficient while maintaining high levels of light transmission (Figure 3-22). Unfortunately, in colder weather, low-solar-gain coatings reduce the beneficial solar gain that could be used to offset heating loads (Figure 3-23). Low-E coatings can be formulated to have a broad range of solar control characteristics while maintaining a low U-factor.

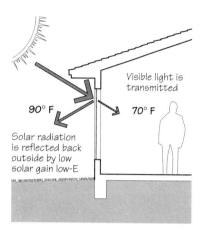

Figure 3-22. Low-solar-gain low-E glass reduces summer cooling loads without reducing daylight.

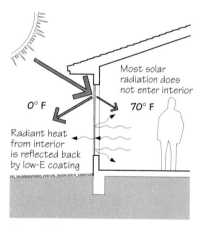

Figure 3-23. Low-solar-gain low-E glass reduces winter heat loss but also reduces beneficial passive solar heat gain.

Coating Types

There are two basic manufacturing processes for making low-E coatings—sputtered and pyrolytic. The best of each type of coating is colorless and optically clear. Some coatings may have a slight hue or subtle reflective quality, particularly when viewed in certain lighting conditions or at oblique angles.

A sputtered coating is multilayered (typically, three primary layers, with at least one layer of metal) and is deposited on glass or plastic film in a vacuum chamber. The total thickness of a sputtered coating is only 1/10,000 of the thickness of a human hair. Sputtered coatings often use a silver layer and must be protected from humidity and contact. For this reason they are sometimes referred to as "soft coats." Since sputtering is a low-temperature process, these coatings can be deposited on flat sheets of glass or thin plastic films. While sputtered coatings are not durable in themselves, when placed into a sealed double- or triple-glazed assembly they should last as long as the sealed glass unit. Sputtered coatings typically have lower emittances than pyrolytic coatings. They are available commercially with emittance ratings of e = 0.20 to as low as e = 0.04 (e = 0.15 means that 85 percent of the long-wavelength radiant energy received by the surface is reflected, while e = 0.04 means 97 percent is reflected). For uncoated glass, e = 0.84, which means only 16 percent of the radiant energy received by the surface is reflected. Low-solar-gain sputtered coatings are created by increasing the number of coating layers and altering their thicknesses, which causes the coating to reflect more of the sun's near-infrared energy as well as the long-wave infrared while still transmitting visible light.

A typical pyrolytic low-E coating is a metallic oxide, most commonly tin oxide with some additives, which is deposited directly onto a glass surface while it is still hot. The result is a baked-on surface layer that is quite hard and thus very durable, which is why this is sometimes referred to as a "hard coat." A pyrolytic coating can be ten to twenty times thicker than a sputtered coating but is still extremely thin. Pyrolytic coatings can be exposed to air, cleaned with normal cleaning products, and subjected to general wear and tear without losing their low-E properties.

Because of their greater durability, pyrolytic coatings are available on single-pane glass and separate storm windows, but not on plastics, since they require a high-temperature process. In general, though, pyrolytic coatings are used in sealed, double-glazed units with the low-E surface inside the sealed air space. While there is considerable variation in the specific properties of these coatings, they typically have emittance ratings in the range of e = 0.40 to e = 0.15. Pyrolytic coatings with lower solar gain properties have also been introduced to the market. These use a modified version of the pyrolytic process that reduces the solar gain while maintaining the low emissivity surface. The spectral selectivity of these coatings is not as sharp as the multilayer sputtered coatings so the visible transmittance is reduced somewhat as the SHGC is lowered but these glazings still appear clear to the eye.

Low-solar-gain low-E coatings on plastic can also be applied to existing glass as a retrofit measure, thus reducing the SHGC of an existing clear glass considerably while maintaining a high visible transmittance. Other conventional tinted and reflective films will also reduce the SHGC but at the cost of lower visible transmittance. Reflective mirror-like metallic films can also lower the U-factor, since the surface facing the room has a lower emittance than uncoated glass.

Low-E glazing technology has been called the most important breakthrough in window technology in the last 30 years. The technology to produce low-E coatings has continued to evolve, with further improvements in quality and diversity of product, and associated reductions in the market price. Once the initial hurdle of making a substantial investment in the necessary production machinery was met, there is a continued market incentive for manufacturers to provide low-E and related high-performance coatings on as much of the glass produced as possible. Thus, windows with low-E coatings have become the standard residential window product in most parts of the U.S. Approximately 60 percent of window residential products now sold in the United States have low-E coatings, and the figure will continue to rise.

Coating Placement

The placement of a low-E coating within the air gap of a double-glazed window does not affect the U-factor but it does influence the solar heat gain coefficient (SHGC). That is why, in heating-dominated climates, placing a low-E coating on the #3 surface (outside surface of the inner pane) is recommended to maximize winter passive solar gain at the expense of a slight reduction in the ability to control summer heat gain (Figure 3-24). In cooling climates, a coating on the #2 surface (inside surface of the outer pane) is generally best to reduce solar heat gain and maximize energy efficiency. Manufacturers sometimes place the coatings on surfaces for other reasons, such as minimizing the potential for thermal stress (e.g., #2

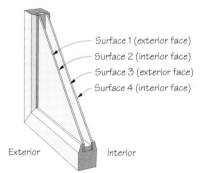

Surface 1 (exterior face)
Surface 2 (interior face)
Surface 3 (exterior face)
Surface 4 (interior face)

Exterior   Interior

Figure 3-24. Low-E coatings are placed on different surfaces to achieve different effects. Whether the coating is placed on surface 2 or surface 3 does not affect the U-factor. A coating placed on the outside of the inner glazing surface (#3) is most effective for maximizing passive solar gain. A coating placed on the inside of the outer glazing surface (#2) is most effective for minimizing solar gain.

surface in a heating climate). Multiple low-E coatings are also placed on surfaces within a triple-glazed window assembly, or on the inner plastic glazing layers of multipane assemblies with a cumulative effect of further improving the overall U-factor. In many skylights, the interior pane is laminated for safety reasons making it easier to place the coating on the #2 surface.

Typical low-E coatings available on the market today can be placed in three categories: high solar gain, moderate solar gain and low solar gain. Their properties are given in Figures 3-25 through 3-28.

High-Solar-Gain Low-E Coatings

Figure 3-25 illustrates the characteristics of a typical double-glazed window with a high-transmission, low-E glass, and argon gas fill (see next section). The properties presented here are typical of some low-E glass product designed to reduce heat loss but admit solar gain. High-solar-gain products are best suited to buildings located in heating-dominated climates and particularly to south-facing windows in passive solar designs.

Moderate-Solar-Gain Low-E Coatings

Figure 3-26 illustrates the characteristics of a typical double-glazed window with a moderate-solar-gain low-E glass and argon gas fill. Such coatings reduce heat loss, maintain high light transmittance, and allow a reasonable amount of solar gain, and are suitable for climates with both heating and cooling concerns.

Low-Solar-Gain Low-E Coatings

Figure 3-27 illustrates the characteristics of a typical double-glazed window with a low-solar-gain low-E glass and argon gas fill. This type of low-E product, using a highly "spectrally selective" low-E glass, reduces heat loss in winter but also reduces heat gain in summer. Compared to most tinted and reflective glazings, this low-E glass transmits visible light, but blocks a large fraction of the solar infrared energy, thus reducing cooling loads. A similar effect can be achieved by combining a high-solar-gain low-E coating (for insulating value) with a high-performance tinted glass (for solar control).

Until recently all of the low- to moderate-solar-gain low-E options were produced by sputtering. Newer pyrolytic coatings are available from several manufacturers which are colorless and provide spectral selectivity in addition to emittances typical of the existing pyrolytic low-E products. These coated glazings can withstand handling and long-term storage, and can be used in non-sealed IG units.

Low-solar-gain low-E glazings are ideal for buildings located in cooling-dominated climates. In heating-dominated climates with a modest amount of cooling or climates where both heating and cooling are required, low-E coatings with high, moderate, or low solar gains may result in similar annual energy costs depending on the house design and operation. While the high-solar-gain glazing performs better in winter, the low-solar-gain performs better in summer. Look at the energy use comparisons in Chapter 6 to see how different glazings perform in particular locations.

Variants on low-solar-gain low-E coatings have also been developed which lower solar gains even further. However this further decrease in solar gains is achieved by reducing

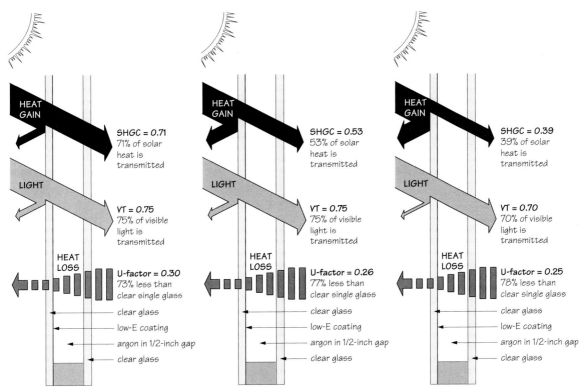

Figure 3-25. Center-of-glass properties for double glazing with a high-solar-gain low-E coating.

Figure 3-26. Center-of-glass properties for double-glazing with a moderate-solar-gain low-E coating.

Figure 3-27. Center-of-glass properties for double-glazing with a low-solar-gain low-E coating.

Note: These values are for the center of glass only. They should only be used to compare the effect of different glazing types, not to compare total window products. Frame choice can drastically affect performance.

the visible transmittance as well—such coatings, which may appear slightly tinted, are best suited for applications where cooling is the dominant factor and where a darker appearing glass is acceptable or desired.

Window manufacturers' product information may not list emittance ratings. Rather, the effect of the low-E coating is incorporated into the U-factor for the unit or glazing assembly. The type and properties of low-E coatings will affect not only the U-factor, but also the transmittance and solar heat gain coefficient of a glass. All these properties (U-factor, VT, and SHGC) need to be taken into consideration in selecting a particular glazing product.

Gas Fills and Gap Width in Multiple-Glazed Units

Another improvement that can be made to the thermal performance of insulating glazing units is to reduce the conductance of the air space between the layers. Originally, the space was filled with air or flushed with dry nitrogen just prior to seal-

Figure 3-28. Whole window properties for different frames using double glazing with 3 types of low-E coatings.

Frame Type	U-factor	SHGC	VT
High-Solar-Gain Low-E Coating (Fig. 3-26)			
aluminum	0.61	0.64	0.62
aluminum with thermal break	0.50	0.58	0.58
wood or wood-clad	0.37	0.53	0.54
vinyl or wood/vinyl hybrid	0.37	0.53	0.54
insulated vinyl or fiberglass	0.29	0.56	0.58
Moderate-Solar-Gain Low-E Coating (Fig. 3-27)			
aluminum	0.60	0.53	0.65
aluminum with thermal break	0.48	0.48	0.60
wood or wood-clad	0.35	0.44	0.56
vinyl or wood/vinyl hybrid	0.35	0.44	0.56
insulated vinyl or fiberglass	0.27	0.46	0.60
Low-Solar-Gain Low-E Coating (Fig. 3-28)			
aluminum	0.59	0.37	0.59
aluminum with thermal break	0.47	0.33	0.55
wood or wood-clad	0.34	0.30	0.51
vinyl or wood/vinyl hybrid	0.34	0.30	0.51
insulated vinyl or fiberglass	0.26	0.31	0.55

Note: The data presented here are averages of similar (but not identical) products from several manufacturers. Specific products will have performance properties slightly higher or lower. Users are encouraged to check with specific manufacturers for product specific NFRC performance properties. All glass is 1/8-inch (3 mm) thick. Skylight U-factors will be higher because of slope and exposure.

ing. In a sealed glass insulating unit, air currents between the two panes of glazing carry heat to the top of the unit and settle into cold pools at the bottom. Filling the space with a less conductive, more viscous, or slow-moving gas minimizes the convection currents within the space, conduction through the gas is reduced, and the overall transfer of heat between the inside and outside is reduced.

Manufacturers have introduced the use of argon and krypton gas fills, with measurable improvement in thermal performance (see Figure 3-29). Argon is inexpensive, nontoxic, nonreactive, clear, and odorless. The optimal spacing for an argon-filled unit is the same as for air, about 1/2 inch (12 mm). Krypton has better thermal performance, but is more expensive to produce. Krypton is particularly useful when the space between glazings must be thinner than normally desired, for example, 1/4 inch (6 mm). A mixture of krypton and argon gases is also used as a compromise between thermal performance and cost.

Filling the sealed unit completely with argon or krypton presents challenges that manufacturers continue to work on. A typical gas fill system adds the gas into the cavity with a pipe inserted through a hole at the edge of the unit. As the gas is pumped in, it mixes with the air, making it difficult to achieve 100 percent purity. Recent research indicates that 90 percent is the typical concentration achieved by manufacturers

Characteristics of Gas Fills

- Thermal resistance is increased with argon and krypton gas fills, reducing winter heat loss and summer heat gain through conduction.

- Higher temperatures in winter on the interior glass surface contribute to greater comfort and less condensation.

- Visible transmittance is not affected.

Figure 3-29. U-factor as a function of air-space thickness and emittance.

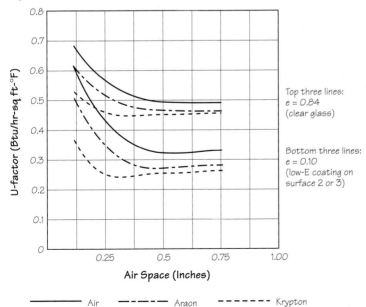

Top three lines:
e = 0.84
(clear glass)

Bottom three lines:
e = 0.10
(low-E coating on surface 2 or 3)

————— Air   —·—·— Argon   ------- Krypton

97

today. Some manufacturers are able to consistently achieve better than 95 percent gas fill by using a vacuum chamber. An uncoated double-pane unit filled with 90 percent argon gas and 10 percent air yields a slightly more than 5 percent improvement in the insulating value at the center of the glass, compared to the same unit filled with air. However, when argon and krypton fills are combined with low-E coatings and multipane glazings, more significant reductions of 15 to 20 percent can be achieved.

The gases are inert, nontoxic, and occur naturally in the atmosphere, but maintaining long-term thermal performance requires that the seals maintain their integrity over time. Studies have shown less than 0.5 percent leakage per year in a well-designed and well-fabricated unit, or a 10 percent loss in total gas over a twenty-year period. The effect of a 10 percent gas loss would only be a few percent change in U-factor on an overall product basis. Keeping the gas within the glazing unit depends largely upon the quality of the glazing design, materials, and, most important, quality control in the assembly of the glazing unit seals. Comparing manufacturers' warranties is one method to help find a quality, long lasting product.

Comparison of Insulating Glazing Units

The human eye is not able to see the heat that radiates from all objects. By using infrared thermography, researchers can "see" and measure the heat that radiates from every surface. This technique can be used to create images, called thermograms, that reflect the temperature of objects.

Infrared thermography is a testing technique that provides detailed maps of surface temperatures and can visually indicate the specific location of design or materials defects that can cause additional heat loss. The glazings are mounted in a test chamber, the temperature on the outdoor side is lowered, and the special infrared detector in the imager observes the indoor warm side of the glazing, recording its surface temperature, or thermogram. The four images (Figures 3-30 through 3-33) show graphically the effects of warm edge spacer design and high-performance insulating glazings with low-E coatings. These images show the insulating glass unit only—there is no sash or frame.

Figures 3-30 and 3-31 compare an aluminum spacer to a foam spacer, both in a clear double-glazed IGU. The aluminum spacer shows very low temperatures around the entire edge, with the lowest at the bottom as expected, since cold air currents in the IGU settle to the bottom. The unit with

Figure 3-30. Thermogram of a double-glazed window with clear glass and aluminum edge spacers.

Figure 3-31. Thermogram of a double-glazed window with clear glass and foam edge spacers.

20 24 28 32 36 40 44 48 52 56 60 64 68
Temperature (°F)

Figure 3-32. Thermogram of a double-glazed window with a low-E coating and foam edge spacers.

Figure 3-33. Thermogram of quadruple-glazed window with three low-E coatings and low conductance edge spacers.

a foam spacer shows a similar top-to-bottom trend, but the temperatures at the edge are all substantially higher and the width of the glass edge effect is reduced. Note that the coldest point at the bottom edge of the foam unit (32°F/0°C) is warmer than the warmest upper edge of the unit with the aluminum spacer (20°F/-6.5°C).

A comparison of Figures 3-31 and 3-32 shows the benefit of replacing a clear uncoated glass with a low-E coated glazing in IGUs with identical foam edge spacers. Under these test conditions, the low-E center-of-glass temperature is 8°F (4.3°C) warmer than the uncoated glazing. Both glazings show the expected top-to-bottom temperature gradient, and illustrate visually where condensation would probably occur first if it were cold enough outdoors.

Comparing Figures 3-32 and 3-39 shows the added benefit of going to a quadruple-glazed unit with three low-E coatings and krypton gas fill. There is a significant increase in center-of-glass temperature, to 64°F (18°F) from the 53°F (11.8°C) of the low-E unit. Note that the heat loss through the center of the glazing of Figure 3-33 is much lower than at the edge, suggesting that more development work is still needed to improve the edge design.

Thermally Improved Edge Spacers

The layers of glazing in an insulating unit must be held apart at the appropriate distance by spacers. The spacer system must serve a number of functions in addition to keeping the glass units separated by the proper dimension:

- accommodate stress induced by thermal expansion and pressure differences;
- provide a moisture barrier that prevents passage of water or water vapor that would fog the unit;
- provide a gas-tight seal that prevents the loss of any special low-conductance gas in the air space;
- create an insulating barrier that reduces the formation of interior condensation at the edge.

Older double-pane wood windows used a wood spacer that could not be hermetically sealed and thus was vented to the outside to reduce fogging in the air gap. Modern versions of this system function well but, because they are not hermetically sealed, cannot be used with special gas fills or some types of low-E coatings. Early glass units were often fabricated with an integral welded glass-to-glass seal. These units did not leak

---

Characteristics of Thermally Improved Spacers

- Overall U-factor is improved because heat loss at the glass edges is reduced.

- Higher temperatures on the glass edges produce less condensation.

but were difficult and costly to fabricate, and typically had a less-than-optimal narrow spacing. The standard solution for insulating glass units (IGUs) that accompanied the tremendous increase in market share of insulating glass in the 1980s was the use of metal spacers and sealants. These spacers, typically aluminum, also contain a desiccant that absorbs residual moisture. The spacer is sealed to the two glass layers with organic sealants that both provide structural support and act as a moisture barrier. There are two generic systems for such IGUs: a single-seal spacer and a double-seal system.

In the single-seal system (Figure 3-34), an organic sealant, typically a butyl material, is applied behind the spacer and serves both to hold the unit together and to prevent moisture intrusion. These seals are normally not adequate to contain special low-conductance gases.

In a double-seal system (Figure 3-35), a primary sealant, typically butyl, seals the spacer to the glass to prevent moisture migration and gas loss, and a secondary backing sealant, often silicone, provides structural strength. When sputtered low-E coatings are used with double-seal systems, the coating may be removed from the edge first ("edge deletion") to provide a better edge seal.

Since aluminum is an excellent conductor of heat, the aluminum spacer used in most standard edge systems represented a significant thermal "short circuit" at the edge of the IGU, which reduces the benefits of improved glazings. As the industry has switched from standard double-glazed IGUs to units with low-E coatings and gas fills, the effect of this edge loss becomes even more pronounced. Under winter conditions, the typical aluminum spacer would increase the U-factor of a low-E, gas fill unit slightly more than it would increase the U-factor of a standard double-glazed IGU. The smaller the glass area, the larger the effect of the edge on the overall product properties. In addition to the increased heat loss, the colder edge is more prone to condensation. The temperature effect at the edge can be clearly seen in a series of infrared images later in this chapter.

Window manufacturers have developed a series of innovative edge systems to address these problems, including solutions that depend on material substitutions as well as radically new designs. One approach to reducing heat loss has been to replace the aluminum spacer with a metal that is less conductive, e.g., stainless steel, and change the cross-sectional shape of the spacer (Figures 3-36 and 3-37). These designs are widely used in windows today.

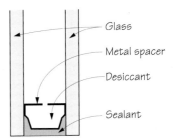

Figure 3-34. Single-seal metal spacer.

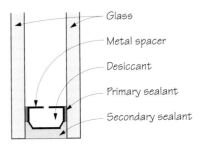

Figure 3-35. Double-seal metal spacer.

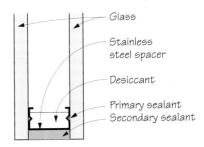

Figure 3-36. Stainless steel spacer.

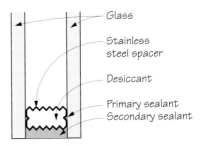

Figure 3-37. Stainless steel spacer.

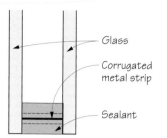

Figure 3-38. Butyl tape spacer with metal.

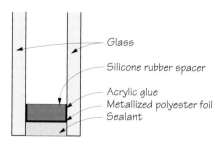

Figure 3-39. Silicone foam spacer.

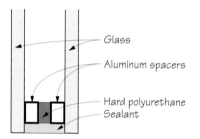

Figure 3-40. Aluminum spacer with thermal break.

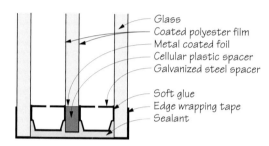

Figure 3-41. Aluminum spacer with thermal break.

Another approach is to replace the metal with a design that uses materials that are better insulators. The most commonly used design incorporates spacer, sealer, and desiccant in a single tape element. The tape includes a solid, extruded thermoplastic compound that contains a blend of desiccant materials and incorporates a thin, fluted metal shim of aluminum or stainless steel (Figure 3-38). Another approach uses an insulating silicone foam spacer that incorporates a desiccant and has a high-strength adhesive at its edges to bond to glass (Figure 3-39). The foam is backed with a secondary sealant. Both extruded vinyl and pultruded fiberglass spacers have also been used in place of metal designs.

There are several hybrid designs that incorporate thermal breaks in metal spacers or use one or more of the elements described above. Some of these are specifically designed to accommodate three- and four-layer glazings or IGUs incorporating stretched plastic films. All are designed to interrupt the heat transfer pathway at the glazing edge between two or more glazing layers (Figures 3-40 and 3-41).

Warm edge spacers have become increasingly important as manufacturers switch from conventional double glazing to higher-performance glazing. For purposes of determining the overall window U-factor, the edge spacer has an effect that extends beyond the physical size of the spacer to a band about 2-1/2 inches (64 mm) wide. The contribution of this 2-1/2-inch-wide "glass edge" to the total window U-factor depends on the size of the window. Glass edge effects are more important for smaller windows, which have a proportionately larger glass edge area. For a typical residential-size window (3 by 4 feet/0.8 by 1.2 meters), changing from a standard aluminum edge to a good-quality warm edge will reduce the overall window U-factor by approximately .02 Btu/hr-sq ft-°F.

A more significant benefit may be the rise in interior surface temperature at the bottom edge of the window, which is most subject to condensation. With an outside temperature of 0°F, a thermally improved spacer could result in temperature increases of 6–8°F (3–4°C) at the window sightline—or 4–6°F (2–4°C) at a point one inch in from the sightline, which is an important improvement. As new highly insulating multiple layer windows are developed, the improved edge spacer remains an important design element of high-performance window system.

Multiple Panes or Films

By adding a second pane, the insulating value of the window glass alone is doubled (the U-factor is reduced by half). As expected, adding a third or fourth pane of glass further increases the insulating value of the window, but with diminishing effect.

Triple- and quadruple-glazed windows became commercially available in the 1980s as a response to the desire for more energy-efficient windows. There is a trade-off with this approach, however. As each additional layer of glass adds to the insulating value of the assembly, it also reduces the visible light transmission and the solar heat gain coefficient, thereby reducing the window's value for providing solar gains or daylighting. In addition, other complications are encountered. Additional panes of glass increase the weight of the unit, which makes mounting and handling more difficult and transportation more expensive.

Because of the difficulties discussed above, it is apparent there are physical and economic limits to the number of layers of glass that can be added to a window assembly. However, multiple-pane units are not limited to assemblies of glass. One popular innovation is based on substituting an inner plastic film for the middle layer of glass. The plastic film is very lightweight, and because it is very thin, it does not increase the thickness

---

Characteristics of Multiple Panes or Films

- Thermal resistance is further increased (more than for double glazing), which reduces winter heat loss and summer heat gain.

- Higher temperatures on the interior glass surface contribute to greater comfort and less condensation in winter.

- Visible transmittance decreases with each additional layer.

- Solar heat gain coefficient decreases with each additional layer, which reduces cooling loads in summer but reduces beneficial gains in winter as well.

- Additional glass panes increase weight, but plastic films achieve the same purpose without adding much weight.

of the unit. The glass layers protect the inner layer of plastic from scratching, mechanical abuse, corrosion, weathering, and visual distortions caused by wind pressure. Thus, the strength and durability of plastic as a glazing material are no longer issues when the plastic is protected from physical abuse and weathering by inner and outer layers of glass. The plastic films are specially treated to resist UV degradation and they are heat shrunk so they remain flat under all conditions.

The plastic inner layer serves a number of important functions. It decreases the U-factor of the window assembly by dividing the inner air space into multiple chambers. Units are offered with one or two inner layers of plastic. Secondly, a low-E coating can be placed on the plastic film itself to further lower the U-factor of the assembly. Also, the plastic film can be provided with spectrally selective coatings to reduce solar gain in hot climates without significant loss of visible transmittance.

Triple Glazing with Moderate-Solar-Gain Low-E Coatings

Figures 3-42 and 3-43 illustrate the performance of a window with a very low heat loss rate (low U-factor). In this case there are three glazing layers and two low-E coatings, 1/4-inch krypton gas fill (or 1/2-inch argon) between glazings, and low-conductance edge spacers. The middle layer is glass in the figure but similar performance can be attained with coated plastic film. Both low-E coatings in this unit have high visible transmittance. The use of three layers, however, reduces the beneficial solar heat gain. This product is suited for homes located in very cold climates.

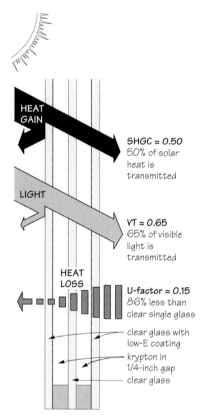

SHGC = 0.50
50% of solar heat is transmitted

VT = 0.65
65% of visible light is transmitted

U-factor = 0.15
86% less than clear single glass

clear glass with low-E coating

krypton in 1/4-inch gap

clear glass

Figure 3-42. Triple glazing with two high-solar-gain low-E coatings. Resulting unit has a moderate solar gain.

Note: These values are for the center of glass only. They should only be used to compare the effect of different glazing types, not to compare total window products. Frame choice can drastically affect performance.

Figure 3-43. Whole window properties for different frames using triple glazing with moderate-solar-gain low-E coating.

Frame Type	U-factor	SHGC	VT
aluminum	–	–	–
aluminum with thermal break	–	–	–
wood or wood-clad	0.29	0.38	0.47
vinyl or wood/vinyl hybrid	0.29	0.38	0.47
insulated vinyl or fiberglass	0.18	0.40	0.50

Note: The data presented here are averages of similar (but not identical) products from several manufacturers. Specific products will have performance properties slightly higher or lower. Users are encouraged to check with specific manufacturers for product specific NFRC performance properties. All glass is 1/8-inch (3 mm) thick. Skylight U-factors will be higher because of slope and exposure.

Triple Glazing with Low-Solar-Gain Low-E Coatings

Figures 3-44 and 3-45 illustrate the performance of another window with a very low heat loss rate (low U-factor) as well as low-solar-heat-gain properties. Similar to the previous example, there are three glazing layers and two low-E coatings, 1/4-inch krypton gas fill (or 1/2-inch argon) between layers, and low-conductance edge spacers. In this case the middle glazing layer is a plastic film. The low-E coatings can be placed on the glass or plastic. Some windows use four glazing layers (two glass layers and two suspended plastic films). With this window, both low-E coatings have low-solar-gain properties in order to reduce cooling loads.

Laminated Glazing

Laminated glass consists of a tough plastic interlayer made of polyvinyl butyral (PVB) bonded between two panes of glass under heat and pressure. Once sealed, the glass sandwich behaves as a single unit and looks like normal glass. Laminated glass provides durability, high performance, and multifunctional benefits while preserving aesthetic appearance.

Similar to car windshield glass, laminated glass may crack upon impact, but the glass fragments tend to adhere to the plastic interlayer rather than falling free and potentially causing injury. Building codes in hurricane-prone areas now require higher impact-resistant standards. Laminated glass is often the best option to meet these requirements.

Single-pane laminated glass with a spectrally selective low-E sputtered coating on plastic film sandwiched between two panes of glass offers the same solar heat gain properties of single-pane, spectrally selective glass and

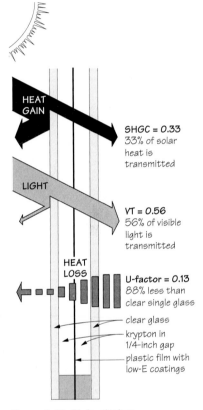

SHGC = 0.33
33% of solar heat is transmitted

VT = 0.56
56% of visible light is transmitted

U-factor = 0.13
88% less than clear single glass

— clear glass
— krypton in 1/4-inch gap
— plastic film with low-E coatings

Figure 3-45. Triple glazing with low-solar-gain low-E coating.

Note: These values are for the center of glass only. They should only be used to compare the effect of different glazing types, not to compare total window products. Frame choice can drastically affect performance.

Figure 3-44. Whole window properties for different frames using triple glazing with low-solar-gain low-E coating.

Frame Type	U-factor	SHGC	VT
aluminum	–	–	–
aluminum with thermal break	–	–	–
wood or wood-clad	0.28	0.25	0.40
vinyl or wood/vinyl hybrid	0.28	0.25	0.40
insulated vinyl or fiberglass	0.18	0.26	0.43

Note: The data presented here are averages of similar (but not identical) products from several manufacturers. Specific products will have performance properties slightly higher or lower. Users are encouraged to check with specific manufacturers for product specific NFRC performance properties. All glass is 1/8-inch (3 mm) thick. Skylight U-factors will be higher because of slope and exposure.

the safety protection of laminated glass. However, in this configuration, since the low-E surface is not exposed to an air space, the lower emittance has no effect on the glazing U-factor. With double-pane laminated glass (Figures 3-46 and 3-47), the full benefit of the low-E coating can be realized by placing the coating on one of the glass surfaces facing the air space.

PERFORMANCE COMPARISON OF DIFFERENT GLAZING TYPES

Figure 3-48 illustrates the impact of glazing type alone on total house energy performance. The total cost of heating and cooling for a typical 2000-square-foot house is shown with ten different window glazing units using the same frame (standard wood or vinyl).

In the heating-dominated climate (Minneapolis), the single glazed cases have the poorest performance. Reductions in energy costs occur by changing to double glazing. With both single and double glazing, adding tinted glass makes the performance worse. Generally, adding low-E coatings to double glazing represents further improvement, and energy costs are even lower using a triple-glazed unit with low-E coatings results in the lowest energy costs. Looking at the different types of low-E coatings, the high-solar-gain coatings result in the lowest heating cost but are a little higher on cooling cost compared to the low-solar-gain coatings. In a cold climate where heating predominates, the high-solar-gain coatings perform slightly better on an annual basis, but all low-E coatings represent very good performance. The relative ranking of the different low-E windows fluctuates depending on your utility prices.

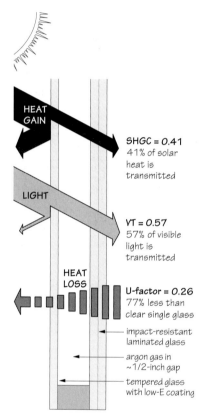

Figure 3-46. Double-pane laminated glazing.

Note: These values are for the center of glass only. They should only be used to compare the effect of different glazing types, not to compare total window products. Frame choice can drastically affect performance.

Figure 3-47. Whole window properties for different frames using laminated glazing.

Frame Type	U-factor	SHGC	VT
aluminum	–	–	–
aluminum with thermal break	0.68	0.42	0.56
wood or wood-clad	0.35	0.33	0.47
vinyl or wood/vinyl hybrid	0.35	0.33	0.47
insulated vinyl or fiberglass	–	–	–

Note: The data presented here are averages of similar (but not identical) products from several manufacturers. Specific products will have performance properties slightly higher or lower. Users are encouraged to check with specific manufacturers for product specific NFRC performance properties. All glass is 1/8-inch (3 mm) thick. Skylight U-factors will be higher because of slope and exposure.

Figure 3-48. Annual energy performance for a 2000-square-foot house with different glazing types using a wood or vinyl frame in two U.S. climates.

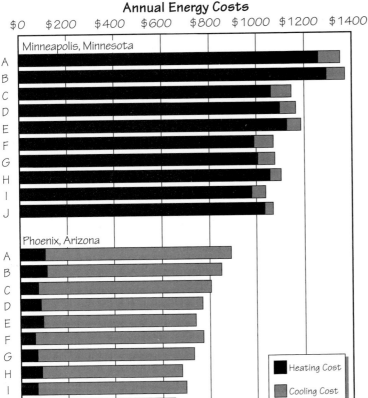

Note: The annual energy performance figures shown here were generated using RESFEN for a typical (new construction) 2000 sq ft house with 300 sq ft of window area. The windows are equally distributed on all four sides of the house and include typical shading (interior shades, overhangs, trees, and neighboring buildings). U-factor, SHGC, and VT are for the total window including frame. The costs shown here are annual costs for space heating and space cooling only and thus will be less than total utility bills. Costs for lights, appliances, hot water, cooking, and other uses are not included in these figures. The mechanical system uses a gas furnace for heating and air conditioning for cooling. The gas and electric prices used in these figures are provided by the Energy Information Administration (EIA) (www.eia.doe.gov). RESFEN is a computer program for calculating the annual cooling and heating energy use and costs due to window selection and is available from Lawrence Berkeley National Laboratory (windows.lbl.gov/software/resfen). See Appendix A for pricing and modeling assumptions.

Window	Glazing	U-factor	SHGC	VT
A	single, clear	0.84	0.64	0.65
B	single, tint	0.84	0.54	0.49
C	double, clear	0.49	0.56	0.59
D	double, tint	0.49	0.47	0.44
E	double, high-performance tint	0.49	0.39	0.50
F	double, high-solar-gain low-E	0.37	0.53	0.54
G	double, moderate-solar-gain low-E	0.35	0.44	0.56
H	double, low-solar-gain low-E	0.34	0.30	0.51
I	triple, moderate-solar-gain low-E	0.29	0.38	0.47
J	triple, low-solar-gain low-E	0.28	0.25	0.40

In the cooling-dominated climate (Phoenix), the clear single glazing also has the poorest performance. Reductions in energy costs occur by changing to double glazing and using tinted glass. The high-performance tint with double glazing represents an improvement over the bronze tint. Adding low-E coatings to double glazing in a hot climate does not necessarily represent further improvement—the type of low-E coating can affect performance greatly. High-solar-gain low-E coatings are not much better than clear double glazing since there is little solar control. Low-solar-gain low-E coatings, on the other hand, result in excellent performance. Using triple-glazed units with low-E coatings can result in the low energy costs as long as the low-solar-gain coatings are used.

COMPARING SKYLIGHT PERFORMANCE

Improved glazing options are also available for skylights and roof windows. Figure 3-45 illustrates the impact of different skylight glazings on total house energy performance in Phoenix, Arizona, and Minneapolis, Minnesota. The total cost of heating and cooling for a typical 2000-square-foot house is shown with four different skylight glazing units. Skylights with low-solar-gain low-E coatings result in the best energy performance compared to clear single- and double-glazed skylights.

EMERGING AND FUTURE DEVELOPMENTS

Innovation is a continuous process in the window market. The advanced glazing technologies discussed above are on the market already, but there are many other technologies continuously emerging from the research and development pipeline. Several promising technologies and systems are described below.

Evacuated Windows

The most thermally efficient gas fill would be no gas at all—a vacuum. For many years, researchers around the world have been pursuing the development of insulating window units in which the space between the glazings is evacuated. If the vacuum is low enough, there would be no conductive or convective heat exchange between the panes of glass, thus lowering the U-factor. However, a vacuum glazing must have a good low-E coating to reduce radiative heat transfer—the vacuum effect alone is not adequate. This principle has been used in

Information on New Technologies

Lawrence Berkeley National Laboratory conducts research on new technologies for windows and glazing. For current information see their web site at:

windows.lbl.gov

Figure 3-49. Annual energy performance for a 2000-square-foot house with different skylight glazings in two cities.

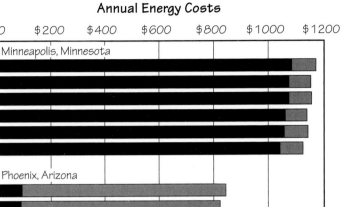

Annual Energy Costs

Skylight	Glazing	Frame	U-factor	SHGC	VT
A	double, clear	aluminum	0.94	0.68	0.70
B	double, low-solar-gain low-E	aluminum	0.75	0.40	0.55
C	double, clear	aluminum w/break	0.80	0.68	0.70
D	double, low-solar-gain low-E	aluminum w/break	0.70	0.40	0.55
E	double, clear-	wood/vinyl	0.75	0.68	0.70
F	double, low-solar-gain low-E	wood/vinyl	0.53	0.40	0.55

Note: The annual energy performance figures shown here were generated using RESFEN for a typical (new construction) 2000 sq ft house with 45 sq ft of skylights. The base house is unshaded and has 300 sq ft of window area. The windows are equally distributed on all four sides of the house and are low-solar-gain low-E in all cases. RESFEN assumes skylights are placed in a typical well which reduces solar heat gain effects by 50%. U-factor, SHGC, and VT are for the total skylight including frame. Skylight U-factors are greater than window U-factors for the same glazing type because of the slope and greater exposure of the frame. The costs shown here are annual costs for space heating and space cooling only and thus will be less than total utility bills. Costs for lights, appliances, hot water, cooking, and other uses are not included in these figures. The gas and electric prices used in these figures are provided by the Energy Information Administration (EIA) (www.eia.doe.gov). RESFEN is a computer program for calculating the annual cooling and heating energy use and costs due to window selection and is available from Lawrence Berkeley National Laboratory (windows.lbl.gov/software/resfen). See Appendix A for pricing and modeling assumptions.

the fabrication of thermos bottles for many years, where the silver coating serves as the low-emittance surface.

Evacuated window assemblies present a number of practical engineering and manufacturing problems. One major issue is the structural requirement to resist normal air pressure and variable pressures caused by wind and vibration. There can be large thermal stresses between large, window-sized panes of glass. A thermos bottle resists these forces easily because of its strong circular shape. However, the large, flat surfaces of a window tend to bow and flex with changing pressures. Minute glass pillars or spheres have been used in prototypes to maintain the separation between the panes. The pillars are very small but are still somewhat visible, reducing the clarity of the window. Figure 3-50 is a thermographic image of an evacuated window in which the pattern of the pillars is evident. The grid of pillars shows up because of the glass-to-glass conduction through the pillars.

The maintenance of an airtight seal around the edge of the unit is critical. The seal must be maintained to eliminate gaseous conduction by keeping the air density within the unit to less than one millionth of normal atmospheric pressure. An air density of only ten times this amount is sufficient to re-establish conduction to its normal value. This vacuum seal must remain intact for the life of the window, through manufacture, transportation, installation, and normal operation and weathering. Special solder glass seals have been used successfully by researchers in the development of large prototypes.

Vacuum glazing has been commercially available in Japan for several years. The center-of-glass U-factors are typically 0.26, with the possibility of even lower values, while maintaining a high SHGC. This unit also has the advantage of being thin and thus suitable for many glazing retrofits. However, since edge condition losses are larger than for conventional IG designs, the design of the sash should accommodate these effects so as not to increase the U value. It is possible that the success of this technology in Japan and continued development in the U.S. and Europe will result in commercially available options in the U.S.

Aerogel

Aerogel is a silica-based, open-cell, foam-like material composed of about 4 percent silica and 96 percent air. The microscopic cells of the foam entrap gas, thereby preventing convection, while still allowing light to pass. The particles that make up the thin cell walls slightly diffuse the light passing through, creating a bluish haze similar to that of the sky.

Aerogel has received research attention for its ability to be both highly transparent and insulating, making it one of a number of materials that are generically referred to as "transparent insulation." It should be technically possible to produce windows made of aerogel with a center-of-glass U-factor as low as 0.05. However, so far solid sheets of aerogel have only been produced in small quantities and small sizes, so that only tile-sized samples of clear aerogel have been used as windows for research purposes.

However aerogel can also be produced in granular form and it is commercially available in Europe and the U.S. in products as a translucent, granular filler for windows and translucent glazing panels. The granules typically range from .02 to .16 inch and are densely packed in the glazing unit. European manufacturers have produced double-glazed windows filled with small beads of aerogel. Since the units are diffusing and do not provide a view, they are mainly used as part of daylighting designs. In the U.S. the translucent granules are packaged within translucent fiberglass-skinned building panels as insulating, daylight-admitting structural panels. A nominal 1 inch thickness of aerogel would have an R8 insulating value (U=0.12) with a light transmittance of 53 percent. When utilized in a standard 2.75-inch thick structural panel the nominal insulating values are U=0.05 with a 20 percent light transmittance and a 0.10 SHGC. Although developed primarily for commercial buildings products of this type might be used in larger spaces in homes as translucent wall panels or roof panels.

Glazings for Light Control

The most interesting new work on glazings with optical control involves the use of smart windows described in the next section. But there is also significant development work in the area of daylight control on commercial buildings that is relevant for homeowner use. This includes a variety of products that are used to control light transmission into buildings. The most widely known are simple diffusers that redirect and scatter sunlight throughout a space as with the aerogel described in the section above. These materials typically block views but provide privacy and redistribute the incident direct sunlight, thus improving the appearance and functionality of the space. These diffusers can be fabricated by placing light-scattering elements within an IG unit, by incorporating a diffusing layer within a laminated glass assembly, by applying a film to the surface, or by otherwise altering the glass surface, e.g., with etching or silkscreening. A more sophisticated control of incident sunlight can be provided using more expensive optical control materials such as prismatic devices or holographic gratings that are designed to redirect light upwards to the ceiling. These types of systems are still in a prototype development phase in the U.S. and performance is very sensitive to several design and installation parameters.

Smart Windows for Dynamic Light and Solar Gain Control

The ideal window would be one whose optical properties could readily change in response to changing climatic conditions or occupant preferences. Researchers have been hard at work on new glazing technologies for the next generation of "smart windows." After many years of development, various smart window technologies are now in prototype testing phases and several are now commercially available. As with other window technologies, the homeowner, architect, or contractor will need to understand these new systems in order to properly specify them.

These new materials and devices can be classified in several different ways. We choose to look at them in terms of how they are actuated or switched. There are two basic types of smart windows—passive devices that respond directly to environmental conditions such as light level or temperature, and active devices that can be directly controlled in response to occupant preferences or heating and cooling system requirements. The main passive devices are photochromics and thermochromics; active devices include liquid crystal, dispersed particle, and electrochromics.

Photochromics

Photochromic materials change their transparency in response to changes in the intensity of light. Photochromic materials are commonly used in sunglasses that change from clear in the dim indoor light to dark in the bright outdoors. Photochromics may be useful in conjunction with daylighting, allowing just enough light through for lighting purposes, while cutting out excess sunlight that creates glare and overloads the cooling system. Although small units have been produced in volume as a consumer product, cost-effective, large, durable glazings for windows are not yet commercially available.

Thermochromics

Thermochromics change transparency in response to changes in temperature. The materials currently under development are gels sandwiched between glass and plastic that switch from a clear state when cold to a more diffuse, white, reflective state when hot. In their switched-on state, the view through the glazing is lost. Such windows could, in effect, turn off the sunlight when the cooling loads become too high. Thermochromics could be very useful to control overheating for passive solar heating applications. The temperature of the glass, which is a function of solar intensity and outdoor and indoor temperature, would regulate the amount of sunlight reaching the thermal storage element. Thermochromics would be particularly appropriate for skylights because the obscured state would not interfere with views as much as with a typical vision window. Such units would come with a preset switching temperature, which would have to be selected carefully for the application in mind. New materials systems are being developed and prototype glazings have been tested but are not yet commercially available.

Liquid Crystal Glazing

A variant of the liquid crystal display technology used in wristwatches is now serving as a privacy glazing for new windows. A very thin layer of liquid crystals is sandwiched between two transparent electrical conductors on thin plastic films and the entire package is laminated between two layers of glass. When the power is off, the liquid crystals are in a random and unaligned state. They scatter light and the glass appears as a diffusing layer, which obscures direct view and provides privacy. The material transmits most of the incident sunlight in a diffuse mode; thus its solar heat gain coefficient remains high. When power is applied, the electric field in the device aligns the liquid crystals and the glazing becomes clear in a fraction of a second, permitting view in both directions. Most such devices have only two states, clear and diffusing, and the power must be continuously applied for the glazing to remain in the clear state. This technology is commercially available for architectural applications. It requires standard household voltage (120v) and is relatively costly but may meet a need where automatic control of privacy or glare from direct sun are needed.

Particle Dispersed Glazing

This electrically controlled film utilizes a thin gel layer in which numerous microscopic particles are suspended. In its unpowered state the particles are randomly oriented and thus partially block sunlight transmission and view. Transparent electrical conductors allow an electric field to be applied to the dispersed particle film, aligning the particles and raising the transmittance in a fraction of a second. This glazing system can be partially transmissive between its clear and dark states. The basic switchable film technology has been licensed to several window manufacturers who offer products to the residential and commercial market.

Electrochromic Glazing

Base on a survey of existing and emerging technologies the most promising smart window technology appears to be devices based on electrochromic coating technology. Just now becoming commercially available in window sized units, they appear to have a good chance to meet performance, cost, and manufacturing requirements that would result in a widely marketable window system with good energy savings potentials.

Electrochromics can change transparency over a wide continuous range, from about 4 to 70 percent light transmittance over a time period of minutes, with a corresponding wide range of control over solar heat gain. The coating darkens as it switches and provides a view out under all switching conditions. Switching occurs at very low DC voltage (1–3 volts), so power supplies and wiring should not be expensive. Removing the voltage stops the electrochromic process without affecting the window's present state of transmittance, although a trickle charge may be needed to maintain a constant state. Reversing the voltage returns the window to its original state. The reversible process has been demonstrated successfully over the tens of thousands of cycles needed for a long lifetime window (Figure 3-51).

Electrochromic technology has been actively researched for over 20 years throughout the world, and promising laboratory results have led to prototype window development and demonstration, and now to commercial sales. Electrochromic window prototypes have been demonstrated in a number of buildings in Japan and more recently in Europe and the United States. Millions of small electrochromic mirrors are sold each year for use as rear-view mirrors in automobiles and trucks. Electrochromic glazings are also now commercially available as sunroofs in several types of cars. So the underlying technology for electrochromic windows has already seen extensive use in other commercial products.

In contrast to thermochromic or photochromic glazings, electrochromic windows offer more flexibility in control. Thermochromics and photochromics must have a preset threshold point at which they will change state. Although a range of thresholds or setpoints could be specified, the specified threshold becomes a permanent feature of that window. Electrochromics, on the other hand, could be dynamically operated by computer, by occupant signal, or by simple thermostat or photocell controls. This offers the potential for occupant

Figure 3-50. Test facilities of electrochromic glazing technologies. (Photo: Lawrence Berkeley National Laboratory.)

adjustments and calibration to changing local conditions and changing personal needs.

Initial studies show that smart windows are likely to have the greatest energy benefits in commercial buildings where lighting and cooling energy costs as well as related mechanical equipment costs are significant. By increasing the use of daylighting and reducing the cooling loads, smart windows not only reduce annual energy costs, but may also reduce the peak electric demand charges and the required size of the cooling equipment, both of which can be very substantial costs in commercial buildings. Similar benefits can be captured in homes. In residences in hot climates the greatest value will be reduction in cooling loads and improved thermal comfort, and greater protection from glare for a home office or when viewing a television. In moderate and cold climates the greatest energy savings occur when cooling loads are managed and windows are used to admit sunlight in winter but reject it in summer. A smart window can be controlled to achieve these objectives, on a seasonal or even hourly basis

Extensive lab and field testing of electrochromic performance has been carried out in office test facilities over the last 10 years with prototype window systems. The tests have demonstrated significant energy savings and improvements and satisfaction in comfort in these spaces. Many of these same benefits may also be of value in homes, especially in more

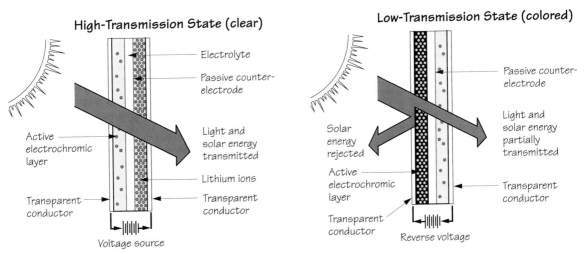

Figure 3-51. Schematic diagram of a five-layer electrochromic coating (not to scale). A reversible low-voltage source moves ions back and forth between an active electrochromic layer and a passive counterelectrode. When the lithium ions migrate into the active electrochromic layer, an electrochemical reaction causes that layer to darken. When the voltage is reversed and the ions are removed, the electrochromic layer returns to its clear state.

extreme climates. In principle, most of the benefits of smart windows might be captured by the intelligent and consistent use of existing manual or automated window control technology. But experience shows that people are often inconsistent and unpredictable in drawing curtains or adjusting blinds, and the cost of motorized controls is an obstacle. By making these control features an integral and dependable part of the building, smart windows can make potential energy savings predictable and guaranteed.

Electrochromic glazings are now commercially available in the U.S. for both skylight and window applications. When incorporated into an insulating glass unit they have the ability to switch from light transmissions in the range of 4 percent to 60 percent, with an associated SHGC range from 0.10 to 0.45. As with other early products, costs will initially be high and it is important to work with suppliers to address the added complexity of the controls needed for successful application. But these installations follow the growing trend for increased use of motorized shades and motorized openable windows and skylights so they are building on an emerging theme of adding smart controls for comfort and energy efficiency in homes. As with any new technology the early introduction of products will start off slowly as manufacturers, installers, and homeowners gain experience in their specification and use. Some of the first applications in homes are likely to find application in skylights and other specialty or high-value window products. To make best use of the technology the

Figure 3-52. Electrochromic glazings are now commercially available for both windows and skylights in the residential market. The skylight on the left is switched to the "on" position—reducing glare and reducing solar heat gain. The skylight on the right is switched to the "off" position.
(Photo: VELUX-America, Inc. and Sage Electro-chromics, Inc.)

windows must be linked to some type of control system. This might involve a light sensor with the product itself, a link to a home automation system, and/or a hand-held remote controller much like that used to control a TV or a garage door. By linking the operational control of the window transparency to a home automation system a wide range of time-dependent, climate-dependent and user-dependent operation can be accommodated. These emerging smart window products will provide added functionality, comfort, and amenity in homes in the 21st century.

Low Maintenance and Self-Cleaning Glass

As much as people love windows, no one likes to clean them. That might become a chore of the past if newly introduced low-maintenance and self-cleaning coatings are successful in the marketplace. Several manufacturers now offer new coatings that incorporate a very thin layer of titanium dioxide on the exterior of glass that make it easy to keep them clean. There are two related effects that help perform these functions. Most glass surfaces are hydrophobic meaning that water beads up on the surface and dries with visible water spots. These newer surface coatings are hydrophilic which encourages water to sheet and flow off, leaving less residue behind, thus reducing the "maintenance" needed to keep them clean. In addition, in the presence of the UV component of sunlight the coatings are also photo-catalytic meaning that the UV in sunlight triggers a reaction on the coating surface that will help digest and destroy many organic material that cause haze and smudges on window glazings. The combination of the two effects means that periodic rain can do a better job of keeping the exterior surface of windows cleaner without the scrubbing and rinsing needed today.

CHAPTER 4

The Complete Window Assembly

Although glazing materials have traditionally been the focus of much of the innovation and improvement in windows, the overall performance of any unit is determined by the complete window assembly. The assembly includes the operating and fixed parts of the window sash and frame as well as associated hardware and accessories. The first section of the chapter defines and illustrates the different options available for window sash operation. In the next section, new advances in frame materials designed to improve window energy efficiency are discussed, along with the traditional window frame materials of wood, aluminum, and more recently, vinyl. A complete range of window frame materials with performance comparisons in four typical U.S. climates is also shown. Proper installation of windows is an important aspect of their performance as well. The final section of this chapter discusses installation issues.

Figure 4-1. Window frame materials can have a substantial impact on energy performance as well as on appearance.

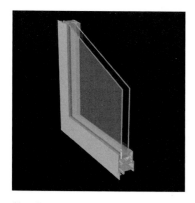

Aluminum frame

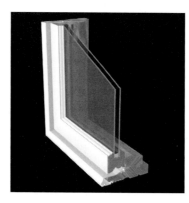

Wood frame with cladding

Vinyl frame

WINDOW SASH OPERATION

When you select a window, there are numerous operating types to consider. Traditional operable window types include the projected or hinged types such as casement, awning, and hopper, and the sliding types such as double- and single-hung and horizontal sliding (Figure 4-2). In addition, the current window market includes fixed windows, storm windows, sliding and swinging patio doors, skylights and roof windows, and window systems that can be added to a house to create bay or bow windows, miniature greenhouses, or full sun rooms.

Figure 4-2. Common window operating types.

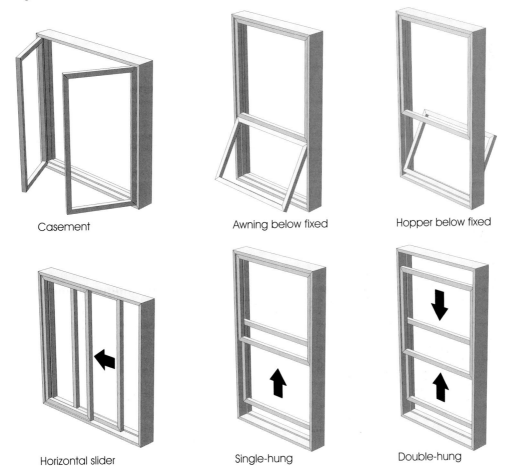

Casement

Awning below fixed

Hopper below fixed

Horizontal slider

Single-hung

Double-hung

Figure 4-3. Casement windows can create large expanses of glazing and can be opened fully to provide ventilation.
(Photo: JELD-WEN, Inc.)

Figure 4-4. Double-hung windows can be opened at the top and bottom to ventilate a room.
(Photo: JELD-WEN, Inc.)

Projected or Hinged Windows

Hinged windows include casements, awnings, and hoppers—hinged at the side, top, and bottom, respectively. Some manufacturers also make pivoting and combination windows that allow for easier cleaning of the exterior surfaces. Hinged windows, especially casements, generally project outward, providing significantly better ventilation than sliders of equal size. Because the sash protrudes from the plane of the wall, it can be controlled to catch passing breezes, but screens must be placed on the interior side. Virtually the entire casement window area can be opened, while sliders are limited to less than half of the window area.

Sliding Windows

Sliders are the most common type of residential windows and include horizontal sliders and single-hung and double-hung windows. Ventilation area can vary from a small crack to an opening of one-half the total glass area. Screens can be placed on the exterior or interior of the window unit.

In double-hung or double-sliding units, both sashes can slide. The same net amount of glass area can be opened for ventilation as in single sliders, but it can be split between the top and bottom or two ends of the window for better control of the air flow. Some sashes can swing in for cleaning.

Sliding Glass Doors

Sliding glass doors (patio doors) are essentially big sliding windows. As extremely large expanses of glass, patio doors exaggerate all of the issues related to comfort and energy performance. Since the proportion of glass to frame is very high for a glass sliding door, the selection of high-performance glass can have significant benefits.

French Doors and Folding Patio Doors

French doors and folding glazed doors are growing in popularity. A basic double French door consists of two hinged doors with no center mullion, resulting in a 5- to 6-foot-wide (1.5 to 1.8 m) opening. Folding doors are typically made of pairs of hinged doors, so that a double folding door with two pairs of doors can create an opening of 12 feet (3.7 m) or more.

Skylights and Roof Windows

The vast majority of skylights are permanently fixed in place, mounted on a curb above a flat or sloped roof. However, hatch-style skylights that can be opened with an extended crank, push latch, or remote control motor are becoming more common. Typical skylights include flat insulated glass units with coatings and tints as well as domed profiles with single or double layers of clear, tinted or diffusing plastic.

Roof windows have become increasingly popular as homeowners and designers seek to better utilize space in smaller houses by creating more habitable rooms under sloping roofs. They are glazed with glass rather than plastic and are available with most of the glazing and solar control options of standard windows. Operable roof windows can be opened manually or by a motorized system. In addition, some manufacturers offer special venting mechanisms that allow some ventilation air flow without actually opening the window. Operable roof windows, or vents allow hot air that rises to the ceiling level to be effectively exhausted from the space. Roof windows have rotating sashes to allow cleaning of the exterior pane. Most roof windows can be equipped with operable interior shading systems to diffuse or reject intense sunlight.

Light Tubes

Light tubes are another method for providing overhead sunlight in a room. A clear plastic dome is mounted on the roof and is connected to a small light diffuser in the ceiling by a highly reflective tube. The tube is relatively small (10 to 14 inches in diameter) and is bendable making it easy to install in difficult places without reframing the roof and constructing a light well as required with a traditional skylight.

Greenhouse (Garden) Windows

Greenhouse windows, also known as garden windows, are typically prefabricated frame and glass kits that can be inserted into a new or existing window opening. They may include shelves for plants or simply be used as a means of creating a greater sense of spaciousness. Greenhouse windows generally have higher heat loss and heat gain than a regular window of the same size because they contain more glazing than a conventional window that fills the same wall opening.

Figure 4-5. Operable skylights provide light as well as ventilation in high spaces.
(Photo: Velux-America Inc.)

Figure 4-6. Tubular daylighting devices capture sunlight and redirect it through a reflective shaft.
(Photo: Solatube International, Inc.)

Figure 4-7. Efficient glazing materials are important in sun rooms and solariums. (Photo: Pella Corporation.)

Sun Rooms and Solariums

Sun rooms and solariums are glazed spaces attached to a house that are used for sitting or eating areas as well as growing plants. Sometimes they are furnished in the form of prefabricated kits and have the appearance of a greenhouse. They may also be built with the same construction and window types found in the rest of the house. Sun rooms and solariums may be fully heated and air-conditioned living spaces, or they may be used only seasonally where they are either semi-conditioned or unconditioned. Because they contain such a large amount of glazing area, it is essential to select efficient glazing solutions, especially if the space is fully air-conditioned.

Combining Windows for Special Effects

In the simplest form, individual windows can be placed top to bottom and side by side to create the feeling of one larger expanse of window area. This results in a much greater feeling of connection to the outdoors, with more extensive views and daylight than an individual unit provides. Window manufacturers also provide special window configurations such as bay or bow windows. Different window operator types may be combined as needed—for example, fixed windows to enhance light and view with operable windows to provide ventilation and emergency egress. Large window walls may require spe-

Figure 4-8. Combining windows can create larger expanse of window area. (Photo: Associated Materials, Inc.)

cial features to ensure structural integrity. These groupings of windows provide a feeling of openness and light, helping to define the architectural character of the exterior and interior of the house. With the almost unlimited array of window types and sizes, designers can create window combinations that are innovative and create the architectural character and spatial relationships they desire.

Performance Implications of Basic Window Types

There are subtle performance differences between a fixed and operable window that fills an identical rough opening. The fixed unit will typically have a smaller fraction of frame and proportionately more glass than the similar operable unit. Thus, fixed windows with high-performance glass will have a better, lower U-factor, but a higher SHGC due to a smaller frame area and larger glass area. Fixed windows have very low air-leakage rates when installed properly, but then they also do not provide natural ventilation and do not satisfy building code requirements for fire egress.

For operating windows, the type of operation has little direct effect on the U-factor or SHGC of the unit, but it can have a significant effect on the air leakage and ventilation characteristics. Window operation can be broken into two basic types: sliding windows and hinged windows. The comments below are a general characterization of American window stock; however, they may or may not apply to a specific window produced by a given manufacturer.

Hinged Windows

Hinged windows such as casements, awnings, and hoppers generally have lower air-leakage rates than sliding windows from the same manufacturer because the sash closes by pressing against the frame, permitting the use of more effective compression-type weatherstripping. In most types, the sash swings closed from the outside, so when windows are exposed to strong prevailing winds the sash is pushed shut more tightly. Hinged windows require a strong frame to encase and support the projecting sash. Also, because projecting-type sash must be strong enough to swing out and still resist wind forces, the stiffer window units do not flex as readily in the wind. In addition, hinged windows have locking mechanisms that force the sash against the weatherstripping to maximize compression. These design details tend to reduce air leakage of hinged windows in comparison to sliders.

Figure 4-9. The traditional bay window is one way to combine smaller windows to enhance light and view. (Photo: Simonton Windows.)

Effect of Window Type on Air Leakage

Hinged windows (casements, awnings, and hoppers) generally have lower air-leakage rates than sliding windows (horizontal sliding and double-hung windows). A compressive latch increases the effectiveness of the weather-stripping in preventing air leakage through hinged windows.

Effect of Window Type on Ventilation

Hinged units can provide natural ventilation through the entire window area. Sliding units can provide ventilation only through half the area or less. Double sliding units provide more control of ventilation than single sliders.

Sliding Windows

Sliding windows, whether single-hung, double-hung, or horizontal sliders, generally have higher air-leakage rates than projecting or hinged windows. Sliding windows typically use a brush-type weatherstripping that allows the sash to slide past. This type is generally less effective than the compression gaskets found in projecting windows. The weatherstrip effectiveness also tends to be reduced over time due to wear and tear from repeated movement of the sliding sash. The frames and sashes of sliding units can be made with lighter, less rigid frame sections since they only need to support their own weight. This lightness may permit the sliding frames to flex and can allow more air leakage under windy conditions. Manufacturers can choose to engineer greater stiffness in their products by design and material selection.

Slider window performance can also be improved with latching mechanisms that compress the sash to the fixed frame and by the addition of compression weatherstripping at the head and sill of double-hung windows or the end jamb of horizontal sliders.

Sliding Glass and French Doors

As previously noted, sliding doors are essentially big sliding windows. However, they are more complicated because of their size and weight and because the sill is also a door threshold, which must keep water out while allowing easy passage of people and objects. The threshold is typically the most difficult part of the frame to weatherstrip effectively.

French doors benefit from being much more like traditional doors than sliding doors. French doors can use weatherstripping and operating hardware designed for similar nonglazed doors. However, when there are large openings with multiple-hinged doors, it is more difficult to positively seal the joints between door leaves and to create the stiffness that will resist air leakage.

Weatherstripping

Weatherstripping is an essential component of the operable part of a window. It must be able to flex each time the window is opened, and return to its original shape each time the window is closed. The quality of weatherstripping on a window is one of the main factors that distinguishes the quality of the window. Cheaper windows tend to save on cost by using poorer-quality, less expensive weatherstripping. Ideally,

Figure 4-10. Sliding glass doors are much like sliding windows and can provide almost uninterrupted views. (Photo: Marvin Windows and Doors.)

weatherstripping must survive thousands of operational cycles and years of exposure to sun, temperature change, and water without serious degradation of performance.

There are two basic strategies for weatherstrip design: brush or wiper types and compression types. Brush weatherstripping, made of felt, nylon, or polyester brushes, or synthetic rubber wipes similar to the wiper blades on a car windshield, sweeps against the window sash as it moves (Figure 4-11). Compression weatherstripping squeezes and expands with window operation (Figure 4-12). Materials used for compressible weatherstripping include felts, springy metal or plastic strips shaped into V-flaps, and synthetic rubber gaskets.

Each material has some disadvantages to be considered. Organic felts age fairly quickly, and all felts absorb moisture, reducing their effectiveness. Brush or wiper-type weatherstripping eventually gets matted down like a carpet that has had too much traffic. Metal strips are easily dented or bent and eventually lose their ability to recover their shape. Early synthetic plastics and rubber age quickly, becoming brittle or sticky. Recently, progress has been made in developing synthetic plastic weatherstripping that is more durable and can be expected to last longer.

Window air-leakage properties are measured under controlled environmental conditions as described in Chapter 2. These properties are typically determined for new windows under conditions that are not as severe as those the window will experience in a building. The window industry has developed additional test procedures that account for a wider range of environmental conditions, but these tests are more time-consuming and costly, and are not widely utilized. Actual performance may thus vary from the rated properties for many reasons. The air leakage may be different at different environmental conditions—e.g., very cold temperature may distort a window shape or change the properties of the weatherstrip. Air leakage will change over time as materials age, or as a wall settles and distorts a window frame.

From the perspective of comfort and energy use, the ability of the window to limit air leakage is an important performance capability. Window designers must select the right weatherstrip designs and materials to minimize air leakage, without adverse effects such as increasing the force required to open or close a sliding sash.

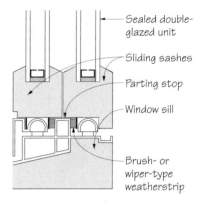

Figure 4-11. Brush- or wiper-type weatherstripping is suitable for sliding windows.

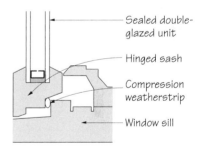

Figure 4-12. Compression-type weatherstripping is typically used for hinged windows.

Emergency Egress and Security

Windows have long been used as alternate escape routes during emergencies, especially during fires. Recognizing this, most codes regulate the size of free openings in windows, which must allow a person to escape from a bedroom or permit a fire fighter to enter.

While emergency egress from the inside is desired, most people want to restrict the entry from the outside. Latches should be quick and easy to operate from the inside, but difficult to see or reach from the outside. Screen or security bars must not restrict egress. Special security glazings, such as tempered and laminated glass or some plastic glazings, cannot be as easily broken as conventional glass and thus delays illegal entry. Operating windows can be wired into security systems to signal when the unit is opened. Windows can also incorporate sensors that report vibration or breakage to a monitoring unit.

FRAME MATERIALS

At the beginning of the century, most residential windows were built on site by local carpenters. Millwork suppliers then started to manufacture window sash and even entire window units. Prefabricated steel-framed "factory" windows became popular for a while in the 1920s. Prefabricated wood-framed windows finally became big business with the tract home building that started during World War II and mushroomed in the 1950s. After the war, aluminum manufacturers turned their plants to domestic production and quickly found a large market with prefabricated, aluminum-framed windows. Until the mid-1980s, well over one-half of all residential windows in the United States were aluminum-framed. Aluminum frames have been losing residential market share, initially to wood-framed windows and more recently to vinyl frames (Figure 4-13). During the 1990s new frames have been introduced made from fiberglass and engineered thermoplastics and new composite materials.

The material used to manufacture the frame governs the physical characteristics of the window, such as frame thickness, weight, and durability, but it also has a major impact on the thermal characteristics of the window. Increasingly, manufacturers are producing hybrid or composite sash and frames, in which multiple materials are selected and combined to best meet the overall required performance parameters.

Figure 4-13. Total U.S. Conventional Residental Window Demand: Historic and Forecasted Window Usage by Framing Material 2001–2009F (includes both new construction and remodeling).

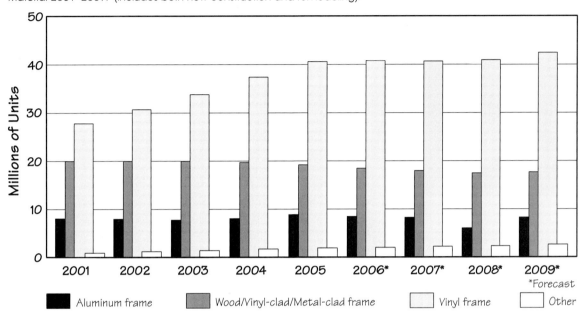

*Forecast

■ Aluminum frame   ▨ Wood/Vinyl-clad/Metal-clad frame   □ Vinyl frame   □ Other

Source: "Study of the U.S. Market for Windows, Doors and Skylights" by Ducker Research Co., Inc. for the American Architectural Manufacturers Association (AAMA) and the Window and Door Manufacturers Association (WDMA), 2006.

Thus, a simple inspection of the inner or outer surface of the frame is no longer an accurate indicator of the total material or its performance.

Figure 4-14 indicates the U-factors of various standard frame types. Since the actual U-factor depends on specific dimensions and design details, these values are only for illustrative purposes. While it is useful to understand the role that frame type plays in window thermal performance, the frame U-factor is not normally reported by manufacturers. The window U-factor, as given on an NFRC certified rating or label, incorporates the thermal properties of the frame, as well as the glazing. Since the sash and frame represent from 10 to 30 percent of the total area of the window unit, the frame properties will definitely influence the total window performance.

The remainder of this section describes aluminum, wood, and vinyl frames, and introduces some new frame materials that are commercially available.

Frame Material	U-factor
	(Btu/hr-sq ft-°F)
Aluminum (no thermal break)	1.7–2.4
Aluminum (with thermal break)	0.8–1.3
Aluminum-clad wood/ reinforced vinyl	0.4–0.6
Wood and vinyl	0.3–0.5
Insulated vinyl/ Insulated fiberglass	0.2–0.4

Figure 4-14. Typical U-factors for frame materials.

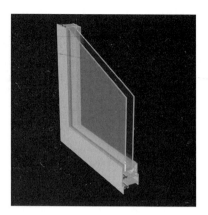

Aluminum frame with thermal break

Aluminum Frames

After World War II, aluminum became one of the most common residential window frame materials. Light, strong, durable, and easily extruded into the complex shapes required for window parts, it can be fabricated to extremely close tolerances, to create special forms for the insertion of glazing, weatherstripping, and thermal breaks. Aluminum frames are available in anodized and factory-baked enamel finishes that are extremely durable and low-maintenance. Aluminum is widely used for storm window units because of its light weight and corrosion resistance, and for sliding glass doors because of its strength.

The biggest disadvantage of aluminum as a window frame material is its high thermal conductance. It readily conducts heat, greatly raising the overall U-factor of a window unit. Because of its high thermal conductance, the thermal resistance of an aluminum frame is determined more by the amount of surface area of the frame than by the thickness or the projected area, as with other frame materials. Thus, an aluminum frame profile with a simple compact shape will perform better than a profile with many fins and undulations.

In cold climates, a simple aluminum frame can easily become cold enough to condense moisture or frost on the inside surfaces of window frames. Even more than the issue of heat loss, condensation problems have spurred development of better insulating aluminum frames.

Figure 4-15. Whole window properties for different glazings with aluminum frames with and without thermal breaks.

Glazing	Type	Aluminum			Aluminum with Thermal Break		
		U-factor	SHGC	VT	U-factor	SHGC	VT
single	clear	1.16	0.76	0.75	1.00	0.70	0.70
single	bronze or gray tint	1.16	0.65	0.56	1.00	0.59	0.53
double	clear	0.76	0.68	0.68	0.63	0.62	0.63
double	bronze or gray tint	0.76	0.56	0.51	0.63	0.52	0.48
double	high-performance tint	0.76	0.47	0.57	0.63	0.43	0.54
double	high-solar-gain low-E	0.61	0.64	0.62	0.50	0.58	0.58
double	moderate-solar-gain low-E	0.60	0.53	0.65	0.48	0.48	0.60
double	low-solar-gain low-E*	0.59	0.37	0.59	0.47	0.33	0.55
triple	moderate-solar-gain low-E	–	–	–	–	–	–
triple	low-solar-gain low-E*	–	–	–	–	–	–

*also known as "spectrally selective"

Note: The data presented here are averages of similar (but not identical) products from several manufacturers. Specific products will have performance properties slightly higher or lower. Users are encouraged to check with specific manufacturers for product specific NFRC performance properties.

The most common solution to the heat conduction and condensation problem of aluminum frames is to provide a "thermal break" by splitting the frame components into interior and exterior pieces and using a less conductive material to join them (Figure 4-16). There are many designs available for thermally broken aluminum frames. The most prevalent technique used in residential windows is called "pouring and debridging." The window frame part is first extruded as a single piece with a hollow trough in the middle. This is filled with a plastic that hardens into a strong intermediate piece. The connecting piece of aluminum is then milled out, leaving only the plastic to join the two halves of aluminum. Functionally, the resulting piece is cut, mitered, and assembled like a simple aluminum extrusion. Thermally, the plastic slows the heat flow between the inside and outside. There are other manufacturing techniques for producing a thermal break, but the thermal results are similar.

Current technology with standard thermal breaks has improved aluminum frame U-factors from roughly 2.0 to about half of that. This is difficult to achieve throughout the entire product, though. While easier to insert in the bulkier main frame, it is problematic to include thermal breaks in the thinner sash components that hold the glazing. In addition, as glazing systems with higher insulating values are developed, a frame with a U-factor of 1.0 or above may not be consistent with the energy efficiency of the other window components. However, innovative new thermal break designs combined with changes in frame design have been used in Europe to achieve U-factors lower than 0.5, but at a higher cost than current thermally broken frames. In hot climates, where solar gain is often more important than conductive heat transfer,

Characteristics of Aluminum Frames
• High thermal conductance resulting in poor U-factors. Thermal breaks are necessary in most climates.
• High strength-to-weight ratio.
• Lightweight compared to wood.
• Durable and low mainten-ance.

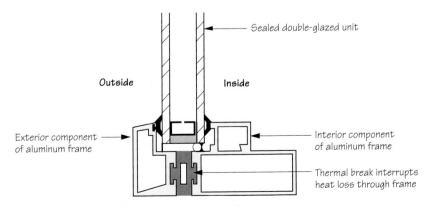

Figure 4-16. A thermal break in an aluminum frame.

improving the insulating value of the frame is less important than using a solar control glazing system.

The residential market share of aluminum windows has declined since the early 1980s. This reduction in market share has been seen for both new construction and renovation projects. Many of the companies that fabricated aluminum windows have switched to fabricating vinyl windows.

Wood Frames

The traditional window frame material is wood, because of its availability and ease of milling into the complex shapes required to make windows. Today, wood units tend to be thought of as "high end" windows because competing products are often less expensive. Wood is not intrinsically the most durable window frame material, because of its susceptibility to rot and of high maintenance requirements, but well-built and well-maintained wood windows can have a very long life.

Wood is easy to repair and maintain with simple tools and materials well understood by the average householder. A coat of paint protects the surface and allows an easy change in color schemes. Frames are generally made of kiln-dried lumber to reduce shrinkage, which results in better operation and weathertightness over their lifetime. Water-repellent and/or chemical treatments can be applied in the factory to reduce swelling and warping, improve paint retention, and increase wood's resistance to decay and insect attack.

Wood or wood-clad frame

Figure 4-17. Whole window properties for different glazings with wood and wood-clad frames.

Glazing	Type	U-factor	SHGC	VT
single	clear	0.84	0.64	0.65
single	bronze or gray tint	0.84	0.54	0.49
double	clear	0.49	0.56	0.59
double	bronze or gray tint	0.49	0.47	0.44
double	high-performance tint	0.49	0.39	0.50
double	high-solar-gain low-E	0.37	0.53	0.54
double	moderate-solar-gain low-E	0.35	0.44	0.56
double	low-solar-gain low-E*	0.34	0.30	0.51
triple	moderate-solar-gain low-E	0.29	0.38	0.47
triple	low-solar-gain low-E*	0.28	0.25	0.40

*also known as "spectrally selective"

Note: The data presented here are averages of similar (but not identical) products from several manufacturers. Specific products will have performance properties slightly higher or lower. Users are encouraged to check with specific manufacturers for product specific NFRC performance properties.

Wood windows are manufactured in all configurations, from sliders to swinging windows. Wood is favored in many residential applications because of its appearance and traditional place in house design.

Cladding the exterior face of a wood frame with either vinyl or aluminum creates a permanent weather-resistant surface. Clad frames thus have lower maintenance requirements, while retaining the attractive wood finish on the interior.

Newer vinyl and enameled metal claddings offer much longer protection to wood frames. However, they are generally available in a limited number of colors, and refinishing these surfaces may be a difficult task. Dark-colored finishes absorb more of the sun's energy, so they tend to be more susceptible to aging from heat and ultraviolet damage. Many vinyl and plastic finishes and frame materials require special solvents and bonding agents for repair or refinishing. Given the specialized nature of repairing or refinishing many of these low-maintenance frame materials, it is best to contact the manufacturer to determine if repairs are feasible or replacement is the preferred option.

From a thermal point of view, wood-framed windows perform well, with frame U-factors in the range of 0.3 to 0.5 Btu/hr-sq ft-°F. The thicker the wood frame, the more insulation it provides. However, metal cladding, metal hardware, or the metal reinforcing often used at corner joints can lower the thermal performance of wood frames. If the metal extends through the window from the cold side to the warm side of the frame, it creates a thermal short circuit, conducting heat more quickly through that section of the frame.

Vinyl Frames

Plastics are relative newcomers as window frame materials in North America. Vinyl, also known as polyvinyl chloride (PVC), is a very versatile plastic with good insulating value, high impact resistance, and excellent resistance to abrasion, corrosion, air pollutants, and termites. Because the color goes all the way through, there is no finish coat that can be damaged or deteriorate over time. Recent advances have improved dimensional stability and resistance to degradation from sunlight and temperature extremes.

Developed and marketed for more than thirty years in Europe, vinyl frames first became available in the U.S. in the 1960s. In 1983, vinyl windows constituted about 3 percent of all residential window sales in the United States, mostly for remodeling and replacement. Since then, the use of vinyl

---

Characteristics of Wood Frames

- Good thermal performance.

- Easy to mill into complex shapes suitable for windows.

- Exterior paint and maintenance required unless clad with vinyl or aluminum.

- Attractive interior appearance.

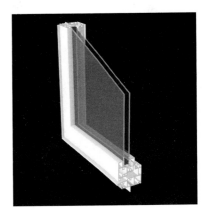

Vinyl frame

Characteristics of Vinyl Frames

- Thermal performance depends on design features. Generally, energy performance is improved by separating cavities to prevent convection around the frame and by filling cavities with insulating material.

- Can be fabricated to custom sizes.

- Low maintenance.

windows has risen steadily in new construction and more dramatically in the remodeling and replacement market. Vinyl windows now represent about 58 percent of all residential windows sold (Figure 4-13).

Similar to aluminum windows, vinyl windows are fabricated by cutting standard lineal extrusions to size and assembling the pieces into complete sash and frame elements. A small number of companies produce the standard lineal extrusions, and a much larger number of companies assemble window units by combining the sash and frame with glazing, weatherstripping, and hardware. This process lends itself to readily fabricating the custom sizes needed for the replacement window market.

Vinyl window frames require very little maintenance. They do not require painting and have good moisture resistance. To provide the required structural performance, vinyl sections often need to be larger than aluminum window sections, closer to the dimensions of wood frame sections. Larger vinyl units will often need to incorporate metal or wood stiffeners.

Since vinyl has a higher coefficient of expansion than either wood or aluminum, vinyl window frame profiles should be designed and assembled to eliminate excessive movement caused by thermal cycles. Vinyl frames with heat-welded joints are stiffer than mechanically joined vinyl frames, so they provide excellent resistance to temperature and handling stresses both at the job site and during shipping. In some cases, a vinyl window

Figure 4-18. Whole window properties for different glazings with hollow vinyl frames.

Glazing	Type	U-factor	SHGC	VT
single	clear	0.84	0.64	0.65
single	bronze or gray tint	0.84	0.54	0.49
double	clear	0.49	0.56	0.59
double	bronze or gray tint	0.49	0.47	0.44
double	high-performance tint	0.49	0.39	0.50
double	high-solar-gain low-E	0.37	0.53	0.54
double	moderate-solar-gain low-E	0.35	0.44	0.56
double	low-solar-gain low-E*	0.34	0.30	0.51
triple	moderate-solar-gain low-E	0.29	0.38	0.47
triple	low-solar-gain low-E*	0.28	0.25	0.40

*also known as "spectrally selective"

Note: The data presented here are averages of similar (but not identical) products from several manufacturers. Specific products will have performance properties slightly higher or lower. Users are encouraged to check with specific manufacturers for product specific NFRC performance properties.

assembly consists of both welded and mechanically fastened components. Interior webs also strengthen the frame, while improving its thermal performance. AAMA (American Architectural Manufacturers Association) has developed standards for vinyl extrusions to ensure impact resistance, dimensional stability, and color retention. New vinyls are being developed that are more resistant to heat and ultraviolet radiation and a variety of new colors are being developed as well.

In terms of thermal performance, most vinyl frames are comparable to wood. Large hollow chambers within the frame can allow unwanted heat transfer through convection currents. Creating smaller cells within the frame reduces this convection exchange, as does adding an insulating material. Most manufacturers are conducting research and development to improve the insulating value of their vinyl window assemblies.

New energy codes in some western states have spurred the sales of vinyl frames in those areas. These codes specifically require windows that have low overall U-factors, giving wood and vinyl frame windows a competitive advantage over metal frames. Given the recent rapid market penetration of plastic frames, much more development in the area of insulating frames is expected.

Insulated Vinyl

Insulated vinyl frames are identical in most of their characteristics to standard vinyl frames. The major difference between insulated vinyl and standard vinyl frames is improved thermal performance. In insulated vinyl frames, the hollow cavities of the frame are filled with insulation, making them thermally superior to standard vinyl and wood frames. Usually these high-performance frames are used with high-performance glazings (see Figure 4-19).

Hybrid Frames and New Materials

Manufacturers are increasingly turning to hybrid frame designs that use two or more of the frame materials described above to produce a complete window system. The wood industry has long built vinyl- and aluminum-clad windows to reduce exterior maintenance needs. Vinyl manufacturers and others offer interior wood veneers to produce the finish and appearance that many homeowners desire. Split-sash designs may have an interior wood element bonded to an exterior fiberglass element. We are likely to see an ever-increasing selection of

Insulated fiberglass or vinyl frame

133

Figure 4-19. Whole window properties for different glazings with insulated fiberglass or vinyl frames.

Glazing	Type	U-factor	SHGC	VT
single	clear	–	–	–
single	bronze or gray tint	–	–	–
double	clear	0.44	0.60	0.63
double	bronze or gray tint	0.44	0.49	0.48
double	high-performance tint	0.44	0.41	0.54
double	high-solar-gain low-E	0.29	0.56	0.58
double	moderate-solar-gain low-E	0.27	0.46	0.60
double	low-solar-gain low-E*	0.26	0.31	0.55
triple	moderate-solar-gain low-E	0.18	0.40	0.50
triple	low-solar-gain low-E*	0.18	0.26	0.43

*also known as "spectrally selective"

Note: The data presented here are averages of similar (but not identical) products from several manufacturers. Specific products will have performance properties slightly higher or lower. Users are encouraged to check with specific manufacturers for product specific NFRC performance properties.

such composite designs as manufacturers continue to try to provide better-performing products at lower cost. It may be important for a homeowner to learn about these materials from the perspective of maintenance requirements and options for interior finishes. However, it becomes increasingly difficult to estimate the thermal properties of such a frame from simple inspection. The best source of information is an NFRC label that provides the thermal properties of the overall window.

Wood Composites

Most people are familiar with composite wood products, such as particle board and laminated strand lumber, in which wood particles and resins are compressed to form a strong composite material. The window industry has now taken this a step further by creating a new generation of wood/polymer composites that are extruded into a series of lineal shapes for window frame and sash members. These composites are very stable, and have the same or better structural and thermal properties as conventional wood, with better moisture resistance and more decay resistance. They can be textured and stained or painted much like wood. They were initially used in critical elements, such as window sills and thresholds in sliding patio doors, but are now being used for entire window units. This approach has the added environmental advantage of reusing a volume of sawdust and wood scrap that would otherwise be discarded. Since wood composites are produced

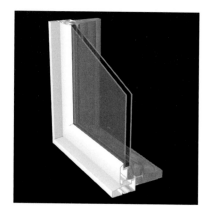

Hybrid wood and vinyl frame

Figure 4-20. Whole window properties for different glazings with typical hybrid and composite frames.

Glazing	Type	U-factor	SHGC	VT
single	clear	0.84	0.64	0.65
single	bronze or gray tint	0.84	0.54	0.49
double	clear	0.49	0.56	0.59
double	bronze or gray tint	0.49	0.47	0.44
double	high-performance tint	0.49	0.39	0.50
double	high-solar-gain low-E	0.37	0.53	0.54
double	moderate-solar-gain low-E	0.35	0.44	0.56
double	low-solar-gain low-E*	0.34	0.30	0.51
triple	moderate-solar-gain low-E	0.29	0.38	0.47
triple	low-solar-gain low-E*	0.28	0.25	0.40

*also known as "spectrally selective"

Note: The data presented here are averages of similar (but not identical) products from several manufacturers. Specific products will have performance properties slightly higher or lower. Users are encouraged to check with specific manufacturers for product specific NFRC performance properties.

as lineals, they have all the manufacturing advantages of vinyl and aluminum in terms of fabricating custom sizes.

Fiberglass

Vinyl windows have captured a large share of the new and retrofit window market in the last fifteen years in part because of the ability to produce a wide range of lineal extrusions that can be assembled into windows. Other polymer-based technologies are beginning to challenge this market, although to date they have captured only a small market share. Windows can be made of glass-fiber-reinforced polyester, or fiberglass, which is pultruded into lineal forms and then assembled into windows. These frames are dimensionally stable and have good insulating value by incorporating air cavities (similar to vinyl). Because the material is stronger than vinyl, it can have smaller cross-sectional shapes and thus less area. Fiberglass windows are typically more expensive than vinyl windows.

Engineered Thermoplastics

Another alternative to vinyl is extruded engineered thermoplastics, a family of plastics used extensively in automobiles and appliances. Like fiberglass, they have some structural and other advantages over vinyl but are also more expensive and have not yet captured a large market share. These high-performance frames are typically used with high-performance glazings.

PERFORMANCE COMPARISON OF DIFFERENT FRAME TYPES

While the overall window performance is often dominated by the glazing type, there are some notable differences in thermal performance between frame materials. Figure 4-21 illustrates the impact of frame type alone on total house energy performance. The total cost of heating and cooling for a typical 2000-square-foot house is shown with five different window frame types using the same glazing (double glazing with a low-solar-gain low-E coating).

In all four cities, the worst performance is attributed to the case with aluminum frame windows with no thermal break. Some reductions in energy costs occur by substituting a thermally broken aluminum frame. Wood and vinyl frames represent further improvement and using an insulated vinyl or fiberglass frame results in the lowest energy costs. In heating-dominated cities, such as Minneapolis and St. Louis, improving the frame reduces the U-factor and thus the heating load. In cities with significant cooling costs and smaller heating requirements, such as Phoenix and Miami, changing the frame material has less of an effect since U-factor has less influence. Nevertheless, Figure 4-19 shows definite improvement in performance in the warmer cities by using a wood or vinyl frame compared to an aluminum frame. This improvement occurs in part because of the improved U-factor, but also because wood and vinyl frames are wider than aluminum. Consequently, for the same window opening size, there is less total glass area with the wider frames. This results in better cooling performance because of the reduction in glazing area. Normally, using a high-performance frame material is not a separate strategy in any climate, but is usually combined with high-performance glazing to maximize energy savings.

Figure 4-21. Annual energy performance for a 2000-square-foot house with different frame types using identical low-E glass in four U.S. climates.

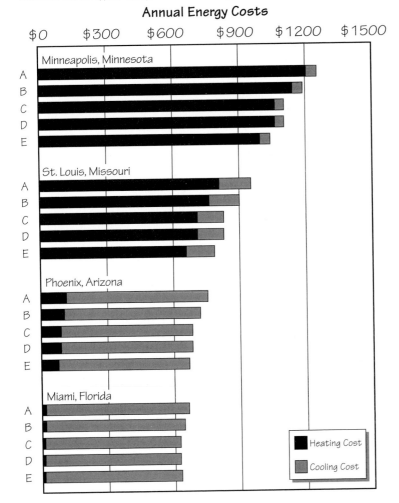

Annual Energy Costs

Note: The annual energy performance figures shown here were generated using RESFEN for a typical (new construction) 2000 sq ft house with 300 sq ft of window area. The windows are equally distributed on all four sides of the house and include typical shading (interior shades, overhangs, trees, and neighboring buildings). U-factor, SHGC, and VT are for the total window including frame. The costs shown here are annual costs for space heating and space cooling only and thus will be less than total utility bills. Costs for lights, appliances, hot water, cooking, and other uses are not included in these figures. The mechanical system uses a gas furnace for heating and air conditioning for cooling. The gas and electric prices used in these figures are provided by the Energy Information Administration (EIA) (www.eia.doe.gov). RESFEN is a computer program for calculating the annual cooling and heating energy use and costs due to window selection and is available from Lawrence Berkeley National Laboratory (windows.lbl.gov/software/resfen). See Appendix A for pricing and modeling assumptions.

Window	Glazing	Frame	U-factor	SHGC	VT
A	double, low-solar-gain low-E	aluminum	0.59	0.37	0.59
B	double, low-solar-gain low-E	aluminum w/break	0.47	0.33	0.55
C	double, low-solar-gain low-E	wood/wood clad	0.34	0.30	0.51
D	double, low-solar-gain low-E	vinyl	0.34	0.30	0.51
E	double, low-solar-gain low-E	insulated fiberglass	0.26	0.31	0.55

WINDOW INSTALLATION

No matter how advanced the glazing and frame materials may be in a window unit, the ultimate performance also depends on the quality of its installation. Improper installation can contribute to air leakage, unnecessary heat loss, condensation, and water leakage. This not only may lead to diminished energy performance but deterioration of walls, insulation, and the window unit itself.

Essentially, installing a window creates a break in several important aspects of the building envelope. A properly installed window must maintain barriers keeping air and water from penetrating the wall and it must restrict vapor flow. It must also reduce heat loss and condensation around the window unit. In addition, the installation must meet several structural and functional requirements. Building loads cannot rest on the window frame, the installation must allow for movement, the window must protect against forced entry, and yet it must maintain ease of operation.

The installation of a window and any treatments added to its exterior or interior can affect the energy efficiency of the total assembly, no matter how advanced the window unit. There are important differences in the details of how a window is installed, depending on the type of construction (wood versus masonry) or exterior cladding material (i.e., wood siding, stucco, brick veneer). In addition, each operator type, frame material, and individual manufacturer may have its own recommended installation practices. It is important to refer to the appropriate manufacturer's instructions and not to rely solely on general guidelines.

Given the importance of proper installation, however, there are some emerging guidelines for installation. AAMA has developed an installer training and registration program and ASTM has developed a Window Installation Standard Practice. The EEBA Water Management Guide is another excellent resource (Lstiburek, 2004). These and other information sources are listed here and in Appendix D.

Water Tight Installation

While there are many wall materials and construction assemblies, there are two fundamental approaches to water control—the surface barrier system and the membrane/drainage system. Determining which of these systems is used in the wall affects the window installation approach.

Installation Information

E 2112: Standard Practice of the Installation of Exterior Windows, Doors and Skylights
American Society for Testing and Materials (ASTM)
100 Barr Harbor Drive
West Conshohocken, PA 19428
Phone: (610) 832-9585
Fax: (610) 832-9555
www.astm.org

Water Management Guide
Joseph W. Lstiburek
Energy & Environmental Building Association (EEBA)
www.eeba.org

InstallationMasters™ Training and Certification Program
Developed by American Architectural Manufacturers Association and administered by Architectural Testing, Inc.
www.installationmastersusa.com

See Appendix D for other installation programs and information.

Surface Barrier System

A wall with a surface barrier system relies on the outermost surface to be weather resistant. Solid walls of masonry, concrete or brick with no cavities are surface barrier systems. Some types of stucco walls are barrier systems if they make no provision for drainage within the wall. Windows placed into a wall with a surface barrier system rely on a sealant joint between the frame and opening in the wall (Figure 4-22). With this type system, there is only one line of defense against water intrusion requiring very careful installation. There is no provision for drainage of moisture that enters the wall.

Membrane/Drainage System

A wall with a membrane/drainage system accepts that small amounts of water may penetrate the outermost wall surface. The system is designed to control and drain away any residual water that penetrates the wall. Typically there is a weather resistant barrier such as house wrap or building paper placed behind the exterior cladding material (wood siding, brick veneer, or stucco). This drainage plane must be overlapped shingle-style and open at the base so that water drains to the

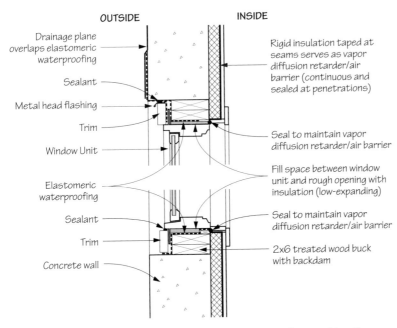

Figure 4-22. Installation of a block frame window in a wall assembly with a surface barrier system.

General Installation Guidelines

- Always follow manufacturer's instructions.

- Meet all codes regarding energy efficiency, structure, proper egress, safety glass, and grade (design pressure).

- Size the rough opening properly to accommodate thermal expansion and movement.

- Install the window unit level, plumb, and square.

- Maintain the continuity of the weather-resistant barrier. In a barrier system, this is achieved with sealants on the outermost surface of the wall. In a membrane/drainage system, residual water must drain freely on the drainage plane. Use flashings overlapped shingle style and drip caps where needed. Avoid trapping water within the wall.

- Do not leave thermal bridges between the interior and exterior. Carefully insulate all voids left between window and wall, but only use foam insulation that expands at a minimum rate.

- Maintain the integrity of air and vapor retarders.

- Avoid using incompatible materials such as certain metal combinations and only apply caulks and sealants that are compatible with the substrate.

exterior. In some cases, this requires flashing and weep holes at the base of the wall. It is important to use caution when sealing a window unit to the exterior cladding of a membrane/drainage wall system so that water within the drainage plane is not blocked and is allowed to escape (Figure 4-23).

In membrane/drainage systems, a window with a mounting flange (nail fin) is typically used to attach the frame to the wall. Block frame windows with brick mold may also be used with a membrane/drainage system. The integrity of the drainage membrane must be preserved by the proper use of flashings and sealants in this type of installation. The placement of flashings must follow a careful sequence resulting in the overlapping of all materials in weather-board (shingle style) fashion (Figure 4-24). One common procedure recommends that the flashing beneath the sill is placed first, then the jamb flashings, then the window is installed with mounting fins over these flashings, and then the head flashing over the top window fin. There are a number of variations and intricate procedures involving proper flashing depending on the exact wall assembly and construction sequence. Consult manufacturer's instructions and the information resources in Appendix D.

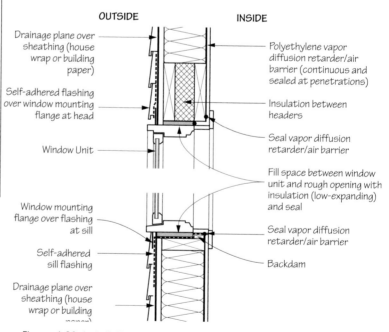

OUTSIDE INSIDE

Drainage plane over sheathing (house wrap or building paper)

Self-adhered flashing over window mounting flange at head

Window Unit

Window mounting flange over flashing at sill

Self-adhered sill flashing

Drainage plane over sheathing (house wrap or building paper)

Polyethylene vapor diffusion retarder/air barrier (continuous and sealed at penetrations)

Insulation between headers

Seal vapor diffusion retarder/air barrier

Fill space between window unit and rough opening with insulation (low-expanding) and seal

Seal vapor diffusion retarder/air barrier

Backdam

Figure 4-23. Installation of a window with a mounting flange in a wall assembly with a membrane/drainage system.

Figure 4-24. Installation sequence of window with housewrap on oriented strand board over a wood framed wall.
Source: Water Management Guide. Used with permission.

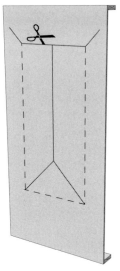  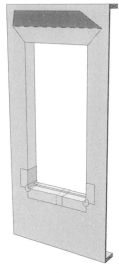

1. In the wood-frame wall with OSB and housewrap, cut a modified "I" in the housewrap.

2. Fold housewrap in at jambs and sill. Temporarily fold housewrap up at head (or tuck under). Install back-dam..

3. Install adhesive-backed sill flashing and corner flashing patches at sill.

4. Install window plumb, level, and square per manufacturer's instructions. A chemically-compatible sealant bead at jambs and head may be optional. Install self-adhered jamb flashing.

5. Install a drip cap (if applicable). Install self-adhered head flashing.

6. Fold down housewrap. Apply corner tape patches at head. Air seal window around entire perimeter on the interior with sealant or non-expanding foam. Expanding foam should not fill the sill pan.

Insulating Around Window Units

Windows are always placed into openings in walls that are sized slightly larger than the window unit itself. This additional space around the window, typically 1/4 to 1/2 inch (6 to 12 mm) on each side, is essential in providing construction tolerances and allowing for any movement of the building over time. However, it also creates a gap between the careful detailing of the window unit and the insulation of the wall.

As window insulating values improve, attention should focus on how to maintain a continuous insulating envelope between window and wall. As much care should be given to preventing infiltration and conduction heat losses at the joint between window unit and wall as is given to insulating the wall or selecting the window unit. The two most important ways to cut heat loss at the perimeter of a window are to place insulation into all voids and to use sealants to close off even the most minute air paths. Special attention must be given to the mounting of thermally broken aluminum frame windows, so that the integrity of the thermal barrier is not compromised.

Many window units are attached to the building with a fin mounting system; a casing placed over the fin provides a visual finish from the exterior. At this joint between the inside and the outside of the building, there is minimum thickness of material and a considerable air space that should be filled with an insulating material. Fiberglass insulation can be manually stuffed into the void, or a foaming insulation can be shot in to provide a tight fit. Foam that expands, however, can exert undue pressure, distorting the window frame and causing even greater air leakage through the window. If insulating foam is used, it is essential that it have low expansion characteristics and that it be applied as directed by the manufacturer.

Air and Vapor Retarders

Any air barrier or water vapor retarder used in residential construction must maintain its integrity at the window opening, as illustrated in Figures 4-22 and 4-23. An interior plastic vapor barrier can be laid continuously across a window opening and cut on the diagonals to form an X cut at the window. The triangular edges are wrapped into the framed opening before the window is inserted. Alternatively, an exterior barrier, such as house wrap or tar paper, is cut in the form of a modified "I" then folded into the window opening at the sill and jambs to make friction contact with the window unit. Caulking then creates a continuous seal from the window unit to the air and/or vapor barrier.

Forming a continuous vapor barrier is essential for extreme climates, either very cold or very hot and humid. Even when condensation has been visibly eliminated from window glazing and frame surfaces by selecting thermally improved products, it can still cause problems. Water vapor will migrate unnoticed from high-pressure areas to low-pressure areas. If a hole in the vapor barrier envelope of a house happens to allow the water vapor to contact a cold surface, it will condense on the cold surface and collect there. If this surface is in the interior of a wall or between a window frame and a wall, the moisture can cause rot or rust damage, or render insulating materials ineffective. Such a condition can go undetected for years.

Replacement Windows and Sashes

Half of all windows sold are installed as replacement windows. Installing replacement windows in an existing building presents a wide range of possible situations and potential problems. Following manufacturers instructions as well as guidelines and standards noted earlier in this section is essential. Replacement windows can be considered in three categories: (1) removal of and complete replacement of the original window, (2) placement of a complete new window within the frame of the existing window, and (3) replacement of the sash only, where the original frame remains in place, and only new glass and operating sash are installed.

Window installation in a remodeling or renovation must address all of the considerations discussed previously for new windows as well as greater concerns over maintaining existing drainage planes and air/vapor barriers. Insulation and air/water vapor barrier continuity should be maintained all around the window. Foam-in-place sealants can be used to fill irregular voids created between old and the new components; however, as with new installations, it is important to use low-expansion foams so that frames are not distorted. Remodeling is often an opportunity to check the interior condition of walls and increase insulation in the opened areas.

In a simpler approach, the old sash and other adjacent trim is removed, leaving the original frame in place. The new window is inserted into this framed opening, following prescribed installation procedures. Then, appropriate trim is installed on the interior and exterior. This provides many of the benefits of a complete window replacement, but at a lower cost. However, the net effect is typically to reduce the total glazing area, since a complete window assembly is basically fitted into the old frame. Caution must be used to avoid diminishing the opening below egress code requirements.

Replacement sashes involve less expense and disruption for a household. They are custom-sized and detailed to fit into existing window frames. Only the glazing and operable sash are new. This is a good approach for upgrading window energy performance when the original window frames are in good shape. At the same time the sash is replaced, new weatherstripping that is most appropriate to the window type and frame details should be installed. Some of the benefits of energy-efficient glazing can be compromised if the new sash is not properly weatherstripped.

Skylight Installation

Installing a skylight or roof window presents the same array of concerns found with windows in vertical walls. The roof window and skylight must maintain continuity with the roof/ roof covering of the building envelope. However, they must also meet much more stringent conditions for shedding water. There are three basic types of skylights:

- Flush Mount: A flush mount skylight is placed on the roof deck with no curb. It is overlapped by and sealed to the roofing material.

- Curb Mount: A curb mounted skylight is placed on a curb raised above the roof plane. This type of curb is not supplied with the skylight. The skylight may be fixed or operable.

- Integral Curb. In this case, the curb is supplied with the skylight as a complete unit. The skylight may also be fixed or operable.

Skylights and roof windows present special installation challenges because they are typically set into the thickest, most heavily insulated framing in the house. Sometimes an insulated well must be created when there is an attic space (Figure 4-25). In all cases, the integrity of the insulating envelope, air and vapor retarders, as well as the exterior water drainage plane must be maintained. Curb-mounted skylights, rising 6 to 12 inches (15 to 30 centimeters) above the roof, create additional heat loss surfaces right where the warmest air of the house tends to collect. Some manufacturers provide curbs prefabricated out of a rigid insulating foam, which can be further insulated at the site (Figure 4-26).

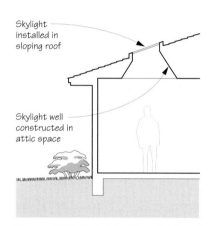

Skylight installed in sloping roof

Skylight well constructed in attic space

Figure 4-25. Skylight with a light well constructed in a flat ceiling with attic roof structure.

The basic flashing methods are installation with mastic, membrane flashing, aluminum/copper sheet, and aluminum/copper step flashing. It is essential to follow good roofing practices and manufacturer's instructions.

Installation at Higher Altitudes

Higher altitudes (over 5000 feet) present transportation and installation issues for window manufacturers who fabricate windows at or near sea level (under 2000' in elevation) and who ship units with sealed insulating glass. The air or gas pressure inside a sealed insulating unit is a function of the atmospheric pressure, barometric pressure, and temperature at the time of manufacture. When the internal pressure differs significantly from the external pressure, the glass will deflect in order to reach a point of equal pressure on both sides. Besides visual distortion, this can also lead to edge stresses (sealant failure and glass cracking).

Changes in elevation are the most significant cause of pressure differentials. Atmospheric pressure at or near sea level is approximately 14.7 psi. As the elevation increases, atmospheric pressure drops to approximately 12.2 psi at 5000 feet, 11.3 psi at 7000 feet, and 10.1 psi at 10,000 feet. A unit manufactured and sealed at sea level (where most windows are made) will bow outwards as the elevation increases.

The surrounding atmospheric pressure will also drop as temperatures drop and will increase as temperatures increase. A 50°F temperature change will result in a change in atmospheric pressure of approximately 1.4 psi. Thus, low temperatures can increase the potential for units to bow out at high elevations.

Transporting windows over high altitudes is one issue of concern for those who live on the west coast and buy windows manufactured east of the Rocky Mountains, or vice-versa. Generally, manufacturers make sure to take routes which do not take windows over extremely high passes, or they make sure their units are shipped quickly over passes and that the units can handle the temporary stress. When buying windows which will be transported over the Rockies, it is prudent to make sure the manufacturer has a proven track record of effectively transporting windows to your area.

A much more significant issue is the installation of windows at high altitudes. Manufacturers have different strategies to address this problem. The stress on a unit is a function of overall unit size, glass thickness, and elevation. Sometimes thicker glass, heat strengthened glass, or tempered glass may

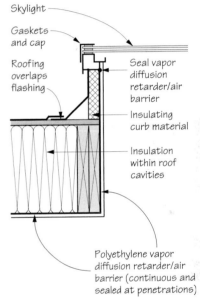

Skylight

Gaskets and cap

Roofing overlaps flashing

Seal vapor diffusion retarder/air barrier

Insulating curb material

Insulation within roof cavities

Polyethylene vapor diffusion retarder/air barrier (continuous and sealed at penetrations)

Figure 4-26. Skylight detail with insulated curb.

be suggested. Another solution is the installation of a capillary tube—an extremely thin and relatively long tube coming out of the IG unit tucked into the sash. Such tubes are designed to allow the unit to come to equilibrium with the atmospheric pressure at the installed site. When installing a window with a capillary tube, make sure to follow manufacturer's installation instructions regarding whether their tube should be left open or crimped shut. Leaving the tube open allows for the optimum pressure equilization but may allow for excessive moisture to enter the unit, leading to condensation between the panes.

The use of capillary tubes (or larger breather tubes) with gas fills presents problems. An insulating glass unit equipped with a capillary tube at the factory and also filled with a gas fill is unlikely to end up at the site with the same fraction of gas as it started out with. Changes in temperature and pressure during transit will most likely cause the unit to "pump" some or all of the gas out and "pull" some or all of the air in. If the tube is not crimped at installation, any gas in the unit will invariably get pumped out over time. As a result, to be safe, gas-filled units looking to capitalize on the performance of the gas fill should not rely on capillary or breather tubes. While cumbersome, the most effective solution is to allow for the units to be gas-filled and sealed at the installation site. Some manufactures have experimented with bladders hooked up to capillary/breather tubes; these bladders expand or contract during transit to account for pressure differences. While such a bladder works in theory, maintaining the bladder and tube in a stable position during transport is challenging in practical terms. Gas-filled units which arrive on site with capillary or breather tubes should be assumed to have the performance of a similar unit with air.

CHAPTER 5

Design Implications with Energy-Efficient Windows

It is clear that the advanced window technologies described throughout this book can have a major effect on comfort and on the annual energy performance of a house. However, there is a broader and possibly more significant impact of the recent revolution in window performance. Because the new glazing technologies provide highly effective insulating value and solar protection, there are important implications for how a house is designed.

There is a long-established set of window design guidelines and assumptions intended to reduce heating and cooling energy use. These are based, in part, on the historical assumption that windows were the weak link in the building envelope. These assumptions frequently created limitations on design freedom or generated conflicts with other performance requirements,

Figure 5-1. High-performance windows make energy-efficient homes possible with greater freedom of design than in the past.
(Photo: Pella Corporation.)

such as view. Traditional considerations include orientation, amount of glazing, and shading requirements for windows. The new technologies, however, challenge the validity of many of these restrictive assumptions. It can be argued that many assumptions developed over the last twenty years about energy-efficient home design require rethinking in light of the new window technologies.

Windows are one of the most multifaceted components of a home. They affect the aesthetics of the home, provide for views, ventilation, and daylight, and have a major impact on the comfort, energy consumption, maintenance requirements, and cost of the home. The designer must determine the amount and placement of glazing to provide natural ventilation in summer, solar heat gain in winter, or simply to allow egress from bedrooms as required. Decisions about window size and placement are also integral to the exterior appearance of the home and the interior aesthetic qualities of the spaces. Possible design objectives include creating a sense of spaciousness and providing natural light or particular views. These architectural decisions are interwoven with site design. Window placement to provide light, solar heating, or ventilation can be enhanced or diminished by landscape elements.

The entire range of window selection considerations is summarized in Chapter 2; this chapter addresses the relationship between window selection and building design. To develop a useful set of guidelines for window sizing, placement, and other building design concerns, it is necessary to consider the multiple design objectives related to windows. These are:

- Providing views.

- Providing daylight.

- Providing fresh air.

- Decreasing summer heat gain.

- Decreasing winter heat loss.

- Providing winter solar heat gain.

The first three of these—providing views, light, and fresh air—represent traditional window functions that do not change fundamentally as new technologies are introduced, although the ability to provide more daylight, for example, without a significant energy penalty is now available. However, the second three objectives—decreasing summer heat gain, decreasing winter heat loss, and providing winter heat gain—are influenced considerably by the ability to select high-performance windows. Guidelines for achieving each of these objectives are discussed in the remainder of this chapter.

PROVIDING VIEWS

When people think of windows, often the immediate association is not with the window unit itself, but rather with the view provided by the window. Views that are highly valued, such as views of oceans, lakes, trees, or mountains, often involve subtle movement and changes in light throughout the day, which can be both mentally restful and stimulating. The view out of a window also contributes to our sense of orientation. Glimpses of familiar scenes or landmarks give a sense of place in the environment and within a building.

Windows provide a connection with the natural environment and a relief from typical interior spaces. An enormous amount of information can be gathered by a simple glance out a window: the time of day, weather conditions, and the coming and going of other people.

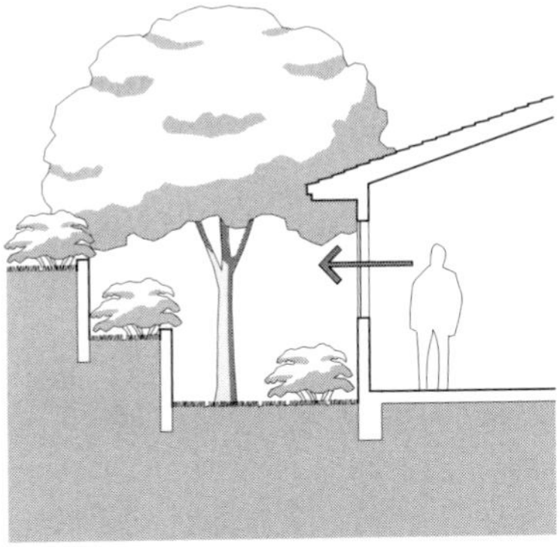

Figure 5-2. View into courtyard.

Connecting Indoor and Outdoor Space

Using one larger window (or group of windows) instead of several smaller, scattered windows can have a powerful effect by visually connecting indoor and outdoor spaces. The picture window, which gained popularity with the availability of plate glass in the 1950s, made it possible to have a wide view without the distortion of many smaller windows. Sliding glass doors provide an even greater sense of openness with the possibility of floor-to-ceiling and wall-to-wall glazing. Creating a sun room that has glazing on two or three walls (and sometimes the roof as well) results in a space that feels as if it is at least partially outdoors.

Guidelines for Providing Views

- Locate and size windows to take advantage of attractive and interesting exterior views and to maximize the connection between indoor and outdoor space.

- Develop attractive views with landscaping or courtyards when expansive views are not available.

- Size and place windows to frame views so that attractive elements are seen and undesirable features are blocked out.

- Place windows to provide surveillance of children's play areas or entry approach.

- Locate windows and use site design elements to maintain privacy.

- Use shades, curtains, or other operable devices to provide privacy when desired.

Figure 5-3. Larger expanses of glazing provide a connection between indoors and outdoors.
(Photo: Associated Materials, Inc.)

As more homes are used for offices, visual relief is an important design consideration for a person sitting at a desk for hours. Exterior views do not have to be large and distant to have a very positive effect. A view of a small courtyard or even a simple garden wall with plantings can be quite attractive at close range.

Careful placement of windows allows for selection and modification of views. A larger window does not always provide a better view. A high sill can cut off the view of an unpleasant parking lot or road. A narrow window can cut the neighbors' house out of the view, leaving only their magnificent garden to be enjoyed. Of course, the position of the viewer on the interior must be considered when framing exterior views through a window. Window placement may be altered if typical viewers are normally seated rather than standing.

Using Windows for Security and Surveillance

In addition to providing attractive views, windows allow visual and verbal communication between the inside and outside of a home. From a window, you can see who is approaching your house, if the neighbors are home, or when the kids arrive home from school. Parents have always valued windows as a way to monitor their children playing outside. The window at the kitchen sink that allows supervision of the backyard while doing kitchen work has become a common pattern in the home-building community. This visual supervision issue is extremely important. A wall of a house with no window in it becomes a "blind spot" in the yard, making supervision difficult.

Maintaining Privacy

A window must provide for just the right level of privacy for the inhabitants. Because a clear glass window is a two-way street, privacy becomes an important issue. A window is one of the main filters between our private world and the public realm beyond. The careful location of a window can resolve many privacy issues: a small window or a window placed high in a wall will restrict the view to the interior, while allowing a view of the outside.

Tinted or reflective glass can provide some degree of privacy, but its effectiveness depends upon a bright exterior and a dim interior. At night, when the relative brightness is reversed, tinted glass no longer offers much privacy. Frosted glass, textured glass, glass block, and stained glass can prevent a full view from the outside while providing daylight, but they

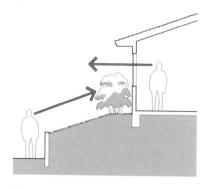

Figure 5-4. Landscape elements such as grade changes, retaining walls, and plantings can be used to ensure privacy while maintaining view out.

just as effectively prevent a view to the outside. Curtains and blinds allow a full range of individual control, and are the primary way most people create the right level of privacy for their homes to accommodate changing privacy needs.

New kinds of window glazing allow the transparency of a window to be controlled electronically. The window is clear with the power on; switching the power off causes the optical material between two panes of glass to change its transparency. This obscured window, which is similar in appearance to frosted glass, still allows the passage of most light.

PROVIDING DAYLIGHT

Letting light into a house is an important function of windows. Even though people have become more reliant on electric light in their houses, good home design can provide most, if not all, the needed daytime light. The qualities of natural light are important even though the amount of energy that can be saved with daylighting is less significant in houses compared to commercial buildings.

The introduction of natural light is also a powerful architectural tool in shaping and defining the interior spaces. However, providing daylight requires thoughtful window placement and interior design that addresses a number of concerns such as visual comfort, balanced light levels, color, and fading of furnishings.

Providing Balanced Lighting

A balance of light is important both for visual comfort and to perform visual tasks. Too much contrast between dark and light, from very bright light to very dark shadows, can be uncomfortable for the eyes. Although the eyes can adjust to changes in light levels very quickly and can simultaneously see a wide range of light intensities, the human eye is more comfortable with a ratio of the brightest to the darkest level of no more than twenty to one. Light levels for reading in the home or office range from 100 to 2000 lux, and an overcast sky can provide outdoor levels of 5000 to 20,000 lux. A beam of bright sunlight will provide up to 100,000 lux on a surface. In order for direct sunlight to be useful visually, it should be diffused and reflected around the room. Most people have experienced the difficulty of reading in bright sunlight. When the sunlight is spread out over a larger area, it provides more comfortable light levels.

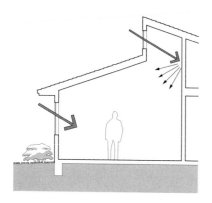

Figure 5-5. A clerestory window enhances architectural volumes with natural light. A light-colored wall acts as a reflector and a diffuser for daylight entering through the clerestory. This approach brings light into the space from two directions, which contributes to more balanced lighting levels.

It is important to recognize that different uses of interior spaces have different ranges of acceptable lighting level. In a corridor, the amount of illumination can range above or below desired levels with little adverse impact. However, in a home office with a computer screen, visual comfort depends on careful control of brightness ratios. Artwork and artifacts, particularly those with paints, dyes, paper, or fabric that are light-sensitive or susceptible to fading, must also be protected from excessive light levels.

The balance of light in a space depends on the overall number and size of windows, their location, and the average reflectance of the interior surfaces of a room. A room with only one window will inevitably have bright areas close to the window and dark areas farther from the window. This gradation in light will be further exaggerated if the room has dark surfaces and furnishings. An improved balance of light can be created by providing light from at least two directions, such as windows located on different walls or a skylight balancing the light from a window. Shadows created from the first window source are balanced by light from the second direction, and the overall contrast is reduced.

As the sun moves through the sky during the day and in different seasons of the year, its angle of penetration into a room changes significantly. In the middle of the day during the summer in the northern hemisphere, for example, the sun

---

Guidelines for Providing Natural Light

- Arrange windows to provide daylight to all occupied rooms.

- Locate windows to define and enhance architectural volumes.

- Provide balanced lighting by introducing daylight from two directions in order to avoid glare and bright visual hot spots.

- Place windows so that direct sunlight, if admitted at all, reflects off interior walls and floors to provide more diffuse, even light.

- Use reflective ground surfaces or walls to increase daylight distribution into south- and north-facing windows.

- Avoid reflective ground surfaces that will increase glare from low sun entering east- and west-facing windows.

- Use translucent glazings on skylights to diffuse direct sunlight. Consider installing shutters or shades to block high midday summer sun while admitting daylight in morning, early evening, and on overcast days.

- Use light pipes to provide bright, diffused sunlight in a particular room location.

- Use landscape elements to block low direct sun into east- and west-facing windows.

- Use shades/curtains/overhangs to block direct sunlight.

- Use light from the north-facing windows to provide less variable, more diffuse illumination when desired.

comes in high overhead and strikes near the sill of a south-facing window. However, the low sun to the east in early morning and to the west during the afternoon will penetrate deep into a room, strike back walls, and shine directly into people's eyes. In the winter, the sun is lower in the sky throughout the day for all orientations, and tends to penetrate more deeply into rooms. This may provide useful heat but must be managed to control glare. In order to be visually useful, direct sunlight must first be reflected off of a floor or wall and then diffused around the room. For instance, east- or west-facing windows can be placed near a corner with a north wall of a room, which will catch and reflect the sunlight before it penetrates too deeply. In addition to designing the room itself properly for glare control, venetian blinds, translucent shades, and drapes can be used to diffuse entering light. In hot climates, it is usually best to avoid direct sun completely during the peak cooling season.

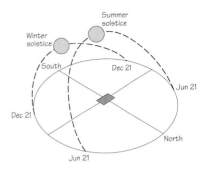

Figure 5-6. Solar path diagram illustrates the range of sun altitude and direction during the year. The maximum altitude at noon in the summer depends on the latitude of the site.

Using Reflective Outdoor Surfaces to Increase Daylight

Direct light from the sun and sky is an important source of daylight, although in hot climates, it is usually best to avoid direct sunlight completely during the cooling season. In all climates there are situations in which the light reflecting off of outside surfaces can be very useful. A view of a light-colored sunlit wall can actually provide more light than a view of the north sky. And large reflective horizontal surfaces outside a window, such as snow, a lake, or a sandy beach, greatly increase the amount of light entering the window.

People often think of south windows as the sunny windows; however, the view from a south window might look out at the dark, shady "back" of a building, which is in stark contrast to the bright, sunlit foreground. On the other hand, a north window can look out onto a brightly sunlit wall or garden, providing both a great deal of reflected light and a cheerful view of sunlit flowers or surfaces.

Figure 5-7. Reflective ground.

Avoiding Glare from the Sun

While sun penetration at south windows in winter can create some glare problems, east- and especially west-facing windows are usually the greatest offenders year round. People inevitably orient windows toward the most interesting view. But when that view includes a reflective surface such as snow, water, or sand, especially if the window faces the east or west, the penetrating low sun problem is intensified. These windows create the most difficult situations for solar control. While the view may be highly desired, the glare and excess heat of the sun and its reflections are not. Typically, these windows require active operation of shades or blinds by the homeowner, and, until recently, the only permanent solar control technology was tinted or reflective glazing, plastic films applied to the glass, or screens.

Direct sun at low angles can be blocked by trees, shrubs, or garden walls. Such landscape elements can be strategically placed to reduce glare as well as heat gain through east- and west-facing windows. The most important time to block low-angled sun is in the summer when the sun rises and sets farther to the north of direct east and west, so plantings should be located to account for this pattern.

Diffusing Direct Sunlight

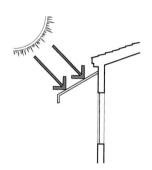

Figure 5-8. Opaque awnings reduce heat gain and glare by blocking most sunlight.

Overhangs and other solid external architectural elements can block direct sunlight completely for some time periods, while more open elements such as lattice structures diffuse the daylight before it enters the windows (Figures 5-8 and 5-9). This can assist in reducing glare from the direct sun or sky, and can illuminate spaces with a larger and more diffuse light source. Dark-colored woven fiberglass or perforated metal screens mounted on the exterior of windows can also reduce glare while still maintaining a high degree of visibility to the outside on sunny days. Light-colored screens diffuse the transmitted light but do not allow as much view to the outside.

Interior shades, drapes, or blinds can block or diffuse direct sunlight. The ideal drapery to reduce glare from bright windows, while still allowing a clear view out, is a loosely woven dark-colored drape. A loosely woven light-colored drape will diffuse the daylight from the window about the room and provide maximum privacy. However, light-colored drapes will appear very bright in direct sunlight and it may be difficult to see through them. Roll-up shades can be translucent, allowing some diffuse light to enter, or opaque, which block all light. Shades can also be made from woven screen materials in varying densities and colors, producing a range of light control and visibility. Reflective and tinted plastic roll-up shades reduce the sun's intensity and provide a clear view out, but do not diffuse or scatter the incoming light. When adjusted to the correct angle, horizontal venetian blinds or miniblinds can block direct sunlight but permit diffuse light to enter the room and often provide views out. Vertical blinds serve a similar function and are particularly useful for controlling low-angle sunlight at east- and west-facing windows.

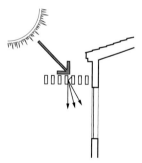

Figure 5-9. Slatted overhangs reduce heat gain and glare but provide diffuse sunlight.

Translucent glazing materials, such as frosted or patterned glass, can diffuse sunlight very evenly. Glass block and translucent fiberglass panels also provide light diffusion and visual privacy. The use of translucent glazings for skylights and clerestory windows, which are not in the visual field, is an excellent way to diffuse sunlight evenly throughout a space. When used on windows at eye level, however, the materials may become too bright for visual comfort. A frosted window in the low afternoon sunlight will seem to glow with the intensity of a searchlight. Because of this effect, clear glass with additional interior shading devices generally allows for better control of the light from sunlit windows.

Skylights and roof windows can provide high levels of daylight, but view is not a concern as it is with conventional windows. The direct light from above can be diffused by using frosted glazing, by using a light well where light-colored vertical surfaces just beneath the skylight reflect and diffuse sunlight, or by using interior shades or blinds operated from below. A single skylight is far more effective at lighting a larger space on a sunny day if the sunlight is diffused either by the glazing or the light well surfaces. The size, shape, and color of light well surfaces influences their ability to diffuse and distribute light (Figures 5-10 and 5-11).

When a skylight and light well are difficult to incorporate into the room design, light tubes are becoming a popular approach to admit sunlight into a room. A clear plastic dome (normally 10–14 inches in diameter) is mounted over a hole in the roof and is connected to a small light diffuser in the ceiling by a highly reflective tube. Sunlight enters through the domed opening and bounces numerous times until it emerges at the ceiling diffuser (Figure 5-12). Although much of the light is lost in the multiple reflections in the tube, these systems can provide as much light as a bright lighting fixture on a sunny day. The overall efficiency of the system depends on the time of day and location of the domed opening as well as the length of the tube and its internal reflectivity.

Using Sky Light

Light from the sky, as distinguished from light from the sun, is cooler, gentler, and diffuse. While sunlight is normally considered to appear white, the early morning and late afternoon sun takes on a yellow or red hue, an effect that can be heightened by dust and pollutants in the atmosphere. Depending upon the position of the sun and type of clouds present, light from the sky will provide illumination levels of 5000 to 20,000 lux,

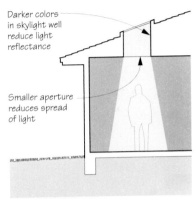

Darker colors in skylight well reduce light reflectance

Smaller aperture reduces spread of light

Figure 5-10. Roof window with smaller, dark-colored light well reduces amount of light and increases contrast.

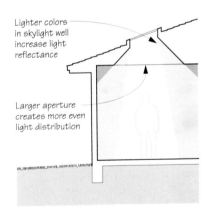

Lighter colors in skylight well increase light reflectance

Larger aperture creates more even light distribution

Figure 5-11. Roof window with larger, light-colored light well increases amount of light and provides more even distribution.

155

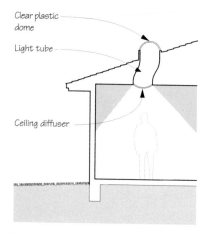

Figure 5-12. Light tube provides daylight through a highly reflective bendable tube.

Figure 5-13. Light tubes capture sunlight from the rooftop, redirect it down a highly reflective shaft, then diffuse it throughout the interior space.
(Photo: Solatube International, Inc.)

or 5 to 20 percent of that provided by bright direct sunlight. Light from a clear blue sky has the additional advantage that there is more visible light, with a significantly smaller infrared component.

In situations where daylight is desired with minimal solar heat gain, north windows can provide the best quality of daylight of any orientation. Artists have long preferred the light from a high north window for their studios because the intensity, quality, and color of the light is most constant throughout the day. While the use of north-facing glass may be desirable in terms of daylighting and avoiding solar heat gain, it is not an effective strategy for providing useful solar gain in winter.

PROVIDING FRESH AIR

Windows provide the primary means to control air flow in most homes. People open windows to provide fresh air, ventilate odors and smoke, dissipate heat and moisture, and create air movement on hot days. While exhaust fans and central air systems can mechanically ventilate a room, opening a room to the outdoors is perceived as more direct and natural. Architects have often found that people will insist upon having operable windows even though they may rarely open them. There seems to be a strong psychological need to know that a window could be opened, if necessary.

In order to ensure that all residences have access to the healthful aspects of natural ventilation, state or local building codes commonly regulate the minimum size of the ventilation opening in a window and the egress opening. Typically, codes require that about 5 percent of the floor area of a "living area," such as a bedroom or living room, be provided in ventilation area. These regulated areas should be carefully checked before sizing or replacing a window.

Guidelines for Providing Fresh Air

- Place operable windows in all rooms to give occupants opportunity for fresh air.

- Provide cross-ventilation by placing window openings on opposite walls in line with the prevailing winds.

- Use casement windows to direct and control ventilation.

- Use operable skylights or roof windows to enhance ventilation.

- Use landscape elements to direct breezes.

The potential value of natural ventilation as an energy efficiency strategy depends on climate and lifestyle. In a mild climate, there may be many hours during the year when outdoor air can be used to improve comfort and save energy for air conditioning. In climates with severe summers and/or winters or in dusty, noisy, or humid locations, the value of natural ventilation may be limited. To the extent that natural ventilation requires occupants to open and close windows, the lifestyle of the occupant may also be a factor. Finally, security concerns may limit the opportunities to provide natural ventilation.

An alternative approach that provides a steady amount of outdoor air is to incorporate a small ventilation element into the frame of the window. This passive approach has been used in the northwest United States to meet state code requirements for a minimum amount of outdoor air in new, tightly built houses that do not use mechanical ventilation. These "trickle ventilators" have been widely used in European houses. The slots go through the window frame, normally on the top or bottom, with screens and flaps that keep out bugs and rain. They can be adjusted by occupants to control the amount of air flow. The peak amount of air exchange can be controlled in each room by properly sizing the ventilators in each window.

Improving Ventilation

Ventilation is maximized by providing for cross-ventilation of as many spaces in the house as is practical. In normal wind conditions, the side of a building facing the wind will have a zone of positive pressure and the opposite side will have a zone of negative pressure (Figure 5-14). By providing adequate ventilation openings on these two sides of the house, a positive flow of air through the interior, from positive to negative pressure, is encouraged. Of course, the interior layout of the house must permit the air to flow through, and interior doors in the ventilation path must remain open.

Ventilation effectiveness depends on wind speed, the angle at which the wind strikes the window, and the location and size of the window. A room with a single opening will have only 12 to 23 percent of the wind velocity. This improves up to 51 percent if windows are located on adjacent walls and as much as 65 percent of the outside air velocity can be reached with windows on opposite walls (Figures 5-15 and 5-16).

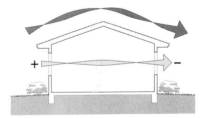

Figure 5-14. House section showing positive/negative air pressure.

Figure 5-15. Ventilation openings arrangement can be optimized to increase the rate of cross ventilation in a room. Source: Sun, Wind & Light: Architectural Design Strategies

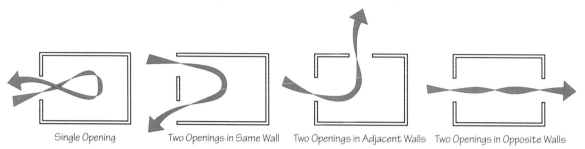

Single Opening   Two Openings in Same Wall   Two Openings in Adjacent Walls   Two Openings in Opposite Walls

window height fraction of wall height	1/3	1/3	1/3
window width fraction of wall width	1/3	2/3	3/3
single opening	12–14%	13–17%	16–23%
two openings in the same wall	—	22%	23%
two openings in adjacent walls	37–45%	37–45%	40–51%
two openings in opposite walls	35–42%	37–51%	47–65%

Figure 5-16. Average interior air velocity as a percentage of the exterior wind velocity. Range = wind 45° to perpendicular to opening.
Source: Sun, Wind & Light: Architectural Design Strategies

If windows cannot be located on opposing walls, high- and low-pressure areas can be induced with the use of casements (Figure 5-17). Of all window types, casements provide the most control of ventilation direction and intensity. Because the sash can be opened into an air stream, breezes that would otherwise pass by can be directed into the room. Window types in which the sash remains flush with the wall ventilate well only with direct pressure differences across the window. In addition, as noted previously, virtually the entire window area of casement units can be opened, while sliders are limited to less than half of the area.

Even without external winds, double-hung windows can sometimes provide natural ventilation caused by stratified air flow within a room. Cooler fresh air enters at the bottom opening, while hotter air at the ceiling level is allowed to exit through the top opening. The taller the windows and the higher the ceiling, the more pronounced is this effect.

Operable skylights or roof windows can aid overall ventilation in a house significantly by creating a similar thermal chimney effect, letting hot air escape from the ceiling level where it accumulates and causing cooler air to be drawn in through lower windows (Figure 5-18).

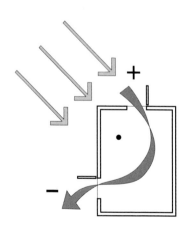

Figure 5-17. Casement windows can be used to deflect air into a room (plan view). Black dot indicates area of static air.

158

Trees, shrubs, exterior walls, and earth berms can all divert wind patterns. These elements can be used to some extent to funnel or direct breezes through a house. Conversely, if these elements are placed without regard for prevailing wind patterns, they can act as obstructions to natural ventilation.

DECREASING SUMMER HEAT GAIN

Orienting Windows to Reduce Heat Gain

Until recently, windows themselves had little inherent capability to reduce solar heat gain, so the layout of energy-efficient houses in hot locations evolved to protect windows from the most significant gains. In predominantly cooling climates, the goal is to face most windows north, where there is little direct exposure, or to the south, where they can easily be designed with overhangs that will keep out most of the hot summer sun (Figure 5-19). Overhangs are much less effective against the lower angles of the east and west sun. Therefore, simply reducing the size and number of east and west windows can be the most direct strategy. West windows are subject to the full force of the strong afternoon sun, at a time of day when temperatures generally climb to their peak. East windows have the same problem in the morning hours, but air temperatures tend to be cooler at that time.

In spite of energy concerns, a house may have an ocean view or other attractive amenity to the east or west of the home. Fortunately, the traditional patterns of avoiding east- and west-facing glazing are not necessarily as critical when better-performing windows with low solar heat gain coefficients are used. Figure 5-20 illustrates the impact of different window orientations on annual energy costs for a typical house in Phoenix, Arizona. As expected, facing windows in different directions has a significant impact when typical clear double-glazed windows are used. The use of bronze-tinted glazing shows little improvement. When higher-performance windows with low-solar-gain low-E coatings are used, however, the window orientation has a diminished impact on energy use. In effect, with these more advanced windows, nearly all of the glazing can face west with the same energy use as more conventional glazings facing north. These computer simulations are done for a house with average shading conditions. If there were no overhangs or interior shades, the less efficient glazing would perform worse in comparison to the low-solar-gain low-E windows.

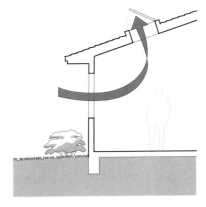

Figure 5-18. Operable skylights or roof windows can enhance natural ventilation.

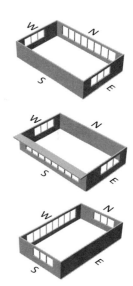

Figure 5-19. North-facing windows are best to reduce heat gain in a hot climate. South-facing windows allow heat gain but can easily be shaded. East- and west-facing windows are worse.

Figure 5-20. Impact of window orientation on annual energy costs for a 2000-square-foot house with three different window types in Phoenix, Arizona.

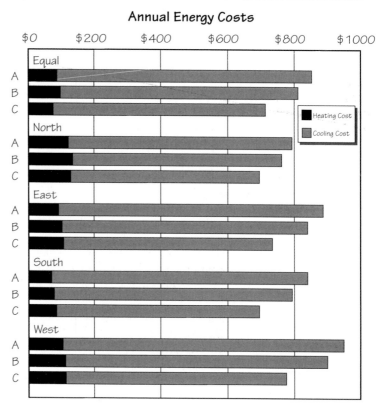

Annual Energy Costs

Window	Glazing	Frame	U-factor	SHGC	VT
A	double, clear	aluminum w/break	0.63	0.62	0.63
B	double, tint	aluminum w/break	0.63	0.52	0.48
C	double, low-solar-gain low-E	aluminum w/break	0.47	0.33	0.55

Note: The annual energy performance figures shown here were generated using RESFEN for a typical (new construction) 2000 sq ft house with 300 sq ft of window area. Where windows are predominately on one side, the distribution is 240 sq ft on that side and 20 sq ft on the others. Typical shading conditions (interior shades, overhangs, trees, and neighboring buildings) are assumed for all windows. U-factor, SHGC, and VT are for the total window including frame. The costs shown here are annual costs for space heating and space cooling only and thus will be less than total utility bills. Costs for lights, appliances, hot water, cooking, and other uses are not included in these figures. The mechanical system uses a gas furnace for heating and air conditioning for cooling. The gas and electric prices used in these figures are provided by the Energy Information Administration (EIA) (www.eia.doe.gov). RESFEN is a computer program for calculating the annual cooling and heating energy use and costs due to window selection and is available from Lawrence Berkeley National Laboratory (windows.lbl.gov/software/resfen). See Appendix A for pricing and modeling assumptions.

Reducing the Glazing Area to Reduce Gain

Another traditional guideline to reduce heat gain is to reduce the total glazing area. Of course, this can be effective with any type of window, but it is particularly important when less efficient windows are used. Figure 5-21 illustrates the impact of three different amounts of glazing on annual energy costs for a house in Phoenix, Arizona. In all cases, the windows are equally distributed on the four orientations. With clear or tinted glazing (Windows A and B), increasing the glazing area has a very significant impact on the cooling load. The annual energy use for a house with low-solar-gain low-E glazing (Windows C) still exhibits the same pattern, but the differences are not nearly as great in relative or absolute terms.

Because of the need for daylighting, views, and ventilation, reducing window area significantly is not a realistic or desirable strategy. This analysis indicates, however, that increasing glazing area for any reason will not have nearly as profound an impact when high-performance windows are used.

Figure 5-21. Impact of window area on annual energy costs for a 2000-square-foot house with three different window types in Phoenix, Arizona.

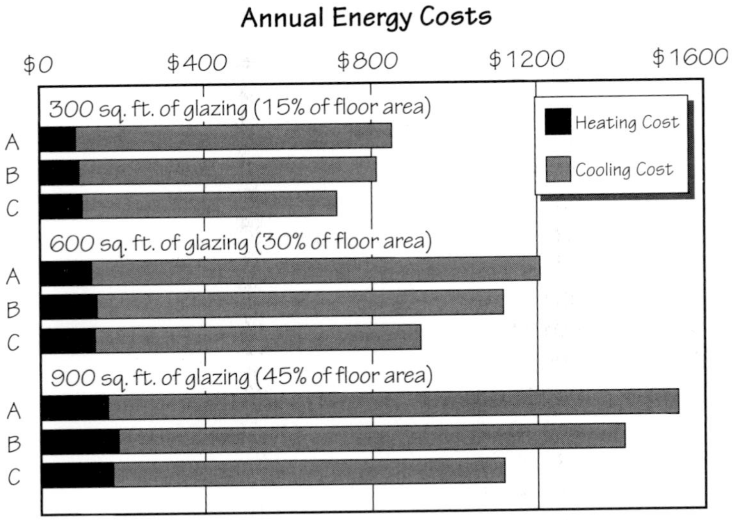

Annual Energy Costs

Note: The annual energy performance figures shown here were generated using RESFEN for a typical (new construction) 2000 sq ft house with 300 sq ft (15%), 600 sq ft (30%) and 900 sq ft (45%) of window area. The windows are equally distributed on all four sides of the house and include typical shading (interior shades, overhangs, trees, and neighboring buildings). U-factor, SHGC, and VT are for the total window including frame. The costs shown here are annual costs for space heating and space cooling only and thus will be less than total utility bills. Costs for lights, appliances, hot water, cooking, and other uses are not included in these figures. The mechanical system uses a gas furnace for heating and air conditioning for cooling. The gas and electric prices used in these figures are provided by the Energy Information Administration (EIA) (www.eia.doe.gov). RESFEN is a computer program for calculating the annual cooling and heating energy use and costs due to window selection and is available from Lawrence Berkeley National Laboratory (windows.lbl.gov/software/resfen). See Appendix A for pricing and modeling assumptions.

Window	Glazing	Frame	U-factor	SHGC	VT
A	double, clear	aluminum w/break	0.63	0.62	0.63
B	double, tint	aluminum w/break	0.63	0.52	0.48
C	double, low-solar-gain low-E	aluminum w/break	0.47	0.33	0.55

Figure 5-22. No shading can result in significant solar heat gain through windows.

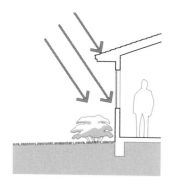

Figure 5-23. Exterior shading devices, such as overhangs, awnings, or screens are effective in reducing heat gain.

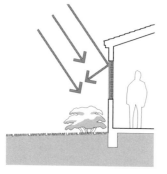

Figure 5-24. Interior blinds, shades, and drapes also reduce heat gain. The most effective have a high reflectance.

When larger windows are desired, the combination of high-performance glazing plus appropriate exterior and interior shading devices can reduce the cooling impact to that of a smaller, unshaded window.

Shading Windows to Reduce Solar Gain

Using Overhangs and Exterior Shading Devices

Since ordinary windows have traditionally been the primary source of heat gain in summer, any effort to shade them has had great benefits in terms of comfort and energy use. The best place to shade a window is on the outside, before the sun strikes the window. Exterior shading devices have long been considered the most effective way to reduce solar heat gain into a home. The most common approach is the fixed overhang. For south-facing windows, overhangs can be sized to block out much of the summer sun but still permit lower-angled winter sun to enter. Compared to other types of shading devices, overhangs have the advantage of reducing heat gain and glare without diminishing the view. Other exterior devices include grills, awnings, roll-down shutters, canopies, Bermuda shutters, and bamboo shades. The choice of shading strategy is often distinctly regional, based on local traditions. The drawback of some shading devices is that they block light and view—a roll down shutter can completely negate the benefits of a window during the day.

Among the possible exterior shading devices are black or dark-colored screens mounted on the exterior of the window. Such a fabric or metal "solar screen" can lower a clear window's solar heat gain coefficient by 30 to 70 percent. The open weave of the screen allows much of the heat from this absorbed radiation to be convected away before it interacts with the window's glazing. While solar screens reduce heat gain, they also can diminish light and view.

Using Interior Shading Devices

Most homeowners use some form of interior window treatment, such as drapes, blinds, or shades, on their windows. In addition to their decorative aspects, drapes and curtains have been traditionally used by homeowners to control privacy and daylight, provide protection from overheating, and reduce the fading of fabrics.

To most effectively reduce solar heat gain, the drapery used to block the sunlight should have high reflectance and low transmittance. A densely woven fabric with a light color would achieve this objective. Drapes can reduce the solar heat gain coefficient of clear glass from 20 to 70 percent, depending upon the color and openness of the drapery fabric. The impact of drapery on the solar heat gain is proportionally lessened as the window is shaded by other methods, such as exterior shading or tinted glass. The main disadvantage of drapes and other interior devices as solar control measures is that once the solar energy has entered the room through a window, a large proportion of the energy absorbed by the shading system will remain inside the house as heat gain. Interior devices are thus most effective when they are highly reflective, with minimum absorption of solar energy.

Blinds and shades primarily provide light and privacy control but they also can have an impact on controlling solar heat gain. They include horizontal venetian blinds, the newer miniblinds, vertical slatted blinds of various materials, a wide variety of pleated and honeycomb shades, and roll-down shades.

White- or silver-colored blinds, coupled with clear glass, have the greatest potential for reducing solar heat gains. Some manufacturers have offered window unit options that include miniblinds mounted inside sealed or unsealed insulating glass. The blinds, in the sealed dust-free environment, can be operated with a magnetic lever without breaking the air seal. Blinds in the unsealed glazing unit are protected as well, but

---

Guidelines for Decreasing Heat Gain in Summer

Using clear single- or double-glazed windows:

- Design the layout so that windows and living areas do not face the hot western sun.
- Minimize window area on sunlit orientations to reduce solar heat gain.
- Use overhangs or other architectural and landscape elements to prevent sunlight from reaching windows.
- Use drapes, blinds, shades, or other interior treatments to reduce heat gain through windows.

Using high-performance windows (low SHGC):

- Orientation is less of a concern.
- Window area can be increased without a significant cooling energy penalty.
- Shading with external devices or landscaping is less of a concern.
- Internal shades are not as critical for solar control purposes.

    Note: Proper orientation and effective use of internal and external shading devices can still be useful in minimizing summer heat gain, but if they are not practical solutions for other reasons, low SHGC windows can largely compensate for their omission.

Figure 5-25. Blinds between the glass help to lower the shading coefficient as well as providing insulating value. (Photo: Pella Corporation)

can be easily removed if needed for cleaning or repair. These "between-glass shading devices" provide a lower shading coefficient than equivalent blinds mounted on the interior (Figure 5-25). They also provide additional insulating value to the double glass by reducing convective loops within the air space.

Unlike other strategies to reduce heat gain, such as overhangs, interior shades generally require consistent, active operation by the occupant. Unfortunately, when shades are down, daylight and view are diminished or excluded completely. It is not uncommon to see shades drawn much of the time on west-facing facades. It is unlikely that anyone would operate all shades in a consistent, optimal pattern as they are often assumed to be operated in computer simulations. Motorized and automated shading systems are now widely available to solve these operational problems, although normally at a significant cost. The control systems can be automated using sensors, time clocks, or a home automation system. They can also be directly controlled by the occupants.

By using high-performance glazing to provide the necessary solar control, there are two important benefits: there is less need for operating the shades, and the window is covered less of the time, resulting in increased daylight and unobstructed views. Of course, shades also provide privacy and darkness when desired, so they may be closed part of the day in any case, but the high-performance glazing means there is less need to operate them in a particular manner to make significant reductions in energy use. If your goal is to minimize cooling energy use, or you live in a house without air-conditioning in a hot climate, then the combination of good shade management with low SHGC windows will be the best strategy.

Using Landscape Elements to Provide Shade

Nothing can be much better at providing cool shade in the summer than a great broad-leafed tree. In addition to shading the building from direct sun, trees have been found to reduce the temperature of air immediately around them by as much as 10°F (5°C) below the temperature of the surrounding air due to evaporation of moisture. A window shaded with a high tree or vine-covered trellis can have full shade in the summer, while enhancing the view and perhaps the ventilation. Trees and bushes can provide strategic shade from low east or west sun angles that are extremely difficult to shade architecturally.

Figure 5-26. Landscape elements provide shade and reduce temperatures.

A Comparison of Shading Conditions

Figure 5-27 illustrates the impact of five different shading conditions on a house in Phoenix, Arizona. When the house has clear glazing (Window A), interior shades and overhangs significantly reduce energy costs. Naturally, a completely shaded house has the best performance in a hot climate. Using tinted glazing (Window B) diminishes energy costs to some degree for all shading conditions, but the difference between shading and no shading is still significant.

Figure 5-27. Impact of different shading conditions on annual energy costs for a 2000-square-foot house with three different window types in Phoenix, Arizona.

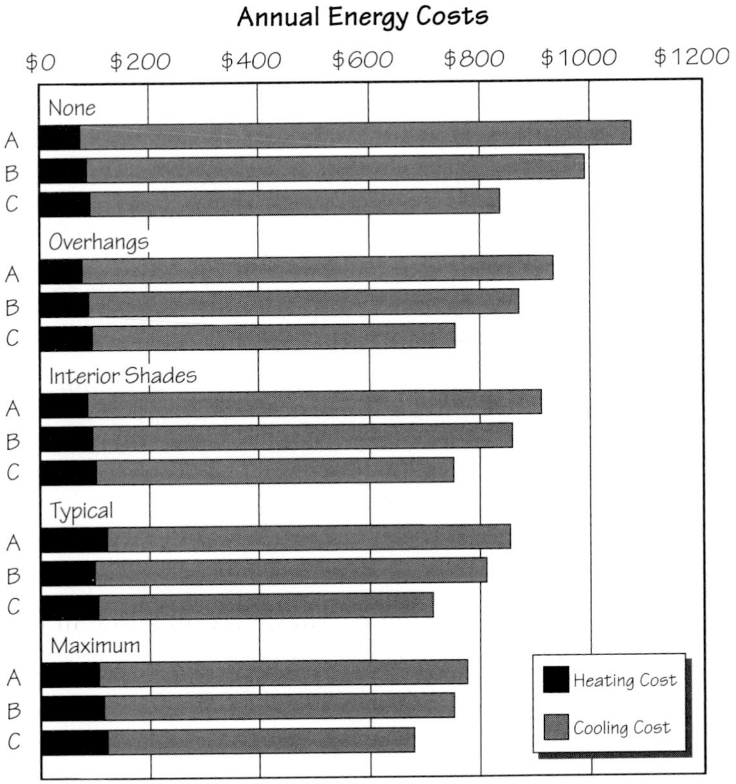

Annual Energy Costs

Note: The annual energy performance figures shown here were generated using RESFEN for a typical (new construction) 2000 sq ft house with 300 sq ft of window area. The windows are equally distributed on all four sides of the house. Typical shading includes (interior shades, overhangs, trees, and neighboring buildings). U-factor, SHGC, and VT are for the total window including frame. The costs shown here are annual costs for space heating and space cooling only and thus will be less than total utility bills. Costs for lights, appliances, hot water, cooking, and other uses are not included in these figures. The mechanical system uses a gas furnace for heating and air conditioning for cooling. The gas and electric prices used in these figures are provided by the Energy Information Administration (EIA) (www.eia.doe.gov). RESFEN is a computer program for calculating the annual cooling and heating energy use and costs due to window selection and is available from Lawrence Berkeley National Laboratory (windows.lbl.gov/software/resfen). See Appendix A for pricing and modeling assumptions.

Window	Glazing	Frame	U-factor	SHGC	VT
A	double, clear	aluminum w/break	0.63	0.62	0.63
B	double, tint	aluminum w/break	0.63	0.52	0.48
C	double, low-solar-gain low-E	aluminum w/break	0.47	0.33	0.55

165

Reliance on any form of shading is not nearly as important, however, when windows with low solar heat gain coefficient are used. Using a low-solar-gain low-E coating (Window C) in Figure 5-27), results in great energy cost reduction for all conditions but shows a more modest benefit from the use of interior shades, overhangs, or vegetation. This is because the glazing itself provides the necessary control of solar radiation, so these additional measures become less important in terms of energy use. The house with no shading and low-solar-gain low-E glazing (Window C) uses about the same energy than the house with typical shading using clear or tinted glazing (Windows A and B).

DECREASING WINTER HEAT LOSS

Determining the Optimal Amount of Glazing

In the 1970s, when energy use was an emerging concern, the high-performance windows of today were not available. One of the obvious architectural design approaches was simple: to reduce heat loss, reduce window area. Furthermore, where windows were used, strategies such as using thermal shades had a major impact. As windows have improved considerably in the last twenty years, very high performance windows can now equal or exceed the performance of even an insulated wall over a complete winter heating season. Consequently, the strategy of reducing window area to reduce energy use is no longer as significant if highly efficient windows are used.

As Figure 5-28 illustrates, total glazing area has a significant impact on heating energy use when clear, double-glazed windows are used (Window A). This difference diminishes with double-glazed low-E windows. With triple-glazed low-E windows (Window C), the glazing area has very little impact on energy use. This indicates that the benefit of more passive solar gain exceeds any losses from more glazing area. It should be noted, however, that cooling energy for the house with high-performance windows increases with greater glazing area resulting in a slight increase in total annual energy costs. Depending on the exact U-factor, SHGC, and climate, energy gains in the heating season may be offset by losses in the cooling season. However, cooling season energy use can be further reduced by shifting the window area to preferred orientations and employing other cooling load reduction strategies for the windows.

Figure 5-28. Impact of window area on annual energy costs for a 2000-square-foot house with three different window types in Minneapolis, Minnesota.

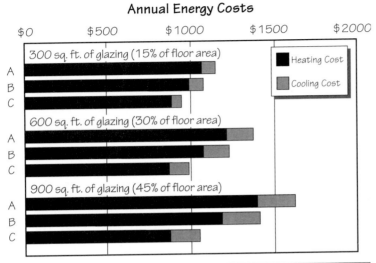

Annual Energy Costs

Note: The annual energy performance figures shown here were generated using RESFEN for a typical (new construction) 2000 sq ft house with 300 sq ft (15%), 600 sq ft (30%) and 900 sq ft (45%) of window area. The windows are equally distributed on all four sides of the house and include typical shading (interior shades, overhangs, trees, and neighboring buildings). U-factor, SHGC, and VT are for the total window including frame. The costs shown here are annual costs for space heating and space cooling only and thus will be less than total utility bills. Costs for lights, appliances, hot water, cooking, and other uses are not included in these figures. The mechanical system uses a gas furnace for heating and air conditioning for cooling. The gas and electric prices used in these figures are provided by the Energy Information Administration (EIA) (www.eia.doe.gov). RESFEN is a computer program for calculating the annual cooling and heating energy use and costs due to window selection and is available from Lawrence Berkeley National Laboratory (windows.lbl.gov/software/resfen). See Appendix A for pricing and modeling assumptions.

Window	Glazing	Frame	U-factor	SHGC	VT
A	double, clear	wood/vinyl	0.49	0.56	0.59
B	double, high-solar-gain low-E	wood/vinyl	0.37	0.53	0.50
C	triple, moderate-solar-gain low-E	insulated	0.18	0.40	0.50

Using Shades and Insulated Shutters

Traditionally, drapes have provided a slight benefit by reducing heat loss and an important contribution by improving thermal comfort as radiant barriers. Because drapes are normally not tightly fitted to the walls and floor, air can circulate around them, making them marginally effective in reducing conductive and convective heat loss. When a heavy drape is pulled across a cold window surface, the occupants of a room can feel considerably warmer because they are no longer radiating their warmth to the cold glass. Studies have suggested that in some cases room air temperatures can be lowered by as much as 5°F (3°C) while still maintaining the same comfort level if cold windows are covered with drapes. Convective air currents, however, can reduce comfort. When a window extends from floor to ceiling, a downdraft of chilled air can be created on the cold interior surface of the glass, which then flows out beneath the drapes and across the floor.

With energy concerns arising in the 1970s, movable insulating panels over windows became a popular strategy. Movable insulation has the advantages of providing high levels of insulation at night when most needed and allowing the greatest transparency for view and solar gain at other times. However, these panels were typically costly, required tight sealing to the window in order to work well, and needed consistent operation to be effective. The value of thermal shades and movable insulation panels is reduced somewhat by high-performance windows. High-performance windows are also more effective than movable insulation since they require no operation and are in place twenty-four hours a day.

Exterior rolling shutters with hollow or insulated slats have been popular in Europe and are available in the United States as well. They provide only modest additional insulating value, but they also reduce wind effects, and provide solar control, privacy, and security. Most are operated manually, which means they are subject to the same inefficiencies of any occupant-operated device, but they can be motorized and controlled automatically.

Minimizing the Effect of Winter Winds

Since air leakage is increased by wind pressure, windows directly facing prevailing winter winds will experience more air leakage than those oriented away from the winds. In many northerly climates, this means minimizing windows toward the north and west, although precise wind patterns depend on many factors, including topography, landscaping, and other site-specific characteristics. Usually this does not conflict with placing windows toward the south for beneficial solar gain.

Guidelines for Decreasing Winter Heat Loss

Using clear single- or double-glazed windows:

- Concentrate glazing on southerly orientations to maximize solar benefits.

- Minimize window area on nonsouth-facing orientations to reduce winter heat loss.

- Use thermal shades or movable insulation over windows to reduce nighttime heat loss.

- Minimize windows facing prevailing winter winds and use landscape elements to block winter winds.

Using high-performance windows (low U-factor and high SHGC):

- Window area can be increased without a significant energy penalty.

- Thermal shades and movable insulation are not necessary to improve energy performance.

When windows do face toward prevailing winter winds, landscape elements such as earth berms, walls, and thick rows of evergreen trees or shrubs can be effective windbreaks. This protection has an impact not only on window air leakage but also on air leakage through the entire building envelope.

Regardless of exact conditions, it is always recommended to select high-performance windows with good weatherstripping and low air-leakage rates. As with other traditional energy-saving strategies, the beneficial impact of wind protection by external elements is reduced as the building and its windows become more airtight.

PROVIDING WINTER SOLAR HEAT GAIN

Strategies to capture winter solar heat gain have a long history in architectural design, and have been promoted in the United States as a specific energy-efficiency strategy since the 1970s. Generally, passive systems have been based on the simple principle that solar gain will be maximized by placing more glazing toward the south and less glazing in other directions. This implies arranging the floor plan along an east-west axis so that more rooms have southern exposure (Figure 5-29). In addition, the amount of south-facing glazing in each room can be sized to optimize solar gain. Simply increasing south-facing window area is not necessarily better. Each additional unit of glass area provides diminishing solar gain benefits while continuing to increase nighttime heat losses. Another characteristic of passive solar design is that, in order to be useful, solar heat admitted through windows must be stored in thermal mass within the house, to be released later in the afternoon and at night. An inadequate ratio of mass to glass area will result in overheating during winter days and less useful solar gain than expected. Finally, the large solar aperture must be carefully protected during the cooling season to avoid increased air-conditioning costs. A number of houses have been designed that successfully use this south-facing glass combined with mass strategy to substantially reduce heating and cooling costs. But this approach has not been adopted widely because it typically involves several departures from traditional design and construction techniques.

The improved insulating value and solar control characteristics of high-performance glazing have modified some traditional energy design assumptions described previously. With passive solar design, the availability of high-performance

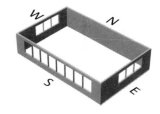

Figure 5-29. South-facing windows provide maximum winter solar heat gain.

glazings requires some rethinking of traditional assumptions as well, but it also presents new opportunities to enhance passive design. For example, east-, west-, and even north-facing windows can become passive solar collectors, meaning that their useful solar contribution exceeds their losses (although they will never provide as much winter solar gain as a south-facing window). This provides more architectural design freedom and should result in greater acceptance of these design approaches.

Orienting Windows to Maximize Solar Gain

It is generally accepted that simply orienting the majority of windows to the south in a heating-dominated climate will result in greater solar gain and less heating energy use. However, it is not always feasible to do so. In these cases east and west windows might be useful as secondary solar collectors using high-performance windows. To test this assumption, a typical house was used in simulating energy use for five different orientation conditions in a cold climate (Minneapolis, Minnesota). The results shown in Figure 5-30 indicate that, as expected, there is a difference between orientations and south-oriented windows perform best. The difference between orientations is more notable when clear double-glazed windows are used (Window A) but is diminished when higher-performance windows with lower U-factors are used (Windows B and C).

Window orientation in a house is often dictated by views and factors other than optimal solar gain. By using high-performance windows, any orientation can result in a very energy-efficient house. For example, when the house in Figure 5-30 has triple-glazed low-E windows (Window A), even a north-facing orientation uses less annual energy than a south-facing orientation with clear double-glazed windows (Window C). All of the cases shown in Figure 5-30 have average shading

---

Guidelines for Providing Winter Heat Gain

- Locate the house so that other buildings or landscape elements do not obstruct winter solar gain. Use deciduous plantings to permit solar gain during winter but block summer sun.

- For houses without air-conditioning, the best strategy is good shading combined with high-performance windows.

- For all types of glazing, face windows to the south to permit maximum solar gain in winter. However, when using high-performance windows, orientation has less impact on energy performance in a typical house without significant thermal mass.

- To maximize useful solar gain, use glazing with high solar heat gain coefficients and suitable thermal mass.

Figure 5-30. Impact of window orientation on annual energy costs for a 2000-square-foot house with two different window types in Minneapolis, Minnesota.

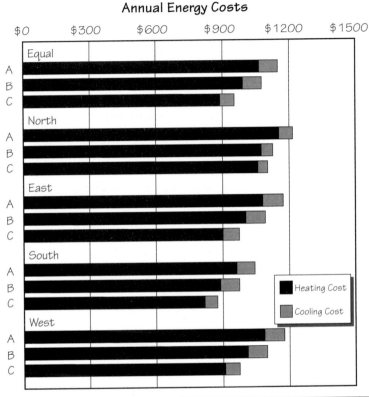

Window	Glazing	Frame	U-factor	SHGC	VT
A	double, clear	wood/vinyl	0.49	0.56	0.59
B	double, high-solar-gain low-E	wood/vinyl	0.37	0.53	0.50
C	triple, moderate-solar-gain low-E	insulated	0.18	0.40	0.50

Note: The annual energy performance figures shown here were generated using RESFEN for a typical (new construction) 2000 sq ft house with 300 sq ft of window area. Where windows are predominately on one side, the distribution is 240 sq ft on that side and 20 sq ft on the others. Typical shading conditions (interior shades, overhangs, trees, and neighboring buildings) are assumed for all windows. U-factor, SHGC, and VT are for the total window including frame. The costs shown here are annual costs for space heating and space cooling only and thus will be less than total utility bills. Costs for lights, appliances, hot water, cooking, and other uses are not included in these figures. The mechanical system uses a gas furnace for heating and air conditioning for cooling. The gas and electric prices used in these figures are provided by the Energy Information Administration (EIA) (www.eia.doe.gov). RESFEN is a computer program for calculating the annual cooling and heating energy use and costs due to window selection and is available from Lawrence Berkeley National Laboratory (windows.lbl.gov/software/resfen). See Appendix A for pricing and modeling assumptions.

conditions. If there was no shading, the difference in energy costs between less efficient and more efficient windows would be greater.

It is likely that in the typical house used in Figure 5-30 the solar gain is not being used optimally. In fact, the house has relatively low thermal mass (just the intrinsic mass of its standard lightweight construction and furnishings), which could be increased to improve the passive solar performance.

Providing Solar Access

In order to receive solar radiation in winter, the house must be located so that it is not in the shadow of other buildings or landscape elements. If possible, locating the building on the north end of the site (in the northern hemisphere) provides a greater assurance of future solar access. Of course, deciduous trees can be located within these limits (Figure 5-31).

As discussed in the previous section, overhangs on south-facing walls can be sized to permit low-angled winter sun to penetrate windows while still blocking much of the higher-angled summer sun. Most other external and internal shading devices such as awnings, shutters, or shades are operable and can be adjusted seasonally or daily to maximize solar gain in winter.

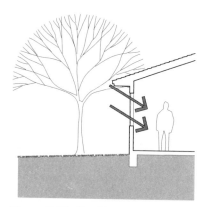

Figure 5-31. Deciduous trees permit solar gain during winter while providing shade in the summer.

The advantage to using deciduous vegetation for shading is that its cycle generally follows the local climate. Trees leaf out in the spring when the weather warms up, just in time to provide shading. They drop their leaves when the cold snap hits, earlier in northern climates than in southern, allowing the sun's heat to penetrate and warm the home. This modulation of shading from trees, shrubs, and vines is wonderfully automatic, but it does require a commitment to landscape maintenance by the homeowner. It should be noted that the branches of a deciduous tree without its leaves still block some sunlight and there may be unseasonably hot or cold weather during which deciduous trees will not perform as intended.

In all cases in Figure 5-32, moving from no shading to more shaded conditions increases heating costs. These increases in heating costs, however, are largely offset by decreased cooling costs if the house is air-conditioned. The benefits of high-performance windows can offset undesirable shading conditions that limit passive solar gain. For example the house with triple-glazed low-E windows (Window C) under typical shading conditions has a lower heating energy cost than the house with clear double-glazed windows (Window A) with no shading (maximum passive solar exposure). Although Figure 5-32 suggests shading makes little difference in energy costs in a heating-dominated climate like Minneapolis, there are still summer comfort and glare control benefits. If the relative cost of cooling increases in comparison to heating, then the cost advantage of shading will become greater.

Figure 5-32. Impact of different shading conditions on annual energy costs for a 2000-square-foot house with three different window types in Minneapolis, Minnesota.

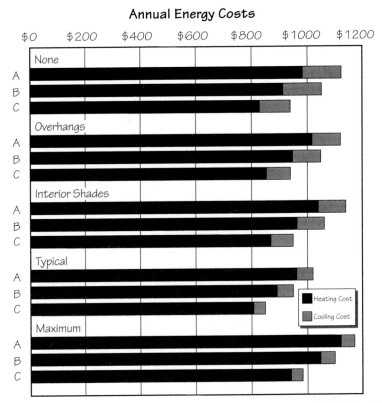

Note: The annual energy performance figures shown here were generated using RESFEN for a typical (new construction) 2000 sq ft house with 300 sq ft of window area. The windows are equally distributed on all four sides of the house. Typical shading includes (interior shades, overhangs, trees, and neighboring buildings). U-factor, SHGC, and VT are for the total window including frame. The costs shown here are annual costs for space heating and space cooling only and thus will be less than total utility bills. Costs for lights, appliances, hot water, cooking, and other uses are not included in these figures. The mechanical system uses a gas furnace for heating and air conditioning for cooling. The gas and electric prices used in these figures are provided by the Energy Information Administration (EIA) (www.eia.doe.gov). RESFEN is a computer program for calculating the annual cooling and heating energy use and costs due to window selection and is available from Lawrence Berkeley National Laboratory (windows.lbl.gov/software/resfen). See Appendix A for pricing and modeling assumptions.

Window	Glazing	Frame	U-factor	SHGC	VT
A	double, clear	wood/vinyl	0.49	0.56	0.59
B	double, high-solar-gain low-E	wood/vinyl	0.37	0.53	0.50
C	triple, moderate-solar-gain low-E	insulated	0.18	0.40	0.50

CHAPTER 6

Energy Performance and Cost Considerations

Often, selecting a window is based on only a few of the many possible considerations. In the simplest case, a decision to purchase a window can be based on the basic style, operating type, and initial cost of the unit. The problem with this approach is that there is no certainty of performance. In many cases, the energy-related aspects of the window are not factored into the decision. While this approach may save money on the initial purchase, it may result in considerably more expense, both directly and indirectly, over the life of the window.

In this chapter, the energy cost and peak demand impacts are shown for different window options in several U.S. cities (Figure 6-1). In each section of the chapter, the performance impact of house design issues such as window area, orientation,

Figure 6-1. Location of cities used in the energy performance analysis in this chapter.

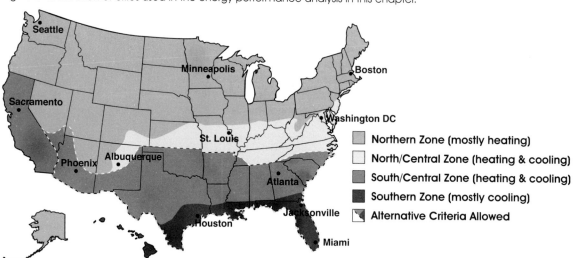

Northern Zone (mostly heating)
North/Central Zone (heating & cooling)
South/Central Zone (heating & cooling)
Southern Zone (mostly cooling)
Alternative Criteria Allowed

and shading are also discussed. Energy impacts of skylight options are shown as well.

Cost issues are addressed in the last section of the chapter. A life cycle cost analysis of a window purchasing decision is recommended. In addition to quantitative issues such as the actual cost of heating fuel or electricity for cooling, energy-performance characteristics are linked to other benefits such as thermal comfort and condensation resistance, discussed in Chapter 2. Choosing a better-performing window to save on fuel costs will also improve comfort and performance in other areas.

ENERGY PERFORMANCE CONSIDERATIONS

One important practical reason to select high-performance windows is to reduce the annual cost of heating and cooling your home. This makes good economic sense for most building owners and it also contributes to national and global efforts to reduce the environmental impacts of nonrenewable energy use. It can be a relatively painless and even profitable way for every homeowner to help improve the environment in which we live.

Until recently, comparing windows based on energy performance was often confusing and difficult. Fortunately, the U.S. Department of Energy has funded the development of a number of programs, tools, and information sources that assist in making more energy-efficient window-purchasing decisions. Beginning with the simplest and least time-consuming and moving to the more complex, here are four basic steps in efficient window selection:

1. Look for the ENERGY STAR label for your climate zone.

2. Compare window properties found on the NFRC label.

3. Compare annual energy costs for different window types on a typical house in your region.

4. Estimate and compare annual energy costs for your house using a computer tool such as RESFEN.

Each of these approaches is described in more detail in Chapter 1 and on the Efficient Windows Collaborative Web site (www.efficientwindows.org).

Efficient Windows

Collaborative

Figure 6-2. The Efficient Windows Collaborative (EWC) Web site (www. efficientwindows.org) provides extensive information on selecting windows including fact sheets and computer simulations for typical houses using a variety of windows in over 90 U.S. cities.

Recommended Window Properties for North U.S. Climates (Mostly Heating)

U-factor: Select windows with a U-factor of 0.35 or less. If air-conditioning loads are minimal, windows with U-factors as high as 0.40 are also energy-efficient if the solar heat gain coefficient is 0.50 or higher. Some double-glazed low-E products have U-factors below 0.30. Some three-layer products have U-factors as low as 0.15.

SHGC: To reduce heating, select the highest SHGC you can find (usually 0.30–0.60 for the U-factor ranges required in colder climates) so that winter solar gains can offset a portion of the heating energy need. If cooling is a significant concern, select windows and skylights with a SHGC lower than 0.55. Use RESFEN to understand trade-offs.

Visible Transmittance: A window with VT above 0.70 for the glass only is desirable to maximize daylight and view assuming glare is not a concern. This translates into a VT above 0.50 for the total window, including a wood or vinyl frame.

Air Leakage: Select a window with an AL of 0.30 or below (units are cfm/sf).

NORTHERN ZONE—MOSTLY HEATING

Comparison of Window Performance

Using the computer simulation program RESFEN, six possible window choices are compared for a typical house in three northern U.S. cities (Figure 6-3). Window A is a clear, double-glazed window with a thermally broken aluminum frame that may be found on older, existing structures but may not be able to be installed under most current codes. Window C has a low-solar-gain low-E coating with a thermally broken aluminum frame. Window D is a typical clear, double-glazed unit—the most common cold-climate window installed in the U.S. during the period from 1970 to about 1985. Window E has a high-solar-gain low-E coating, while Window F has a low-solar-gain low-E coating. Window E is designed to reduce winter heat loss (low U-factor) and provide winter solar heat gain (high SHGC). Window F also reduces winter heat loss (low U-factor) but it reduces solar heat gain as well (low SHGC). Windows D, E and F are in a wood, vinyl or clad frame. Window G, with triple glazing and two low-E coatings in an insulated fiberglass frame, is representative of the most efficient window on the market today with respect to winter heat loss (very low U-factor).

Figure 6-3 illustrates that in northern climates, the highest heating energy costs occur with aluminum-framed windows regardless of glazing type (Windows A and C). Within the wood/vinyl frame group, the low-E windows (E and F) have lower annual energy costs than clear double glazing (Window D). The high-solar-gain low-E unit (Window E) is better than the low-solar-gain low-E unit (Window F) in heating season performance because it allows more passive solar gain, but Window F is clearly better during the cooling season making them close in total energy cost. The fact that Window E has a lower annual cost than Window F in these northern cities is partly a result of higher natural gas costs that tend to emphasize heating savings. If natural gas costs go down (or electricity costs go up) the annual costs of the two windows (Windows E and F) may be equal or even reversed. The triple-glazed unit (Window G), with its very low U-value, results in even greater heating season savings.

To make a window selection based on this energy-performance data, it is necessary to factor in the other issues discussed throughout this book. For example, Window E may have lower total energy costs than Window F, but the low-solar-gain low-E option has advantages of summer comfort and reduced

Figure 6-3. Comparison of annual energy cost with different window types on a typical house in the Northern Climate Zone.

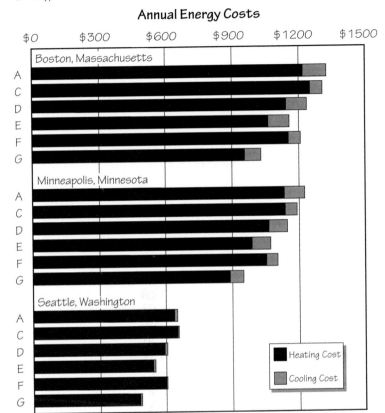

Annual Energy Costs

Note: The annual energy performance figures shown here were generated using RESFEN for a typical (new construction) 2000 sq ft house with 300 sq ft of window area. The windows are equally distributed on all four sides of the house and include typical shading (interior shades, overhangs, trees, and neighboring buildings). U-factor, SHGC, and VT are for the total window including frame. The costs shown here are annual costs for space heating and space cooling only and thus will be less than total utility bills. Costs for lights, appliances, hot water, cooking, and other uses are not included in these figures. The mechanical system uses a gas furnace for heating and air conditioning for cooling. The gas and electric prices used in these figures are provided by the Energy Information Administration (EIA) (www.eia.doe.gov). RESFEN is a computer program for calculating the annual cooling and heating energy use and costs due to window selection and is available from Lawrence Berkeley National Laboratory (windows.lbl.gov/software/resfen). See Appendix A for pricing and modeling assumptions.

Window	Glazing	Frame	U-factor	SHGC	VT
A	double, clear	aluminum w/break	0.63	0.62	0.63
B	double, bronze tint	aluminum w/break	0.63	0.52	0.48
C	double, low-solar-gain low-E	aluminum w/break	0.47	0.33	0.55
D	double, clear	wood/vinyl	0.49	0.56	0.59
E	double, high-solar-gain low-E	wood/vinyl	0.37	0.53	0.54
F	double, low-solar-gain low-E	wood/vinyl	0.34	0.30	0.51
G	triple, moderate-solar-gain low-E	insulated vinyl	0.18	0.40	0.50

Figure 6-4. Peak heating loads for a typical house with different window types in the northern zone.

Figure 6-5. Peak cooling loads for a typical house with different window types in the northern zone.

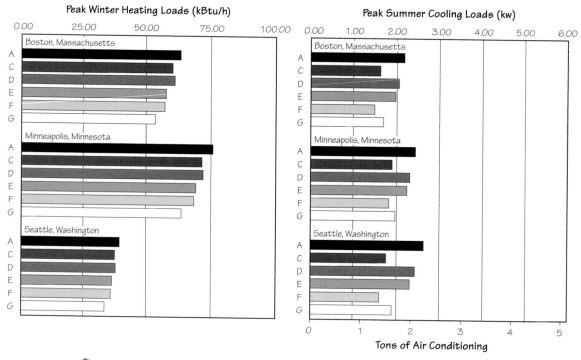

Note: The peak energy performance figures shown here were generated using RESFEN for a typical (new construction) 2000 sq ft house with 300 sq ft of window area. The windows are equally distributed on all four sides of the house and include typical shading (interior shades, overhangs, trees, and neighboring buildings). U-factor, SHGC, and VT are for the total window including frame. The mechanical system uses a gas furnace for heating and air conditioning for cooling. The gas and electric prices used in these figures are provided by the Energy Information Administration (EIA) (www.eia.doe.gov). RESFEN is a computer program for calculating the annual cooling and heating energy use and costs due to window selection and is available from Lawrence Berkeley National Laboratory (windows.lbl.gov/software/resfen). See Appendix A for pricing and modeling assumptions.

peak loads which may reduce equipment costs. The benefit of reducing cooling costs in a heating-dominated climate must be examined in terms of whether air conditioning is installed in the house; however, the increased comfort in summer of a window with a low SHGC is a factor to be considered whether or not the homeowner is paying for cooling.

In applying these typical results to your particular situation, remember that the example is an average house (2000 square feet) with an average amount of window area (300 square feet). Instead of drawing conclusions from average conditions such as these, the best way to compare different windows is by using a computer tool such as RESFEN so you can base decisions on your own house design.

Comparison of Peak Performance

High-performance windows not only provide reduced annual heating and cooling bills; they reduce the peak heating and cooling loads as well. This has benefits for the homeowner, in that the size of the heating or cooling system may be reduced, and it also benefits the electrical utilities, in that load factors are reduced during the peak times in summer.

The peak load for a building is the maximum requirement for heating or cooling at one time. These loads determine the size of the furnace, heat pump, air conditioner, and fans that must be installed. The peak heating load (in kBtu/h) represents how much heat must be delivered from the furnace at the coldest outdoor temperature in order to maintain a given interior temperature (typically, 70°F/21°C). Similarly, the peak cooling load (in kW) represents how much air-conditioning capacity is required to maintain a given interior temperature (typically, 75°F/24°C) during the hottest summer conditions.

Figures 6-4 and 6-5 illustrate typical reductions in peak loads that occur with different window types used in a typical house in a cold climate. In the heating season, there is a steady reduction in peak load as the window U-factor decreases. This may translate into savings from smaller heating equipment size in new construction or when equipment is replaced in existing houses, especially if it is combined with other energy-efficient strategies. Even though the northern zone is not predominantly a cooling climate, there can still be hot, humid days in summer with high peak loads. Low-solar-gain low-E glazing (Windows C and F) reduces the peak cooling load by 20 to 25 percent compared to clear double glazing. This difference would be higher if the windows were unshaded.

The greatest economic benefits come from reduced peak heating loads in cold climates where heat pumps are used to provide space heat. In new construction, reducing peak loads might also lead to using smaller fans and ducts. High-performance windows can be an important part of a larger package of energy-efficiency measures that combine to produce large savings in space conditioning equipment. Any time an air-conditioning unit must be replaced in an existing home, consider upgrading to windows with a lower SHGC at the same time to reduce the size and cost of the replacement cooling equipment.

Lowering the peak cooling load is a goal of most electric utilities. If peak cooling loads are minimized, additional generating capacity is not required. This benefits the utility company directly and the consumer indirectly, by keeping rates down. Some electric utilities provide financial incentives to builders and homeowners to reduce peak loads, which can offset some of the incremental cost of higher-performance windows. Check with your local utility to see if such incentives are available.

Influence of House Design on Energy Performance

All of the energy performance comparisons in this section are based on a typical 2000-square-foot house with a window area of 300 square feet distributed equally on four orientations with typical shading conditions. If these assumptions about the house design are changed, the impact of choosing efficient windows can vary. To illustrate these impacts, the energy performance of several window options is shown for different window areas, orientations, and shading conditions.

As shown in Figure 6-6, increasing the window area in Minneapolis, Minnesota results in increased annual energy costs. The increase is greater, however, for windows with higher U-factors (A, C and D) than for windows with lower U-factors (E, F and G). In fact, when tripled-glazed Window G is used, the annual energy cost increases only slightly even

Note: The annual energy performance figures shown here were generated using RESFEN for a typical (new construction) 2000 sq ft house with 300 sq ft (15%), 600 sq ft (30%) and 900 sq ft (45%) of window area. The windows are equally distributed on all four sides of the house and include typical shading (interior shades, overhangs, trees, and neighboring buildings). U-factor, SHGC, and VT are for the total window including frame. The costs shown here are annual costs for space heating and space cooling only and thus will be less than total utility bills. Costs for lights, appliances, hot water, cooking, and other uses are not included in these figures. The mechanical system uses a gas furnace for heating and air conditioning for cooling. The gas and electric prices used in these figures are provided by the Energy Information Administration (EIA) (www.eia.doe.gov). RESFEN is a computer program for calculating the annual cooling and heating energy use and costs due to window selection and is available from Lawrence Berkeley National Laboratory (windows.lbl.gov/software/resfen). See Appendix A for pricing and modeling assumptions.

Figure 6-6. Glazing area comparison of annual energy costs and summer peak cooling loads for six window types in Minneapolis, Minnesota.

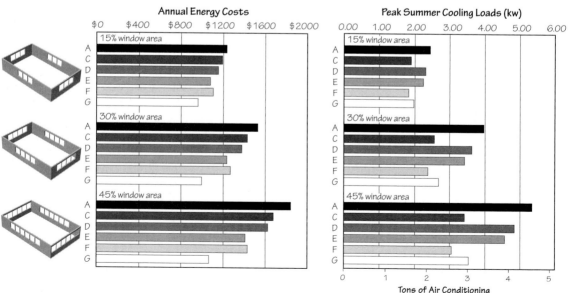

Figure 6-7. Orientation comparison of annual energy costs and summer peak cooling loads for six window types in Minneapolis, Minnesota.

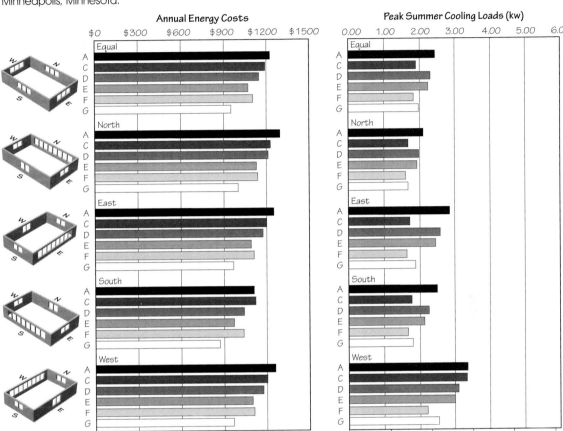

when the glazing area is tripled. Essentially, the benefit of using low-E windows (E and F) in a northern climate is greater with increased glazing area.

Figure 6-6 also shows that peak demand increases with increased glazing area. In this case, solar heat gain coefficient (SHGC) rather than U-factor is the key attribute. The peak demand for higher-SHGC windows (A, D and E) increases significantly as glazing area increases. The increase in peak demand is less with lower-SHGC windows (C, F and G). Window F with low-solar-gain low-E glazing shows the least increase in peak demand as glazing area increases.

In a northern city such as Minneapolis, Minnesota, orienting windows predominantly to the north increases energy costs while orienting them predominantly to the south decreases

Note: The annual energy performance figures shown here were generated using RESFEN for a typical (new construction) 2000 sq ft house with 300 sq ft of window area. Windows are distributed 240 sq ft on one side and 20 sq ft on the others. Typical shading conditions are assumed for all windows. U-factor, SHGC, and VT are for the total window including frame. The costs shown here are annual costs for space heating and space cooling only and thus will be less than total utility bills. Costs for lights, appliances, hot water, cooking, and other uses are not included in these figures. The mechanical system uses a gas furnace for heating and air conditioning for cooling. The gas and electric prices used in these figures are provided by the Energy Information Administration (EIA) (www.eia.doe.gov). RESFEN is a computer program for calculating the annual cooling and heating energy use and costs due to window selection and is available from Lawrence Berkeley National Laboratory (windows.lbl.gov/software/resfen). See Appendix A for pricing and modeling assumptions.

Figure 6-8. Shading comparison of annual energy costs and summer peak cooling loads for six window types in Minneapolis, Minnesota.

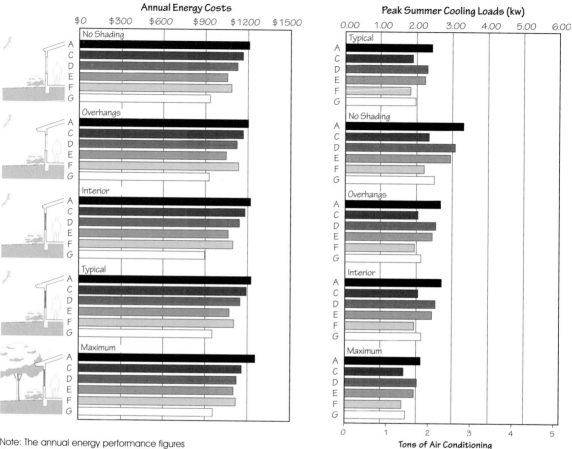

Note: The annual energy performance figures shown here were generated using RESFEN for a typical (new construction) 2000 sq ft house with 300 sq ft of window area. The windows are equally distributed on all four sides of the house. Typical shading includes (interior shades, overhangs, trees, and neighboring buildings). U-factor, SHGC, and VT are for the total window including frame. The costs shown here are annual costs for space heating and space cooling only and thus will be less than total utility bills. Costs for lights, appliances, hot water, cooking, and other uses are not included in these figures. The mechanical system uses a gas furnace for heating and air conditioning for cooling. The gas and electric prices used in these figures are provided by the Energy Information Administration (EIA) (www.eia.doe.gov). RESFEN is a computer program for calculating the annual cooling and heating energy use and costs due to window selection and is available from Lawrence Berkeley National Laboratory (windows.lbl.gov/software/resfen). See Appendix A for pricing and modeling assumptions.

energy costs (Figure 6-7). The difference in costs due to orientation is greatest with higher-SHGC windows (A, D and E) and less with lower-SHGC windows (C, F and G). Similar effects occur with peak demand when window orientation is changed.

Different shading conditions in northern climates do not affect energy costs significantly (Figure 6-8). This occurs because increased shading reduces cooling costs in summer by approximately the same amount as it increases heating costs by blocking passive solar gain in winter. Increased shading significantly affects peak demand, however, with higher-SHGC windows (A, D and E) but has less effect with lower-SHGC windows (C, F and G).

Comparison of Skylight Performance

Six possible skylight choices are compared for a typical house in Minneapolis, Minnesota (Figure 6-9). Skylight A has clear double-glazing and Skylight B has a low-solar-gain low-E coating. Both are in aluminum frames. Skylights C and D have the same two types of glazing in thermally broken aluminum frames. Skylights E and F have the same glazings in wood, wood-clad or vinyl frames.

In a northern climate, a skylight with a lower U-value results in lower annual energy costs. Thus, wood frames (Skylights E and F) outperform aluminum (Skylights A and B) and thermally broken aluminum (Skylights C and D). Skylights with the low-solar-gain low-E coating results in slightly better energy performance compared to the clear double-glazed options. The difference between the worst case and the best is notable considering that skylight areas are often small compared to the total house window area (45 square feet in Figure 6-9).

Figure 6-9. Skylight comparison of annual energy costs for six window types in Minneapolis, Minnesota.

Annual Energy Costs

Skylight	Glazing	Frame	U-factor	SHGC	VT
A	double, clear	aluminum	0.94	0.68	0.70
B	double, low-solar-gain low-E	aluminum	0.75	0.40	0.55
C	double, clear	aluminum w/break	0.80	0.68	0.70
D	double, low-solar-gain low-E	aluminum w/break	0.70	0.40	0.55
E	double, clear-	wood/vinyl	0.75	0.68	0.70
F	double, low-solar-gain low-E	wood/vinyl	0.53	0.40	0.55

Note: The annual energy performance figures shown here were generated using RESFEN for a typical (new construction) 2000 sq ft house with 45 sq ft of skylights. The base house has 300 sq ft of window area and includes typical shading (interior shades, overhangs, trees, and neighboring buildings). The windows are equally distributed on all four sides of the house and are low-solar-gain low-E in all cases. RESFEN assumes skylights are placed in a typical well which reduces solar heat gain effects by 50%. U-factor, SHGC, and VT are for the total skylight including frame. Skylight U-factors are greater than window U-factors for the same glazing type because of the slope and greater exposure of the frame. The costs shown here are annual costs for space heating and space cooling only and thus will be less than total utility bills. Costs for lights, appliances, hot water, cooking, and other uses are not included in these figures. The mechanical system uses a gas furnace for heating and air conditioning for cooling. The gas and electric prices used in these figures are provided by the Energy Information Administration (EIA) (www.eia.doe.gov). RESFEN is a computer program for calculating the annual cooling and heating energy use and costs due to window selection and is available from Lawrence Berkeley National Laboratory (windows.lbl.gov/software/resfen). See Appendix A for pricing and modeling assumptions.

ENERGY STAR Requirements for the North/Central Zone (Heating and Cooling)

U-factor = 0.40 or less
(0.60 or less for skylights)

SHGC = 0.55 or less
(0.40 or less for skylights)

Recommended Window Properties for North/Central U.S. Climates (Heating and Cooling)

U-factor: Select windows with a U-factor of 0.40 or less. The larger your heating bill, the more important a low U-factor becomes.

SHGC: If you have significant air-conditioning costs or summer overheating problems, look for SHGC values of 0.40 or less. If you have moderate air-conditioning requirements, select windows and skylights with a SHGC of 0.55 or less. While windows with lower SHGC values reduce summer cooling and overheating, they also reduce free winter solar heat gain. Use a computer program such as RESFEN to understand heating and cooling trade-offs.

Visible Transmittance: A window with VT above 0.70 for the glass only is desirable to maximize daylight and view assuming glare is not a concern. This translates into a VT above 0.50 for the total window, including a wood or vinyl frame.

Air Leakage: Select a window with an AL of 0.30 or below (units are cfm/sf).

NORTH/CENTRAL ZONE—HEATING AND COOLING

Comparison of Window Performance

As with the northern climates, six possible window choices are compared for a typical house in three U.S. cities in the north/central heating and cooling zone (Figure 6-10). Window A is a clear, double-glazed window with a thermally broken aluminum frame that may be found on older, existing structures but may not be able to be installed under most current codes. Window C has a low-solar-gain low-E coating with a thermally broken aluminum frame. Window D is a typical clear, double-glazed unit, the most common cold-climate window installed in the U.S. during the period from 1970 to about 1985. Window E has a high-solar-gain low-E coating, while Window F has a low-solar-gain low-E coating. Window E is designed to reduce winter heat loss (low U-factor) and provide winter solar heat gain (high SHGC). Window F also reduces winter heat loss (low U-factor) but it reduces solar heat gain as well (low SHGC). Windows D, E and F are in a wood, vinyl or clad frame. Window G, with triple glazing and two low-E coatings in an insulated fiberglass frame, is representative of the most efficient window on the market today with respect to winter heat loss (very low U-factor).

Within the north/central climate zone, cities have both heating and cooling requirements, though many cities are more heating-dominated. St. Louis, and Washington, DC, and Albuquerque are all more heating-dominated. The window comparison in these three cities is similar to the northern zone locations-there are savings in annual heating costs using windows with low-E coatings (Windows E and F) instead of double-glazed, clear units (Windows A and D). As with the northern cities, the high-solar-gain low-E unit (Window E) is better than the low-solar-gain low-E unit (Window F) in heating season performance, but Window E is clearly better during the cooling season. The fact that Window E has a lower annual cost than Window F in these north/central cities is partly a result of higher natural gas costs that tend to emphasize heating savings. If natural gas costs go down (or electricity costs go up) the annual costs of the two windows (Windows E and F) may be equal or even reversed. The triple-glazed unit (Window G), with its very low U-value, results in even greater heating season savings.

Figure 6-10. Comparison of annual energy cost with different window types on a typical house in the North/Central Climate Zone.

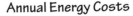

Annual Energy Costs

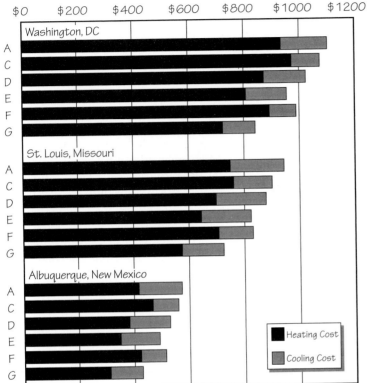

Note: The annual energy performance figures shown here were generated using RESFEN for a typical (new construction) 2000 sq ft house with 300 sq ft of window area. The windows are equally distributed on all four sides of the house and include typical shading (interior shades, overhangs, trees, and neighboring buildings). U-factor, SHGC, and VT are for the total window including frame. The costs shown here are annual costs for space heating and space cooling only and thus will be less than total utility bills. Costs for lights, appliances, hot water, cooking, and other uses are not included in these figures. The mechanical system uses a gas furnace for heating and air conditioning for cooling. The gas and electric prices used in these figures are provided by the Energy Information Administration (EIA) (www.eia.doe.gov). RESFEN is a computer program for calculating the annual cooling and heating energy use and costs due to window selection and is available from Lawrence Berkeley National Laboratory (windows.lbl.gov/software/resfen). See Appendix A for pricing and modeling assumptions.

Window	Glazing	Frame	U-factor	SHGC	VT
A	double, clear	aluminum w/break	0.63	0.62	0.63
B	double, bronze tint	aluminum w/break	0.63	0.52	0.48
C	double, low-solar-gain low-E	aluminum w/break	0.47	0.33	0.55
D	double, clear	wood/vinyl	0.49	0.56	0.59
E	double, high-solar-gain low-E	wood/vinyl	0.37	0.53	0.54
F	double, low-solar-gain low-E	wood/vinyl	0.34	0.30	0.51
G	triple, moderate-solar-gain low-E	insulated vinyl	0.18	0.40	0.50

185

Figure 6-11. Peak heating loads for a typical house with different window types in the north/central zone.

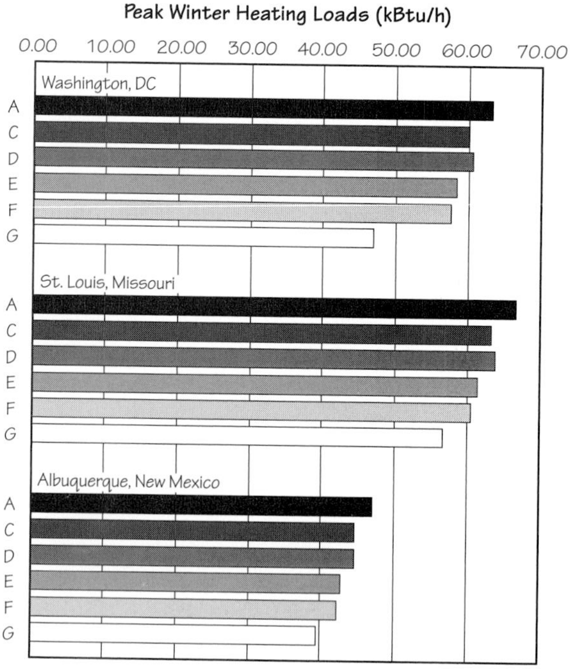

Figure 6-12. Peak cooling loads for a typical house with different window types in the north/central zone.

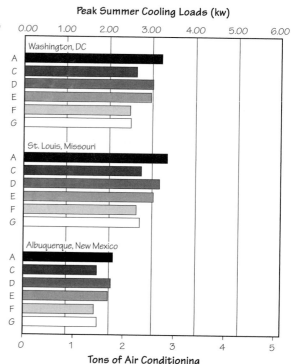

Note: The peak energy performance figures shown here were generated using RESFEN for a typical (new construction) 2000 sq ft house with 300 sq ft of window area. The windows are equally distributed on all four sides of the house and include typical shading (interior shades, overhangs, trees, and neighboring buildings). U-factor, SHGC, and VT are for the total window including frame. The mechanical system uses a gas furnace for heating and air conditioning for cooling. The gas and electric prices used in these figures are provided by the Energy Information Administration (EIA) (www.eia.doe.gov). RESFEN is a computer program for calculating the annual cooling and heating energy use and costs due to window selection and is available from Lawrence Berkeley National Laboratory (windows.lbl.gov/software/resfen). See Appendix A for pricing and modeling assumptions.

Because heating and cooling costs must be balanced in mixed climates and then combined with all of the other selection factors, it is important to use a reliable computer tool such as RESFEN so you can base decisions on your own house design and fuel costs for your area.

Comparison of Peak Performance

High-performance windows not only provide reduced annual heating and cooling bills; they reduce the peak heating and cooling loads as well. This has benefits for the homeowner, in that the size of the heating or cooling system may be reduced, and it also benefits the electrical utilities, in that load factors are reduced during the peak times in summer.

The peak load for a building is the maximum requirement for heating or cooling at one time. These loads determine the size of the furnace, heat pump, air conditioner, and fans that must be installed. The peak heating load (in kBtu/h) represents how much heat must be delivered from the furnace at the coldest outdoor temperature in order to maintain a given interior temperature (typically, 70°F/21°C). Similarly, the peak cooling load (in kW) represents how much air-conditioning capacity is required to maintain a given interior temperature (typically, 75°F/24°C) during the hottest summer conditions.

Figures 6-11 and 6-12 illustrate typical reductions in peak loads that occur with different window types used in a typical house in a north/central climate. In the heating season, there is a steady reduction in peak load as the window U-factor decreases. This may translate into savings from smaller heating equipment size in new construction or when equipment is replaced in existing houses, especially if it is combined with other energy-efficient strategies. Low-solar-gain low-E glazing (Windows C and F) reduces the peak cooling loads by 20 to 25 percent compared to clear double glazing. This difference would be higher if the windows were unshaded.

The greatest economic benefits come from reductions of peak cooling loads in hot climates and peak heating loads in cold climates where heat pumps are used to provide space heat. In new construction, reducing peak loads might also lead to using smaller fans and ducts. High-performance windows can be an important part of a larger package of energy-efficiency measures that combine to produce large savings in space conditioning equipment. Any time an air-conditioning unit must be replaced in an existing home, consider upgrading to windows with a lower SHGC at the same time to reduce the size and cost of the replacement cooling equipment.

Lowering the peak cooling load is a goal of most electric utilities. Low-solar-gain low-E glazing has the ability to lower electric utility load factors during the peak summer use in warmer climates. If peak cooling loads are minimized, additional generating capacity is not required. This directly benefits the utility company, and indirectly the consumer, by keeping rates down. Some electric utilities provide financial incentives to builders and homeowners to reduce peak loads, which can offset some of the incremental cost of higher-performance windows. Check with your local utility to see if such incentives are available.

Influence of House Design on Energy Performance

All of the energy performance comparisons in this section are based on a typical 2000-square-foot house with a window area of 300 square feet distributed equally on four orientations with typical shading conditions. If these assumptions about the house design are changed, the impact of choosing efficient windows can vary. To illustrate these impacts, the energy performance of several window options is shown for different window areas, orientations, and shading conditions.

As shown in Figure 6-13, increasing the window area in St. Louis, Missouri results in increased annual energy costs. The increase is greater, however, for windows with higher U-factors and SHGC (A and D) than for windows with lower U-factors and SHGC (F and G). In fact, when tripled-glazed Window G is used, the annual energy cost increases a relatively small amount even though the glazing area is tripled. Essentially, the benefit of using low-E windows (E, F and G) in this climate zone is greater with increased glazing area.

Figure 6-13 also shows that peak demand increases with increased glazing area. In this case, solar heat gain coefficient (SHGC) rather than U-factor is the key attribute. The peak demand for higher-SHGC windows (A and D) increases significantly as glazing area increases. The increase in peak demand is less with lower-SHGC windows (F and G). Window F with low-solar-gain low-E glazing shows the least increase in peak demand as glazing area increases.

In St. Louis, Missouri, orienting windows predominantly to the north increases energy costs while orienting them predominantly to the south decreases energy costs (Figure 6-14). This holds true for all window types. Similar effects oc-

Note: The annual energy performance figures shown here were generated using RESFEN for a typical (new construction) 2000 sq ft house with 300 sq ft (15%), 600 sq ft (30%) and 900 sq ft (45%) of window area. The windows are equally distributed on all four sides of the house and include typical shading (interior shades, overhangs, trees, and neighboring buildings). U-factor, SHGC, and VT are for the total window including frame. The costs shown here are annual costs for space heating and space cooling only and thus will be less than total utility bills. Costs for lights, appliances, hot water, cooking, and other uses are not included in these figures. The mechanical system uses a gas furnace for heating and air conditioning for cooling. The gas and electric prices used in these figures are provided by the Energy Information Administration (EIA) (www.eia.doe.gov). RESFEN is a computer program for calculating the annual cooling and heating energy use and costs due to window selection and is available from Lawrence Berkeley National Laboratory (windows.lbl.gov/software/resfen). See Appendix A for pricing and modeling assumptions.

Figure 6-13. Glazing area comparison of annual energy costs and summer peak cooling loads for six window types in St. Louis, Missouri.

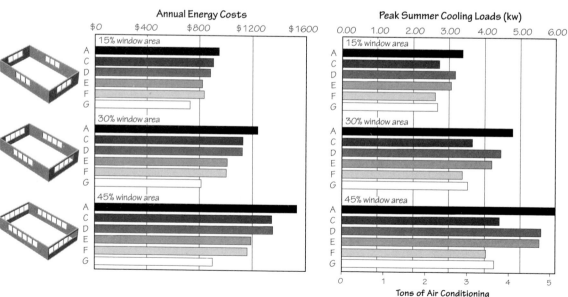

Figure 6-14. Orientation comparison of annual energy costs and summer peak cooling loads for six window types in St. Louis, Missouri.

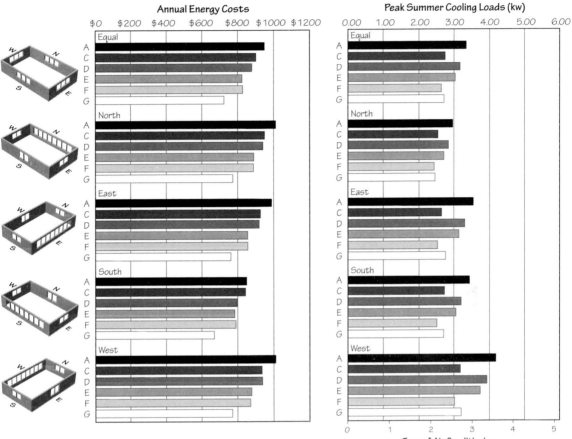

Window	Glazing	Frame	U-factor	SHGC	VT
A	double, clear	aluminum w/break	0.63	0.62	0.63
B	double, low-solar-gain low-E	aluminum	0.75	0.40	0.55
C	double, low-solar-gain low-E	aluminum w/break	0.47	0.33	0.55
D	double, clear	wood/vinyl	0.49	0.56	0.59
E	double, high-solar-gain low-E	wood/vinyl	0.37	0.53	0.54
F	double, low-solar-gain low-E	wood/vinyl	0.34	0.30	0.51
G	triple, moderate-solar-gain low-E	insulated vinyl	0.18	0.40	0.50

Note: The annual energy performance figures shown here were generated using RESFEN for a typical (new construction) 2000 sq ft house with 300 sq ft of window area. Windows are distributed 240 sq ft on one side and 20 sq ft on the others. Typical shading conditions are assumed for all windows. U-factor, SHGC, and VT are for the total window including frame. The costs shown here are annual costs for space heating and space cooling only and thus will be less than total utility bills. Costs for lights, appliances, hot water, cooking, and other uses are not included in these figures. The mechanical system uses a gas furnace for heating and air conditioning for cooling. The gas and electric prices used in these figures are provided by the Energy Information Administration (EIA) (www.eia.doe.gov). RESFEN is a computer program for calculating the annual cooling and heating energy use and costs due to window selection and is available from Lawrence Berkeley National Laboratory (windows.lbl.gov/software/resfen). See Appendix A for pricing and modeling assumptions.

189

Figure 6-15. Shading comparison of annual energy costs and summer peak cooling loads for six window types in St. Louis, Missouri.

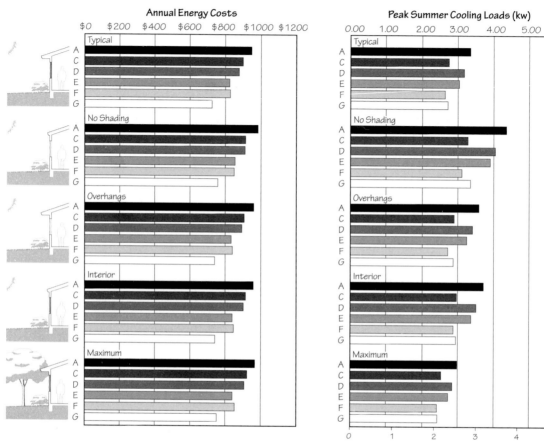

Note: The annual energy performance figures shown here were generated using RESFEN for a typical (new construction) 2000 sq ft house with 300 sq ft of window area. The windows are equally distributed on all four sides of the house. Typical shading includes (interior shades, overhangs, trees, and neighboring buildings). U-factor, SHGC, and VT are for the total window including frame. The costs shown here are annual costs for space heating and space cooling only and thus will be less than total utility bills. Costs for lights, appliances, hot water, cooking, and other uses are not included in these figures. The mechanical system uses a gas furnace for heating and air conditioning for cooling. The gas and electric prices used in these figures are provided by the Energy Information Administration (EIA) (www.eia.doe.gov). RESFEN is a computer program for calculating the annual cooling and heating energy use and costs due to window selection and is available from Lawrence Berkeley National Laboratory (windows.lbl.gov/software/resfen). See Appendix A for pricing and modeling assumptions.

cur with peak demand when window orientation is changed. The difference in cooling peak demand due to orientation is greatest with higher-SHGC windows (A and D) and less with lower-SHGC windows (F and G).

Different shading conditions in the north/central climate zone do not affect energy costs significantly (Figure 6-15). This occurs because increased shading reduces cooling costs in summer by approximately the same amount as it increases heating costs by blocking passive solar gain in winter. Increased shading significantly affects peak demand, however, with higher-SHGC windows but has less effect with lower-SHGC windows.

Comparison of Skylight Performance

Six possible skylight choices are compared for a typical house in St. Louis, Missouri (Figure 6-16). Skylight A has clear, double-glazing and Skylight B has a low-solar-gain low-E coating. Both are in aluminum frames. Skylights C and D have the same two types of glazing in thermally broken aluminum frames. Skylights E and F have the same glazings in wood, wood-clad or vinyl frames.

In this climate, a skylight with a lower U-value results in lower annual energy costs. Thus, wood frames (Skylights E and F) outperform aluminum (Skylights A and B) and thermally broken aluminum (Skylights C and D). Skylights with the low-solar-gain low-E coating result in slightly better energy performance compared to the clear double-glazed options. This improvement is notable, although not large in total savings, considering that skylight areas are often small compared to the total house window area (45 square feet in Figure 6-16).

Figure 6-16. Skylight comparison of annual energy costs for six window types in St. Louis, Missouri.

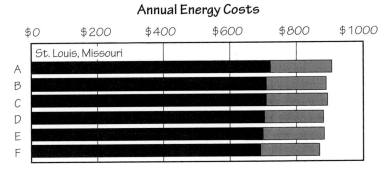

Annual Energy Costs

Note: The annual energy performance figures shown here were generated using RESFEN for a typical (new construction) 2000 sq ft house with 45 sq ft of skylights. The base house has 300 sq ft of window area and includes typical shading (interior shades, overhangs, trees, and neighboring buildings). The windows are equally distributed on all four sides of the house and are low-solar-gain low-E in all cases. RESFEN assumes skylights are placed in a typical well which reduces solar heat gain effects by 50%. U-factor, SHGC, and VT are for the total skylight including frame. Skylight U-factors are greater than window U-factors for the same glazing type because of the slope and greater exposure of the frame. The costs shown here are annual costs for space heating and space cooling only and thus will be less than total utility bills. Costs for lights, appliances, hot water, cooking, and other uses are not included in these figures. The mechanical system uses a gas furnace for heating and air conditioning for cooling. The gas and electric prices used in these figures are provided by the Energy Information Administration (EIA) (www.eia.doe.gov). RESFEN is a computer program for calculating the annual cooling and heating energy use and costs due to window selection and is available from Lawrence Berkeley National Laboratory (windows.lbl.gov/software/resfen). See Appendix A for pricing and modeling assumptions.

Skylight	Glazing	Frame	U-factor	SHGC	VT
A	double, clear	aluminum	0.94	0.68	0.70
B	double, low-solar-gain low-E	aluminum	0.75	0.40	0.55
C	double, clear	aluminum w/break	0.80	0.68	0.70
D	double, low-solar-gain low-E	aluminum w/break	0.70	0.40	0.55
E	double, clear-	wood/vinyl	0.75	0.68	0.70
F	double, low-solar-gain low-E	wood/vinyl	0.53	0.40	0.55

Recommended Window Properties for South/Central U.S. Climates (Heating and Cooling)

U-factor: Select windows with a U-factor of 0.40 or less. The larger your heating bill, the more important a low U-factor becomes.

SHGC: If you have significant air-conditioning costs or summer overheating problems, look for SHGC values of 0.40 or less. A low SHGC is the most important window property in warm climates.

Visible Transmittance: A window with VT above 0.70 for the glass only is desirable to maximize daylight and view assuming glare is not a concern. This translates into a VT above 0.50 for the total window, including a wood or vinyl frame.

Air Leakage: Select a window with an AL of 0.30 or below (units are cfm/sf).

SOUTH/CENTRAL ZONE—HEATING AND COOLING

Comparison of Window Performance

Six possible window choices are compared for a typical house in three U.S. cities in the south/central heating and cooling zone (Figure 6-17). The six windows used are appropriate choices in this region but are different from those shown for the northern and north/central zones. Window A is a clear, double-glazed unit in a thermally broken aluminum frame, still commonly used in this region. Window B, with bronze-tinted glass in a thermally broken aluminum frame, represents a traditional approach to reducing solar heat gain in hot climates (note the somewhat reduced SHGC accompanied by a significant reduction in daylight—lower VT). Window C represents the relatively new technology of using a low-solar-gain low-E coating (a low SHGC combined with a relatively high VT) in an aluminum frame. Window D is a typical clear, double-glazed unit in a wood, vinyl or clad frame. Window E is a low-E glazing in a wood, vinyl or clad frame but it has high-solar-gain characteristics. Window F uses low-solar-gain low-E glazing in a wood, vinyl, or clad frame.

Within the south/central climate zone, cities have both heating and cooling requirements. Atlanta, Georgia represents a south/central zone climate where the annual heating costs are higher than the cooling costs. Because of the heating season loads, windows with wood or vinyl frames (Windows D, E and F) have lower costs than windows with aluminum frames (Windows A, B and C). In Atlanta, the bronze tinted Window B performs worse than any of the low-E options. The comparison between high-solar-gain and low-solar-gain low-E is instructive. Even though the high-solar-gain low-E option (Window E) has a lower annual heating cost than the low-solar-gain low-E case (Window F), it is offset by the greater cooling costs. Phoenix, Arizona is a south/central climate zone city where cooling costs exceed heating costs regardless of frame type. In Phoenix, the low-solar-gain low-E case (Window F) clearly has lower annual energy costs than the high-solar-gain low-E option (Window E). Because the cooling costs are dominant, the frame type has less influence on energy costs.

Because heating and cooling costs must be balanced in mixed climates and then combined with all of the other selection factors, it is important to use a reliable computer tool such as RESFEN where you can base decisions on your own house design and fuel costs for your area.

Figure 6-17. Comparison of annual energy cost with different window types on a typical house in the South/Central Climate Zone.

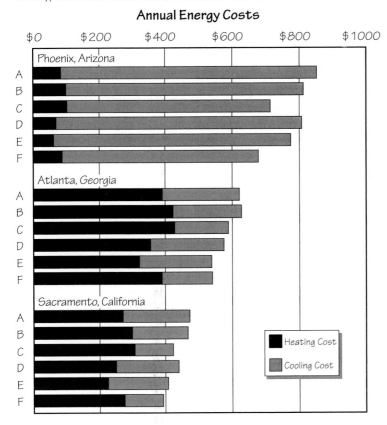

Annual Energy Costs

Note: The annual energy performance figures shown here were generated using RESFEN for a typical (new construction) 2000 sq ft house with 300 sq ft of window area. The windows are equally distributed on all four sides of the house and include typical shading (interior shades, overhangs, trees, and neighboring buildings). U-factor, SHGC, and VT are for the total window including frame. The costs shown here are annual costs for space heating and space cooling only and thus will be less than total utility bills. Costs for lights, appliances, hot water, cooking, and other uses are not included in these figures. The mechanical system uses a gas furnace for heating and air conditioning for cooling. The gas and electric prices used in these figures are provided by the Energy Information Administration (EIA) (www.eia.doe.gov). RESFEN is a computer program for calculating the annual cooling and heating energy use and costs due to window selection and is available from Lawrence Berkeley National Laboratory (windows.lbl.gov/software/resfen). See Appendix A for pricing and modeling assumptions.

Window	Glazing	Frame	U-factor	SHGC	VT
A	double, clear	aluminum w/break	0.63	0.62	0.63
B	double, bronze tint	aluminum w/break	0.63	0.52	0.48
C	double, low-solar-gain low-E	aluminum w/break	0.47	0.33	0.55
D	double, clear	wood/vinyl	0.49	0.56	0.59
E	double, high-solar-gain low-E	wood/vinyl	0.37	0.53	0.54
F	double, low-solar-gain low-E	wood/vinyl	0.34	0.30	0.51
G	triple, moderate-solar-gain low-E	insulated vinyl	0.18	0.40	0.50

Figure 6-18. Peak heating loads for a typical house with different window types in the south/central zone.

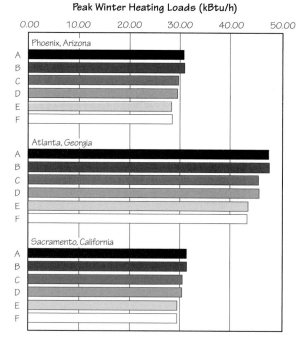

Figure 6-19. Peak heating loads for a typical house with different window types in the south/central zone.

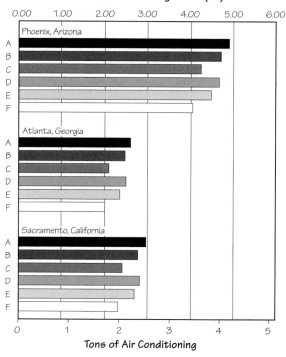

Note: The peak energy performance figures shown here were generated using RESFEN for a typical (new construction) 2000 sq ft house with 300 sq ft of window area. The windows are equally distributed on all four sides of the house and include typical shading (interior shades, overhangs, trees, and neighboring buildings). U-factor, SHGC, and VT are for the total window including frame. The mechanical system uses a gas furnace for heating and air conditioning for cooling. The gas and electric prices used in these figures are provided by the Energy Information Administration (EIA) (www.eia.doe.gov). RESFEN is a computer program for calculating the annual cooling and heating energy use and costs due to window selection and is available from Lawrence Berkeley National Laboratory (windows.lbl.gov/software/resfen). See Appendix A for pricing and modeling assumptions.

Comparison of Peak Performance

High-performance windows not only provide reduced annual heating and cooling bills; they reduce the peak heating and cooling loads as well. This has benefits for the homeowner, in that the size of the heating or cooling system may be reduced, and it also benefits the electrical utilities, in that load factors are reduced during the peak times in summer.

The peak load for a building is the maximum requirement for heating or cooling at one time. These loads determine the size of the furnace, heat pump, air conditioner, and fans that must be installed. The peak heating load (in kBtu/h) represents how much heat must be delivered from the furnace at the coldest outdoor temperature in order to maintain a given interior temperature (typically, 70°F/21°C). Similarly, the peak cooling load (in kW) represents how much air-conditioning capacity is required to maintain a given interior temperature (typically, 75°F/24°C) during the hottest summer conditions.

Figures 6-18 and 6-19 illustrate typical reductions in peak loads that occur with different window types used in a typical house in a south/central climate. As expected, tinted glazing (Window B) does little to lower peak cooling loads but low-solar-gain low-E (Windows C and F) has a significant impact. High-performance windows also reduce peak heating loads although this has less economic payoff in hot climates.

The greatest economic benefits come from reductions of peak cooling loads in hot climates and peak heating loads in cold climates where heat pumps are used to provide space heat. In new construction, reducing peak loads might also lead to using smaller fans and ducts. High-performance windows can be an important part of a larger package of energy-efficiency measures that combine to produce large savings in space conditioning equipment. Any time an air-conditioning unit must be replaced in an existing home, consider upgrading to windows with a lower SHGC at the same time to reduce the size and cost of the replacement cooling equipment.

Lowering the peak cooling load is a goal of most electric utilities. Low-solar-gain low-E glazing has the ability to lower electric utility load factors during the peak summer use in warmer climates. If peak cooling loads are minimized, additional generating capacity is not required. This directly benefits the utility company, and indirectly the consumer, by keeping rates down. Some electric utilities provide financial incentives to builders and homeowners to reduce peak loads, which can offset some of the incremental cost of higher-performance windows. Check with your local utility to see if such incentives are available.

Influence of House Design on Energy Performance

All of the energy performance comparisons in this section are based on a typical 2000-square-foot house with a window area of 300 square feet distributed equally on four orientations with typical shading conditions. If these assumptions about the house design are changed, the impact of choosing efficient windows can vary. To illustrate these impacts, the energy performance of several window options is shown for different window areas, orientations, and shading conditions.

As shown in Figure 6-20, increasing the window area in Phoenix, Arizona results in increased annual energy costs. The increase is greater, however, for windows with higher SHGC (A and D) than for windows with lower SHGC (C and F). In a cooling-dominated climate, the benefit of using low-solar-gain low-E windows is greater with increased glazing area.

Figure 6-20 also shows that peak demand increases with increased glazing area. The peak demand for higher-SHGC windows (A and D) increases significantly as glazing area increases. The increase in peak demand is less with lower-SHGC windows (C and F). Window F with low-solar-gain low-E glazing shows the least increase in peak demand as glazing area increases.

In Phoenix, Arizona, orienting windows predominantly to the north decreases energy costs while orienting them predominantly to the west increases energy costs (Figure 6-21). The difference in costs due to orientation is greatest with higher-SHGC windows (A and D) and less with lower-SHGC windows (C and F). The west orientation has the highest peak demand but low-solar-gain low-E windows mitigate the impact.

Note: The annual energy performance figures shown here were generated using RESFEN for a typical (new construction) 2000 sq ft house with 300 sq ft (15%), 600 sq ft (30%) and 900 sq ft (45%) of window area. The windows are equally distributed on all four sides of the house and include typical shading (interior shades, overhangs, trees, and neighboring buildings). U-factor, SHGC, and VT are for the total window including frame. The costs shown here are annual costs for space heating and space cooling only and thus will be less than total utility bills. Costs for lights, appliances, hot water, cooking, and other uses are not included in these figures. The mechanical system uses a gas furnace for heating and air conditioning for cooling. The gas and electric prices used in these figures are provided by the Energy Information Administration (EIA) (www.eia.doe.gov). RESFEN is a computer program for calculating the annual cooling and heating energy use and costs due to window selection and is available from Lawrence Berkeley National Laboratory (windows.lbl.gov/software/resfen). See Appendix A for pricing and modeling assumptions.

Figure 6-20. Glazing area comparison of annual energy costs and summer peak cooling loads for six window types in Phoenix, Arizona.

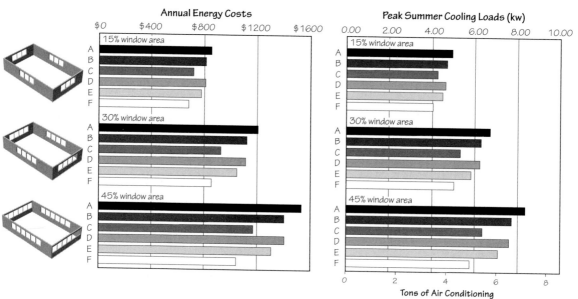

Figure 6-21. Orientation comparison of annual energy costs and summer peak cooling loads for six window types in Phoenix, Arizona.

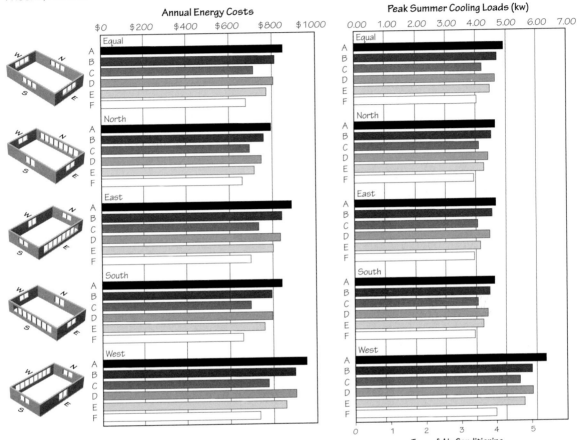

Window	Glazing	Frame	U-factor	SHGC	VT
A	double, clear	aluminum w/break	0.63	0.62	0.63
B	double, bronze tint	aluminum w/break	0.63	0.52	0.48
C	double, low-solar-gain low-E	aluminum w/break	0.47	0.33	0.55
D	double, clear	wood/vinyl	0.49	0.56	0.59
E	double, high-solar-gain low-E	wood/vinyl	0.37	0.53	0.54
F	double, low-solar-gain low-E	wood/vinyl	0.34	0.30	0.51
G	triple, moderate-solar-gain low-E	insulated vinyl	0.18	0.40	0.50

Note: The annual energy performance figures shown here were generated using RESFEN for a typical (new construction) 2000 sq ft house with 300 sq ft of window area. Windows are distributed 240 sq ft on one side and 20 sq ft on the others. Typical shading conditions are assumed for all windows. U-factor, SHGC, and VT are for the total window including frame. The costs shown here are annual costs for space heating and space cooling only and thus will be less than total utility bills. Costs for lights, appliances, hot water, cooking, and other uses are not included in these figures. The mechanical system uses a gas furnace for heating and air conditioning for cooling. The gas and electric prices used in these figures are provided by the Energy Information Administration (EIA) (www.eia.doe.gov). RESFEN is a computer program for calculating the annual cooling and heating energy use and costs due to window selection and is available from Lawrence Berkeley National Laboratory (windows.lbl.gov/software/resfen). See Appendix A for pricing and modeling assumptions.

Figure 6-22. Shading comparison of annual energy costs and summer peak cooling loads for six window types in Phoenix, Arizona.

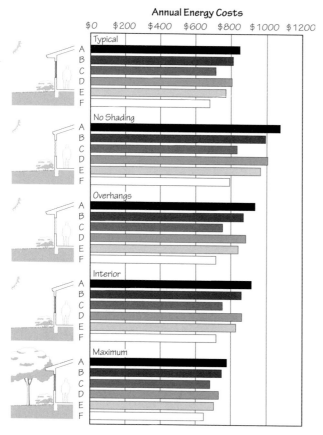

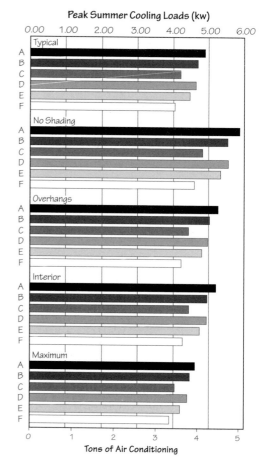

Note: The annual energy performance figures shown here were generated using RESFEN for a typical (new construction) 2000 sq ft house with 300 sq ft of window area. The windows are equally distributed on all four sides of the house. Typical shading includes (interior shades, overhangs, trees, and neighboring buildings). U-factor, SHGC, and VT are for the total window including frame. The costs shown here are annual costs for space heating and space cooling only and thus will be less than total utility bills. Costs for lights, appliances, hot water, cooking, and other uses are not included in these figures. The mechanical system uses a gas furnace for heating and air conditioning for cooling. The gas and electric prices used in these figures are provided by the Energy Information Administration (EIA) (www.eia.doe.gov). RESFEN is a computer program for calculating the annual cooling and heating energy use and costs due to window selection and is available from Lawrence Berkeley National Laboratory (windows.lbl.gov/software/resfen). See Appendix A for pricing and modeling assumptions.

Different shading conditions in cooling-dominated climates can affect energy costs significantly (Figure 6-22). Greater impacts occur with higher-SHGC windows (A and D). Since low-solar-gain low-E windows (C and F) are most effective at reducing heat gain, the need for and impact of shading is less. Increased shading affects peak demand in a similar manner.

Comparison of Skylight Performance

Six possible skylight choices are compared for a typical house in Phoenix, Arizona (Figure 6-23). Skylight A has clear, double-glazing and Skylight B has a low-solar-gain low-E coating. Both are in aluminum frames. Skylights C and D have the same two types of glazing in thermally broken aluminum frames. Skylights E and F have the same glazings in wood, wood-clad or vinyl frames.

In a southern climate, the U-factor of a skylight has little impact on annual energy costs. Most importantly, skylights with a low-solar-gain low-E coating result in better energy performance compared to the clear double-glazed options, regardless of frame type. This improvement is notable, although not large in total savings, considering that skylight areas are often small compared to the total house window area (45 square feet in Figure 6-23).

Figure 6-23. Skylight comparison of annual energy costs for six window types in Phoenix, Arizona.

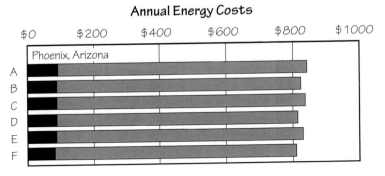

Annual Energy Costs

Note: The annual energy performance figures shown here were generated using RESFEN for a typical (new construction) 2000 sq ft house with 45 sq ft of skylights. The base house has 300 sq ft of window area and includes typical shading (interior shades, overhangs, trees, and neighboring buildings). The windows are equally distributed on all four sides of the house and are low-solar-gain low-E in all cases. RESFEN assumes skylights are placed in a typical well which reduces solar heat gain effects by 50%. U-factor, SHGC, and VT are for the total skylight including frame. Skylight U-factors are greater than window U-factors for the same glazing type because of the slope and greater exposure of the frame. The costs shown here are annual costs for space heating and space cooling only and thus will be less than total utility bills. Costs for lights, appliances, hot water, cooking, and other uses are not included in these figures. The mechanical system uses a gas furnace for heating and air conditioning for cooling. The gas and electric prices used in these figures are provided by the Energy Information Administration (EIA) (www.eia.doe.gov). RESFEN is a computer program for calculating the annual cooling and heating energy use and costs due to window selection and is available from Lawrence Berkeley National Laboratory (windows.lbl.gov/software/resfen). See Appendix A for pricing and modeling assumptions.

Skylight	Glazing	Frame	U-factor	SHGC	VT
A	double, clear	aluminum	0.94	0.68	0.70
B	double, low-solar-gain low-E	aluminum	0.75	0.40	0.55
C	double, clear	aluminum w/break	0.80	0.68	0.70
D	double, low-solar-gain low-E	aluminum w/break	0.70	0.40	0.55
E	double, clear-	wood/vinyl	0.75	0.68	0.70
F	double, low-solar-gain low-E	wood/vinyl	0.53	0.40	0.55

ENERGY STAR Requirements for the Southern Zone (Mostly Cooling)

U-factor = 0.65 or less
(0.75 or less for skylights)

SHGC = 0.40 or less
(0.40 or less for skylights)

Recommended Window Properties for South U.S. Climates (Mostly Cooling)

U-factor: Select windows with a U-factor lower than 0.65 and preferably lower than 0.60.

SHGC: Select windows with a SHGC less than 0.40. A low SHGC is the most important window property in warm climates.

Visible Transmittance: A window with VT above 0.70 for the glass only is desirable to maximize daylight and view assuming glare is not a concern. This translates into a VT above 0.50 for the total window, including a wood or vinyl frame.

Air Leakage: Select a window with an AL of 0.30 or below (units are cfm/sf).

SOUTHERN ZONE—MOSTLY COOLING

Comparison of Window Performance

As with the other climate zones, a computer simulation program was used to compare six possible window choices for a typical house in three southern U.S cities. The six windows used are appropriate choices in this region but are different from those shown for the northern and north/central zones (Figure 6-24). Window A is a clear, double-glazed unit in a thermally broken aluminum frame, commonly used in this region. Window B, with bronze-tinted glass in a thermally broken aluminum frame, represents a traditional approach to reducing solar heat gain in hot climates (note the somewhat reduced SHGC accompanied by a significant reduction in daylight—lower VT). Window C represents the relatively new technology of using a low-solar-gain low-E coating (a low SHGC combined with a relatively high VT) in an aluminum frame. Window D is a typical clear, double-glazed unit in a wood, vinyl or clad frame. Window E is a low-E glazing in a wood, vinyl or clad frame but it has high-solar-gain characteristics. Window F uses a low-solar-gain low-E glazing in a wood, vinyl, or clad frame.

Figure 6-24 illustrates that in Houston, Jacksonville, and Miami there are significant savings in annual cooling costs by using windows with low-solar-heat gain coefficients (Windows C and F) instead of double-glazed, clear units or traditional bronze- or gray-tinted glass (Windows A, B, and D). The windows with comparable glazings but different frames show that wood and vinyl frames perform better than aluminum frames. Some of this effect is because with thicker wood and vinyl frames there is less glazing area and thus less total solar heat gain in the same size window opening. It is important to note that in cooling-dominated climates, high-solar-gain low-E units (Window E) do not perform as well as low-solar-gain low-E units (Window F). All low-E windows are not the same. In Miami, the energy penalty from choosing the wrong kind of low-E glazing is most apparent. The high-solar-gain low-E unit (Window E) uses much more cooling energy than the low-solar-gain low-E option (Window F).

Just as with the colder climate examples, making a window selection in a cooling climate based on this energy-performance data must include the other issues discussed throughout this chapter. Improvements in energy performance must be weighed against both initial and life-cycle costs. In addition, there are benefits of greater comfort in both summer and

Figure 6-24. Comparison of annual energy cost with different window types on a typical house in the Southern Climate Zone.

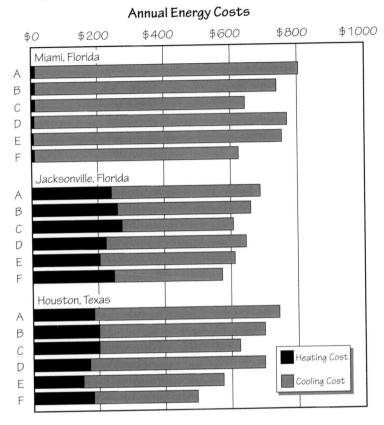

Annual Energy Costs

Note: The annual energy performance figures shown here were generated using RESFEN for a typical (new construction) 2000 sq ft house with 300 sq ft of window area. The windows are equally distributed on all four sides of the house and include typical shading (interior shades, overhangs, trees, and neighboring buildings). U-factor, SHGC, and VT are for the total window including frame. The costs shown here are annual costs for space heating and space cooling only and thus will be less than total utility bills. Costs for lights, appliances, hot water, cooking, and other uses are not included in these figures. The mechanical system uses a gas furnace for heating and air conditioning for cooling. The gas and electric prices used in these figures are provided by the Energy Information Administration (EIA) (www.eia.doe.gov). RESFEN is a computer program for calculating the annual cooling and heating energy use and costs due to window selection and is available from Lawrence Berkeley National Laboratory (windows.lbl.gov/software/resfen). See Appendix A for pricing and modeling assumptions.

Window	Glazing	Frame	U-factor	SHGC	VT
A	double, clear	aluminum w/break	0.63	0.62	0.63
B	double, bronze tint	aluminum w/break	0.63	0.52	0.48
C	double, low-solar-gain low-E	aluminum w/break	0.47	0.33	0.55
D	double, clear	wood/vinyl	0.49	0.56	0.59
E	double, high-solar-gain low-E	wood/vinyl	0.37	0.53	0.54
F	double, low-solar-gain low-E	wood/vinyl	0.34	0.30	0.51
G	triple, moderate-solar-gain low-E	insulated vinyl	0.18	0.40	0.50

Figure 6-25. Peak heating loads for a typical house with different window types in the south zone.

Figure 6-26. Peak heating loads for a typical house with different window types in the south zone.

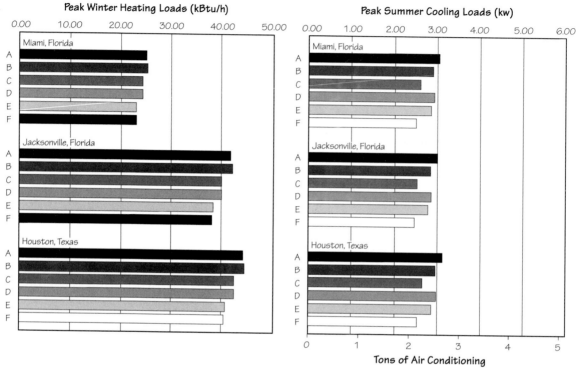

Note: The peak energy performance figures shown here were generated using RESFEN for a typical (new construction) 2000 sq ft house with 300 sq ft of window area. The windows are equally distributed on all four sides of the house and include typical shading (interior shades, overhangs, trees, and neighboring buildings). U-factor, SHGC, and VT are for the total window including frame. The mechanical system uses a gas furnace for heating and air conditioning for cooling. The gas and electric prices used in these figures are provided by the Energy Information Administration (EIA) (www.eia.doe.gov). RESFEN is a computer program for calculating the annual cooling and heating energy use and costs due to window selection and is available from Lawrence Berkeley National Laboratory (windows.lbl.gov/software/resfen). See Appendix A for pricing and modeling assumptions.

winter. In warm climates, the traditional approach of using tinted glass and films will reduce cooling energy somewhat, but an important related factor is the diminished amount of daylight they allow. If controlling heat gain while maximizing light and view is your goal, then a low-solar-gain low-E glazing is the obvious choice in warmer climates.

Comparison of Peak Performance

High-performance windows not only provide reduced annual heating and cooling bills; they reduce the peak heating and cooling loads as well. This has benefits for the homeowner, in that the size of the heating or cooling system may be reduced, and it also benefits the electrical utilities, in that load factors are reduced during the peak times in summer.

The peak load for a building is the maximum requirement for heating or cooling at one time. These loads determine the size of the furnace, heat pump, air conditioner, and fans that must be installed. The peak heating load (in kBtu/h) represents how much heat must be delivered from the furnace at the coldest outdoor temperature in order to maintain a given interior temperature (typically, 70°F/21°C). Similarly, the peak cooling load (in kW) represents how much air-conditioning capacity is required to maintain a given interior temperature (typically, 75°F/24°C) during the hottest summer conditions.

Figures 6-25 and 6-26 illustrate typical reductions in peak loads that occur with different window types used in a typical house in a hot climate. As expected, tinted glazing (Window B) does little to lower peak cooling loads but low-solar-gain low-E (Windows C and F) has a significant impact. High-performance windows also reduce peak heating loads although this has less economic payoff in hot climates.

The greatest economic benefits come from reductions of peak cooling loads in hot climates and peak heating loads in cold climates where heat pumps are used to provide space heat. In new construction, reducing peak loads might also lead to using smaller fans and ducts. High-performance windows can be an important part of a larger package of energy-efficiency measures that combine to produce large savings in space conditioning equipment. Any time an air-conditioning unit must be replaced in an existing home, consider upgrading to windows with a lower SHGC at the same time to reduce the size and cost of the replacement cooling equipment.

Lowering the peak cooling load is a goal of most electric utilities. Low-solar-gain low-E glazing has the ability to lower electric utility load factors during the peak summer use in warmer climates. If peak cooling loads are minimized, additional generating capacity is not required. This directly benefits the utility company, and indirectly the consumer, by keeping rates down. Some electric utilities provide financial incentives to builders and homeowners to reduce peak loads, which can offset some of the incremental cost of higher-performance windows. Check with your local utility to see if such incentives are available.

Influence of House Design on Energy Performance

All of the energy performance comparisons in this section are based on a typical 2000-square-foot house with a window area of 300 square feet distributed equally on four orientations with typical shading conditions. If these assumptions about the house design are changed, the impact of choosing efficient windows can vary. To illustrate these impacts, the energy performance of several window options is shown for different window areas, orientations, and shading conditions.

As shown in Figure 6-27, increasing the window area in Miami, Florida results in increased annual energy costs. The increase is greater, however, for windows with higher SHGC (A and D) than for windows with lower SHGC (C and F). In a cooling-dominated climate, the benefit of using low-solar-gain low-E windows is greater with increased glazing area.

Figure 6-27 also shows that peak demand increases with increased glazing area. The peak demand for higher-SHGC windows (A and D) increases significantly as glazing area increases. The increase in peak demand is less with lower-SHGC windows (C and F). Window F with low-solar-gain low-E glazing shows the least increase in peak demand as glazing area increases.

In Miami, Florida, orienting windows predominantly to the north decreases energy costs compared to other orientations (Figure 6-28). The difference in costs due to orientation is greatest with higher-SHGC windows (A and D) and less with lower-SHGC windows (C and F). The west orientation has the highest peak demand but low-solar-gain low-E windows mitigate the impact.

Note: The annual energy performance figures shown here were generated using RESFEN for a typical (new construction) 2000 sq ft house with 300 sq ft (15%), 600 sq ft (30%) and 900 sq ft (45%) of window area. The windows are equally distributed on all four sides of the house and include typical shading (interior shades, overhangs, trees, and neighboring buildings). U-factor, SHGC, and VT are for the total window including frame. The costs shown here are annual costs for space heating and space cooling only and thus will be less than total utility bills. Costs for lights, appliances, hot water, cooking, and other uses are not included in these figures. The mechanical system uses a gas furnace for heating and air conditioning for cooling. The gas and electric prices used in these figures are provided by the Energy Information Administration (EIA) (www.eia.doe.gov). RESFEN is a computer program for calculating the annual cooling and heating energy use and costs due to window selection and is available from Lawrence Berkeley National Laboratory (windows.lbl.gov/software/resfen). See Appendix A for pricing and modeling assumptions.

Figure 6-27. Glazing area comparison of annual energy costs and summer peak cooling loads for six window types in Miami, Florida.

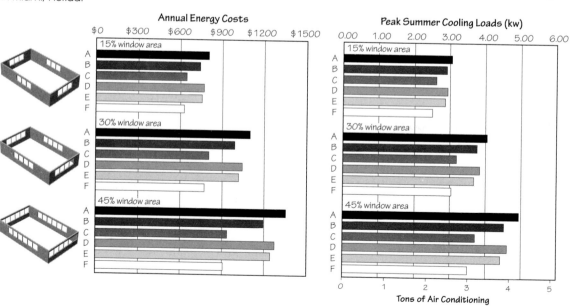

Figure 6-28. Orientation comparison of annual energy costs and summer peak cooling loads for six window types in Miami, Florida.

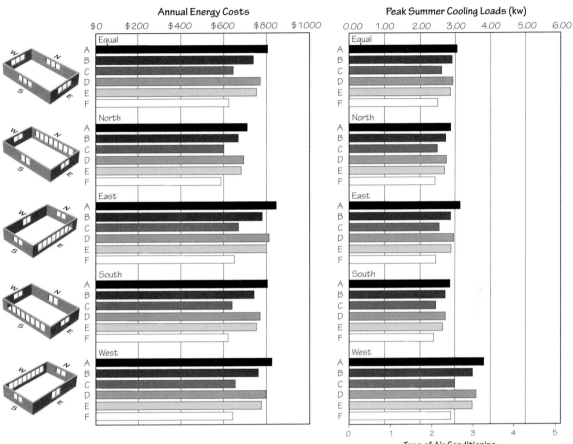

Window	Glazing	Frame	U-factor	SHGC	VT
A	double, clear	aluminum w/break	0.63	0.62	0.63
B	double, bronze tint	aluminum w/break	0.63	0.52	0.48
C	double, low-solar-gain low-E	aluminum w/break	0.47	0.33	0.55
D	double, clear	wood/vinyl	0.49	0.56	0.59
E	double, high-solar-gain low-E	wood/vinyl	0.37	0.53	0.54
F	double, low-solar-gain low-E	wood/vinyl	0.34	0.30	0.51
G	triple, moderate-solar-gain low-E	insulated vinyl	0.18	0.40	0.50

Note: The annual energy performance figures shown here were generated using RESFEN for a typical (new construction) 2000 sq ft house with 300 sq ft of window area. Windows are distributed 240 sq ft on one side and 20 sq ft on the others. Typical shading conditions are assumed for all windows. U-factor, SHGC, and VT are for the total window including frame. The costs shown here are annual costs for space heating and space cooling only and thus will be less than total utility bills. Costs for lights, appliances, hot water, cooking, and other uses are not included in these figures. The mechanical system uses a gas furnace for heating and air conditioning for cooling. The gas and electric prices used in these figures are provided by the Energy Information Administration (EIA) (www.eia.doe.gov). RESFEN is a computer program for calculating the annual cooling and heating energy use and costs due to window selection and is available from Lawrence Berkeley National Laboratory (windows.lbl.gov/software/resfen). See Appendix A for pricing and modeling assumptions.

Figure 6-29. Shading comparison of annual energy costs and summer peak cooling loads for six window types in Miami, Florida.

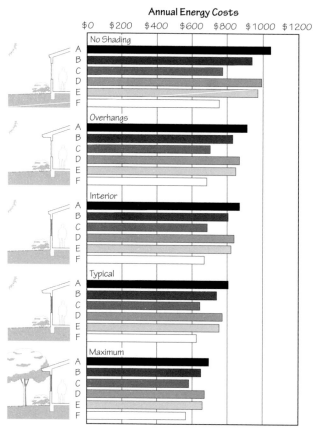

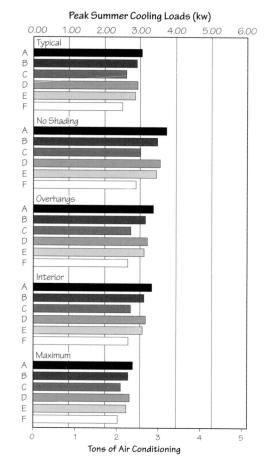

Note: The annual energy performance figures shown here were generated using RESFEN for a typical (new construction) 2000 sq ft house with 300 sq ft of window area. The windows are equally distributed on all four sides of the house. Typical shading includes (interior shades, overhangs, trees, and neighboring buildings). U-factor, SHGC, and VT are for the total window including frame. The costs shown here are annual costs for space heating and space cooling only and thus will be less than total utility bills. Costs for lights, appliances, hot water, cooking, and other uses are not included in these figures. The mechanical system uses a gas furnace for heating and air conditioning for cooling. The gas and electric prices used in these figures are provided by the Energy Information Administration (EIA) (www.eia.doe.gov). RESFEN is a computer program for calculating the annual cooling and heating energy use and costs due to window selection and is available from Lawrence Berkeley National Laboratory (windows.lbl.gov/software/resfen). See Appendix A for pricing and modeling assumptions.

Different shading conditions in cooling-dominated climates can affect energy costs significantly (Figure 6-29). Greater impacts occur with higher-SHGC windows (A and D). Since low-solar-gain low-E windows (C and F) are most effective at reducing heat gain, the need for and impact of shading is less. Increased shading affects peak demand in a similar manner.

Comparison of Skylight Performance

Six possible skylight choices are compared for a typical house in Miami, Florida (Figure 6-30). Skylight A has clear double-glazing and Skylight B has a low-solar-gain low-E coating. Both are in aluminum frames. Skylights C and D have the same two types of glazing in thermally broken aluminum frames. Skylights E and F have the same glazings in wood, wood-clad or vinyl frames.

In a southern climate, the U-factor of a skylight has little impact on annual energy costs. Most importantly, skylights with a low-solar-gain low-E coating result in better energy performance compared to the clear double-glazed options, regardless of frame type. This improvement is notable considering that skylight areas are often not large compared to the total house window area (45 square feet in Figure 6-30).

Figure 6-30. Annual energy performance for a 2000-square-foot house with different skylights in the south zone.

Annual Energy Costs

	$0	$200	$400	$600	$800

Miami, Florida

A
B
C
D
E
F

Skylight	Glazing	Frame	U-factor	SHGC	VT
A	double, clear	aluminum	0.94	0.68	0.70
B	double, low-solar-gain low-E	aluminum	0.75	0.40	0.55
C	double, clear	aluminum w/break	0.80	0.68	0.70
D	double, low-solar-gain low-E	aluminum w/break	0.70	0.40	0.55
E	double, clear-	wood/vinyl	0.75	0.68	0.70
F	double, low-solar-gain low-E	wood/vinyl	0.53	0.40	0.55

Note: The annual energy performance figures shown here were generated using RESFEN for a typical (new construction) 2000 sq ft house with 45 sq ft of skylights. The base house has 300 sq ft of window area and includes typical shading (interior shades, overhangs, trees, and neighboring buildings). The windows are equally distributed on all four sides of the house and are low-solar-gain low-E in all cases. RESFEN assumes skylights are placed in a typical well which reduces solar heat gain effects by 50%. U-factor, SHGC, and VT are for the total skylight including frame. Skylight U-factors are greater than window U-factors for the same glazing type because of the slope and greater exposure of the frame. The costs shown here are annual costs for space heating and space cooling only and thus will be less than total utility bills. Costs for lights, appliances, hot water, cooking, and other uses are not included in these figures. The mechanical system uses a gas furnace for heating and air conditioning for cooling. The gas and electric prices used in these figures are provided by the Energy Information Administration (EIA) (www.eia.doe.gov). RESFEN is a computer program for calculating the annual cooling and heating energy use and costs due to window selection and is available from Lawrence Berkeley National Laboratory (windows.lbl.gov/software/resfen). See Appendix A for pricing and modeling assumptions.)

COST CONSIDERATIONS

In evaluating the cost of a window unit, the aesthetic, functional, and energy-performance characteristics come together. Without the proper understanding of total window performance, costs may be evaluated based on one or two facts—the initial cost of the unit and, possibly, a characteristic such as U-factor (if it is available). To make a better decision about the costs and benefits of a particular window, it is useful to think of the life-cycle cost of the unit. There are both monetary and nonmonetary costs and benefits. Even if the decision is made to base window selection on monetary costs and benefits only, the following factors should be included:

1. Initial Cost

   This is the most obvious of the factors and is included in virtually any analysis. For new construction, initial cost may be defined as only the cost of the window unit itself, since the installation cost will generally be equal for any similar window. In a retrofit situation, the comparison between an existing window and a replacement window usually should include the installation cost as part of the project cost analysis. Installation labor may be half the cost of window replacement so it pays to shop for the best price and check on the reputation of the installer. If the windows must be replaced because of failure of the existing units, then the comparative cost analysis might only include the relative costs of the alternative new window units, not the installation. The cost of a specific window from a particular manufacturer may vary considerably between alternative suppliers. Since window purchases are often large investments, it pays to shop aggressively for the best price and take advantage of any sales or discounts.

2. Cost of Exterior and Interior Window Treatments

   At first glance, window treatments may not seem to be an integral part of comparing the cost of window units. With newer high-performance windows, however, they may be quite relevant to consider. Many of the higher-performance windows (using low-E coatings, gas fills, and low-conductance frames) do the work of various shading and insulating components that were necessary to achieve comfort in the past. If choosing a better window reduces the need for some external shading devices or interior blinds or drapes (or allows the purchase of a simpler, cheaper version), then this is part of the total cost/benefit picture. Of course, elements such as blinds or drapes when operated effectively can further reduce unwanted heat gain as well as have the additional benefits of providing privacy and glare control.

3. Cost of Maintenance

In the past, window maintenance has represented a significant cost and effort. Materials such as vinyl and aluminum, as well as claddings and more durable finishes on wood windows, have greatly reduced exterior maintenance. When choosing between products that have different maintenance requirements (i.e., continued painting of an existing window versus a new, maintenance-free window), consider the cost and frequency of this activity over the life of the window.

4. Frequency of Replacement

Some windows simply last longer than others because of their quality and durability. The life of a window unit is related to its design, materials, and workmanship. In assessing life cycle costs for a window purchase, the frequency of replacement should be included as well.

5. Resale Value

It is well known that special features such as a large bay window, skylights, or a glazed sun porch can add value to a home. High-performance windows may also add to the resale value of a house. Energy-efficient windows can be attractive selling features, and lead to higher appraisals. Homes with lower annual energy costs provide some protection from future fuel cost increases.

6. Cost of Heating and Cooling System

In some cases, choosing a higher-performance window reduces the peak heating and cooling loads sufficiently so that the mechanical system size can be smaller, resulting in initial cost savings on furnaces and air-conditioning units. This is relevant not only in new construction but in any renovation in which HVAC systems are being upgraded or replaced. Utilities may offer rebates as incentives to purchase windows which result in lower cooling loads and thus lower peak electric demand. (See previous section, Peak Heating and Cooling Loads.)

7. Annual Cost of Heating and Cooling Energy

This is a very important but often elusive cost to determine. Earlier in this chapter many examples were given illustrating the impact of window choices on annual energy costs in several U.S. cities. Once energy cost savings are determined for a particular window type, it must be remembered that this is an annually recurring savings.

Windows that are purchased in new homes or as part of a major renovation are typically paid for through a mortgage, home-equity loan, or some other form of long-term financing that distributes the purchase and installation cost over many monthly payments. The monthly energy savings from high-performance windows can offset or even exceed these payments. Here is a simple example:

A homeowner chooses an energy-efficient window upgrade option (low-E, gas-fill glazing) in a new house, at an additional cost of $500 (about $2 per square foot) above the standard cost of windows. This glazing provides energy savings of about $100 per year, or an average of $8.33 per month. The additional purchase cost of $500 is amortized as part of an 8 percent loan over 30 years. The added monthly payment, including interest, is $3.67, which is less than the average monthly energy savings, thus providing a net "profit" on this efficiency investment of $4.66 per month. More important, from the first day the house is occupied and throughout the life of the mortgage, the owner has lower monthly living costs (mortgage plus utilities), as well as the advantage of a more comfortable home.

Our lives are filled with many purchasing decisions. Some are tightly constrained by economic factors, while others may be based more on appearance, style, and comfort. The appropriate balance depends on the unique priorities and circumstances of each individual.

Once a life-cycle analysis that includes initial cost and energy saving benefits has been completed, it is important to recognize that this is only part of the picture. Subjective issues of appearance, comfort, performance, and code compliance are all part of the overall cost/benefit analysis, and homeowners must consider their own values just as they do when making other purchases.

APPENDIX A

Energy Performance Calculation Assumptions

In order to understand the impact of window selection on annual energy use, researchers performed thousands of computer simulations of houses with a wide range of characteristics in several U.S. climates. The simulation program used was RESFEN 5.0 which is based on DOE-2.1E, which is considered one of the standards for building simulation in the United States. The results of these simulations appear throughout the book. The basic assumptions underlying the simulations are described below. A more detailed discussion of these assumptions can be found in the RESFEN 5.0: A PC program for Calculating the Heating and Cooling Energy Use of Windows in Residential Buildings (Mitchell, R. et al., 2005). See References for more information.

The prices shown in the figures in this book are average energy prices projected for the period of 2006-2030, which is the typical effective lifetime of a window installed in 2005. The bases for these prices are average state-specific 2005 prices for electricity during the cooling season and for natural gas during the heating season, adjusted by the projected difference between average national 2005 prices and average national prices between 2006 and 2030. Energy Information Administration (EIA) data (www.eia.doe.gov) is used for the 2005 prices. The 2006-2030 prices are based on EIA projections of future prices in real 2004 dollars that have been adjusted to take into account an estimated future inflation rate of 3 percent annually.

Figure A-1. RESFEN 5.0 modeling assumptions.

PARAMETER	MODELING ASSUMPTION
Floor Area	2,000 sq ft
House Type	New frame construction, single-family, single story
Foundation	Basement, slab-on-grade, or crawlspace; a function of typical construction for location.
Insulation	Envelope insulation levels are based on location. See Table 6-1 of the RESFEN 5.0 User Manual for a list of packages that correspond to each location. See Tables 6-3 and 6-4 for a list of R-values for each building component for each location. See Table 6-5 for a list of U-factors that correspond to the R-value constructions.

PARAMETER	MODELING ASSUMPTION
Structural Mass	3.5 lb/ft² of floor area, in accordance with the Model Energy Code and NFRC Annual Energy Performance Subcommittee recommendation (September 1998).
Internal Mass	8.0 lb/ft² of floor area, in accordance with the Model Energy Code and NFRC Annual Energy Performance Subcommittee recommendation (September 1998).
Solar Gain Reduction	To represent a statistically average solar gain reduction for a generic house, the following are included: • Interior shades (Seasonal SHGC multiplier, summer value = 0.80, winter value=0.90); • 1' overhangs on all four sides; • a 67% transmitting same-height obstruction 20' away intended to represent adjacent buildings. • To account for other sources of solar heat gain reduction (insect screens, trees, dirt, building & window self-shading), the SHGC multiplier was further reduced by 0.1. This results in a final winter SHGC multiplier of 0.8 and a final summer SHGC multiplier of 0.7.
Window Area	300 sq ft (15% of floor area)
Window Type	Variable
Window Distribution	Equal area on north, east, south, and west.
HVAC System	Gas furnace & A/C
HVAC System Sizing	For each climate, system sizes are fixed for all window options. Fixed sizes are based on the use of DOE-2 auto-sizing for the same house as defined in the analysis, with the most representative window for that specific climate. An auto-sizing multiplier of 1.3 used to account for a typical safety factor.
HVAC Efficiency	AFUE = 0.78, A/C SEER=10.0
Duct Losses	Heating: 10% (fixed) / Cooling: 10% (fixed)
Part-Load Performance	Part-load curves (Henderson 1998) for new construction.
Thermostat Settings	Heating: 70°F, Cooling: 78°F Basement (partially conditioned): Heating 62°F, Cooling 85°F
Night Heating Setback	65°F (11 PM – 6 AM)
Internal Loads	Sensible: 43,033 Btu/day + (floor area * 8.42 Btu/ft²-day for lighting) Latent: 12.2 kBtu/day
Natural Ventilation	Enthalpic – Sherman-Grimsrud (78°F / 72°F based on 4 days history)
Weather Data	All TMY2
Number of Locations	48 US cities 4 Canadian cities
Calculation Tool	DOE-2.1E

Figure A-3. Properties of common window assemblies.

Frame Type	# of Glazings	Glazing Description	Gap (inch)	Gas*	U-factor (Btu/hr-ft²-°F)	TOTAL WINDOW SHGC (Solar Heat Gain Coefficient)	VT (Visible Transmittance)
AL	1	Clear	n/a	n/a	1.16	0.76	0.75
AL	1	Bronze	n/a	n/a	1.16	0.65	0.56
AL	2	Clear	0.375	Air	0.76	0.68	0.68
AL	2	Bronze	0.375	Air	0.76	0.56	0.51
AL	2	HP Tint	0.375	Air	0.76	0.47	0.57
AL	2	HS Low-E	0.50	Argon	0.61	0.64	0.62
AL	2	MS Low-E	0.50	Argon	0.60	0.53	0.65
AL	2	LS Low-E	0.50	Argon	0.59	0.37	0.59
ATB	1	Clear	n/a	n/a	1.00	0.70	0.70
ATB	1	Bronze	n/a	n/a	1.00	0.59	0.53
ATB	2	Clear	0.50	Air	0.63	0.62	0.63
ATB	2	Bronze	0.50	Air	0.63	0.52	0.48
ATB	2	HP Tint	0.50	Air	0.63	0.43	0.54
ATB	2	HS Low-E	0.50	Argon	0.50	0.58	0.58
ATB	2	MS Low-E	0.50	Argon	0.48	0.48	0.60
ATB	2	LS Low-E	0.50	Argon	0.47	0.33	0.55
W/V	1	Clear	n/a	n/a	0.84	0.63	0.65
W/V	1	Bronze	n/a	n/a	0.84	0.54	0.49
W/V	2	Clear	0.50	Air	0.49	0.56	0.59
W/V	2	Bronze	0.50	Air	0.49	0.47	0.44
W/V	2	HP Tint	0.50	Air	0.49	0.39	0.50
W/V	2	HS Low-E	0.50	Argon	0.37	0.53	0.54
W/V	2	MS Low-E	0.50	Argon	0.35	0.44	0.56
W/V	2	LS Low-E	0.50	Argon	0.34	0.30	0.51
W/V	3	HT Super	0.50	Argon	0.29	0.38	0.47
W/V	3	SS Super	0.50	Argon	0.28	0.25	0.40
INS	2	Clear	0.50	Air	0.44	0.60	0.63
INS	2	Bronze	0.50	Air	0.44	0.49	0.48
INS	2	HP Tint	0.50	Air	0.44	0.41	0.54
INS	2	HS Low-E	0.50	Argon	0.29	0.56	0.58
INS	2	MS Low-E	0.50	Argon	0.27	0.46	0.60
INS	2	LS Low-E	0.50	Argon	0.26	0.31	0.55
INS	3	HT Super	0.50	Argon	0.18	0.40	0.50
INS	3	SS Super	0.50	Argon	0.18	0.26	0.43

NOTES:

FRAME TYPE CODES:

AL = Aluminum
ATB = Aluminum, Thermally Broken
W/V = Wood/Vinyl
INS = Insulated Frame

ARGON GAS: Consists of 10% air, 90% argon

GLAZING TYPE CODES:

HP = High-performance
HS = High-solar-gain low-E (e=0.15–0.20)
MS = Moderate-solar-gain low-E (e=10)
LS = Low-solar-gain (or "spectrally selective") low-E (e=0.04)
MS Super = 3-layer insulating glazing, two layers with high-solar-gain low-E coatings.
LS Super = 3-layer insulating glazing, two layers with low-solar-gain low-E coatings.

The data presented here and in RESFEN are average properties for several commercially available products. Specific products will perform slightly above or below the average products defined here. Users are encouraged to only use these numbers as a general guide and to use specific manufacturer's product data (i.e. NFRC U-factors and Solar Heat Gain Coefficients) whenever possible. The values in this table may differ slightly from those from RESFEN 3.1 because these windows were calculated with WINDOW 5 using the new ISO 15099 and NFRC modeling assumptions. See the WINDOW5 User Manual for more details.

APPENDIX B

Overview of the NFRC Program

National Fenestration Rating Council

The National Fenestration Rating Council, Inc. (NFRC) was formed in 1989 to respond to a need for fair, accurate, and credible ratings for fenestration products. Fenestration products include all types of windows, skylights, and doors, both glazed and opaque: vertical sliders, horizontal sliders, casements, projecting (awning), fixed (including nonstandard shapes), single door with frame, double and multiple doors with frames, glazed wall systems (including curtain wall, store-front and other site-built systems), tubular daylight devices, skylights and sloped glazing, greenhouse/garden, dual action, and pivoted windows; as well as window films.

NFRC has adopted rating procedures for U-factor (NFRC 100), Solar Heat Gain Coefficient and Visible Transmittance(NFRC 200), Optical Properties (NFRC 300), emittances (NFRC 301), Air Leakage (NFRC 400) and Condensation Resistance (NFRC 500). To provide certified ratings, manufacturers follow the requirements of the NFRC Product Certification Program (PCP), which involves working with laboratories accredited to the NFRC Laboratory Accreditation Program (LAP) and Independent Certification and Inspection Agencies licensed through the NFRC Certification Agency Program (CAP). The complete NFRC program, with various checks to maintain a high degree of confidence and integrity, is summarized below.

NFRC 100, Procedure for Determining Fenestration Product U-Factors, was the first rating procedure approved and thus the first NFRC procedure adopted into state energy codes. Because it is also the most widely adopted, it is a good choice as an example to demonstrate the process. NFRC 100 requires the use of a combination of state-of-the-art computer simulations and improved thermal testing to determine U-factors for the whole product. Manufacturers seeking to acquire energy-performance ratings for their products contact NFRC-accredited simulation laboratories. These simulation laboratories use advanced computer tools to calculate product performance ratings in accordance with NFRC 100. To become accredited, each simulation laboratory must demonstrate competence in the use of the computer programs used in the rating system and must meet strict independence criteria. Following computer simulation, one product within each product line undergoes periodic thermal testing to validate the computer simulations. The testing is performed by an NFRC-accredited testing laboratory. These testing laboratories have demonstrated their ability to conduct NFRC thermal tests. They are periodically inspected and evaluated by the NFRC for continued competence, and are independent of any product manufacturer that they serve. Generally, if the thermal test results are within 10 percent of the simulated U-factor, then the U-factors are considered validated and manufacturers obtain product ratings for that entire product line.

The next step is product certification authorization. NFRC has a series of checks and balances in place to ensure that the rating system is accurately and uniformly employed. Products and their ratings are authorized for certification by an NFRC-licensed independent certification and inspection agency (IA). The IA reviews all simulation and test information, conducts in-plant inspections, and provides secondary oversight to the manufacturer's in-house quality control program. This helps to ensure that the rated products reaching the marketplace are built in the same manner as the product samples simulated and tested, that the appropriate product ratings and labels are put on the correct products, and that the manufacturer maintains an in-house quality assurance program. Licensed IA's must demonstrate their ability to perform these services and meet strict independence criteria.

The authorization for certification means that the manufacturer is able to have the product listed in the NFRC Certified Products Directory. However, this does not mean that a product is certified. The actual act of certification occurs when the manufacturer labels the product. Two labels are required: the temporary label (shown in Chapter 1), which contains the product ratings, and a permanent label, which allows tracking back to the IA and information in the NFRC Certified Products Directory. In addition to informing the buyer, the temporary label provides building inspectors with the information necessary to verify energy code compliance. The permanent label provides access to energy rating information for a future owner, property manager, building inspector, lending agency, or building energy rating organization. In the case of site-built fenestration systems, or for manufactured windows in large building projects, a Label Certificate may be utilized in the place of the temporary label.

This process has a number of noteworthy features that makes it superior to previous fenestration energy rating systems and corrects past problems.

- The procedures provide a means for manufacturers to take credit for all the improvement and refinement to their product design and a common basis for others to compare product claims.

- The involvement of independent laboratories and the IA provides architects, engineers, designers, contractors, consumers, building officials, and utility representatives with greater confidence that the information is unbiased.

- By requiring both simulation and testing, there is an automatic check on accuracy. This also remedies a shortcoming of previous state energy requirements that relied on testing alone.

- The certification and labeling process indicates that the manufacturer is consistently producing the product that was rated and that the product information is communicated in a consistent and uniform manner.

- There is now a readily visible temporary label that can be used by the building inspector to quickly verify compliance with the energy code.

- The permanent label provides future access to energy rating information.

While the program is similar for other fenestration characteristics, there are differences worth pointing out. The solar heat gain coefficient ratings (NFRC 200), which have been referenced in several codes, including ASHRAE 90.1; 90.2 and the International Energy Conservation Code (IECC) are based on simulation and peer-reviewed test data on each glazing layer's solar optical properties. The solar optical properties of glazing materials and systems (NFRC 300) and emittance (NFRC 301) are based on measurements by the glazing manufacturer, with independent verification. The air-leakage ratings (NFRC 400) are based on testing alone. Condensation resistance ratings (NFRC 500) are based on computer simulation and indicate the potential for products to resist the formation of condensation.

The NFRC publishes a directory of products eligible to be certified. For further information and to obtain copies of program documents and publications, contact:

National Fenestration Rating Council
8484 Georgia Avenue, Suite 320
Silver Spring, MD 20910

Phone: 301-589-1776
Fax: 301-589-3884
www.nfrc.org

APPENDIX C

Specifying Product Performance

The National Fenestration Rating Council, Inc. (NFRC) was established in 1989 to develop a fair, accurate, and credible rating system for the energy performance of fenestration products. This was in response to the technological advances and increasing complexity of these products, which manufacturers wanted to take credit for but which could not be easily visually verified. NFRC procedures started to be incorporated in state energy codes in 1992. The 1992 National Energy Policy Act provided for the development of a national rating system. The U.S. Department of Energy has identified the NFRC program as the national rating system for the United States. In addition, the NFRC rating procedures are now referenced as the method for determining energy ratings for windows, doors, and skylights in the International Energy Conservation Code and ASHRAE Standards 90.1 and 90.2. Contractors and homeowners can and should look for the NFRC label when selecting fenestration products as a way of identifying and confirming energy ratings that have been developed to a nationally recognized standard with independent oversight. Designers should specify the NFRC rating program to ensure that their design is implemented on a level playing field with other bidders. Specifications are provided on the next page as an aid to designers.

Sample Specification for Fenestration Products

1. U-factor for all fenestration products (windows, doors, curtain walls, skylights) shall include the effects of glass, sash, and frame and shall be determined in accordance with NFRC 100. The product shall be labeled and certified by the manufacturer for U-factor in accordance with the NFRC Product Certification Program.

2. Solar Heat Gain Coefficient (SHGC) and Visible Light Transmittance for all fenestration products (windows, doors, curtain walls skylights) shall include the effects of glass, sash, and frame and shall be determined in accordance with NFRC 200. The product shall be labeled and certified by the manufacturer for SHGC and VT in accordance with the NFRC Product Certification Program.

3. Air Leakage for all fenestration products (windows, doors, curtain walls skylights) shall include the effects of glass, sash, and frame and shall be determined in accordance with NFRC 400. The product shall be labeled and certified by the manufacturer for Air Leakage in accordance with the NFRC Product Certification Program.

4. Condensation Resistance for all fenestration products (windows, doors, curtain walls skylights) shall include the effects of glass, sash, and frame and shall be determined in accordance with NFRC 500. The product shall be labeled and certified by the manufacturer for Condensation Resistance in accordance with the NFRC Product Certification Program.

APPENDIX D

Resources

This appendix includes a variety of resources that are referred to in the book as well as some additional sources of information related to windows. Lists of organizations are followed by lists of printed material directly relevant to window installation and technical standards for windows.

For information concerning windows and energy-efficiency in general, there are several local resources worth investigating:

- Local utilities
- State or municipal energy agencies
- Regional universities that may have architecture, construction, or extension programs
- Bookstores
- Publications in window sales areas
- Local chapters of the American Institute of Architects
- Local builder's associations

Computer Simulation Programs

RESFEN

RESFEN is a computer program that helps consumers and builders pick the most energy-efficient and cost-effective window for a given application. It calculates heating and cooling energy use and associated costs as well as peak heating and cooling demand for specific window products. Users define a specific "scenario" by specifying house type, geographic location, orientation, electricity and gas cost, and building configuration details. Users also specify size,

shading, and thermal properties of the window they wish to investigate. The thermal properties that RESFEN requires are: U-factor, Solar Heat Gain Coefficient, and air leakage rate. RESFEN calculates the energy and cost implications of the window compared to an insulated wall. Available from:

windows.lbl.gov/software/resfen/resfen.html
RESFENHelp@lbl.gov

WINDOW

WINDOW is a computer program for calculating total window thermal performance indices (i.e. U-values, solar heat gain coefficients, shading coefficients, and visible transmittances). WINDOW provides a versatile heat transfer analysis method consistent with the updated rating procedure developed by the National Fenestration Rating Council (NFRC) that is consistent with the ISO 15099 standard. The program can be used to design and develop new products, to assist educators in teaching heat transfer through windows, and to help public officials in developing building energy codes. Available from:

windows.lbl.gov/software/window/window.html
WindowHelp@lbl.gov

THERM

THERM is a computer program for use by building component manufacturers, engineers, educators, students, architects, and others interested in heat transfer. Using THERM, you can model two-dimensional heat-transfer effects in building components such as windows, walls, foundations, roofs, and doors; appliances; and other products where thermal bridges are of concern. THERM's heat-transfer analysis allows you to evaluate a product's energy efficiency and local temperature patterns, which may relate directly to problems with condensation, moisture damage, and structural integrity. Available from:

windows.lbl.gov/software/therm/therm.html
THERMHelp@lbl.gov

DOE-2.1E

DOE-2 is an up-to-date, unbiased computer program that predicts the hourly energy use and energy cost of a building given hourly weather information and a description of the building and its HVAC equipment and utility rate structure. Using DOE-2, designers can determine the choice of building parameters that improve energy efficiency while maintaining thermal comfort and cost-effectiveness. The purpose of DOE-2 is to aid in the analysis of energy usage in buildings. For a listing of where to purchase the program go to:

gundog.lbl.gov

American Professional and Manufacturer's Organizations

American Architectural Manufacturers
Association (AAMA)
1827 Walden Office Square, Suite 550
Schaumberg, IL 60173-4268
Phone: (847) 303-5664/Fax: (847) 303-5774
www.aamanet.org

American Institute of Architects (AIA)
1735 New York Ave. NW
Washington, DC 20006-5292
Phone: (202) 626-7300/ Fax: 202-626-7547
www.aia.org
infocentral@aia.org

American National Standards Institute (ANSI)
1819 L Street, NW, 6th floor
Washington, DC 20036
Phone: (212) 293-8020/Fax: (212) 298-9287
www.ansi.org

American Society of Heating, Refrigerating and Air Conditioning Engineers, Inc. (ASHRAE)
1791 Tullie Circle, NE
Atlanta, GA 30329-2305
Phone: (404) 636-8400/Fax: (404) 321-5478
www.ashrae.org
ashrae@ashrae.org

American Society for Testing and Materials (ASTM)
100 Barr Harbor Drive
West Conshohocken, PA 19428-2959
Phone: (610) 832-9585 /Fax: (610) 832-9555
www.astm.org

American Solar Energy Society
2400 Central Avenue, Suite A
Boulder, CO 80301-2843
Phone: (303) 443-3130/Fax: (303) 443-3212
www.ases.org
ases@ases.org

Glass Association of North America (GANA)
2945 S.W. Wanamaker Dr., Suite A
Topeka, KS 66614-5321
Phone: (785) 271-0208/Fax: (785) 271-0166
www.glasswebsite.com

International Code Council (ICC)
5203 Leesburg Pike, Suite 600
Falls Church, VA 22041-3401
Phone: (703) 422-7233/Fax: (703) 379-1546
www.iccsafe.org

National Association of Home Builders (NAHB)
1201 15th Street NW
Washington, DC 20005
Phone: (202) 266-8200/Fax: (202) 266-8400
www.nahb.org

National Fenestration Rating Council
(NFRC)
8484 Georgia Avenue, Suite 320
Silver Spring, MD 20910
Phone: (301) 589-1776/Fax: (301) 589-3884
www.nfrc.org
info@nfrc.org

The Responsible Energy Codes Alliance
(RECA)
www.reca-codes.org

Sustainable Buildings Industry Council
(SBIC)
1112 16th Street NW, Suite 240
Washington, DC 20036
Phone: (202) 628-7400/Fax: (202) 393-5043
www.sbicouncil.org
sbic@sbicouncil.org

Window and Door Manufacturers Association (WDMA)
1400 East Touhy Avenue, Suite 470
Des Plaines, IL 60018
Phone: (847) 299-5200/Fax: (847) 299-1286
www.wdma.com
admin@wdma.com

Canadian and International Organizations

Canadian Home Builders' Association
200 Elgin Street, Suite 502
Ottawa, Ontario K2P 1L5
Phone: (613) 230-3060
www.chba.ca
chba@chba.ca

Canadian Standards Association
5060 Spectrum Way
Mississauga, Ontario L4W 5N6
Phone: (416) 747-4000/Fax: (416) 747-2473
www.csa.ca

Canadian Window and Door Manufacturers
Association (CWDMA)
6835 Century Avenue, 2nd Floor
Mississauga, Ontario L5N 2L2
Phone: (905) 286-0660/Fax: (905) 826-4873
www.cwdma.ca

Insulating Glass Manufacturers Alliance
(IGMA)
1500 Bank Street, Suite 300
Ottawa, Ontario K1H 1B8
Phone: (613) 233-1510/Fax: (613) 482-9436
www.igmaonline.org
info@igmaonline.org

International Energy Agency (IEA)
9, rue de la Fédération
75739 Paris Cedex 15, France
Phone: +33 1 40 57 65 00/01
Fax: +33 1 40 57 65 59
www.iea.org
info@iea.org

International Standards Organization (ISO)
1, rue de Varembé, Case postale 56
CH-1211 Geneva 20, Switzerland
Phone: +41 22 749 01 11
Fax: +41 22 733 34 30
www.iso.org

National Research Council of Canada
Institute for Research in Construction (IRC)
1200 Montreal Road
Ottawa, Ontario K1A 0R6
Phone: (613) 993-2607/Fax: (613) 952-7673
irc.nrc-cnrc.gc.ca/index_e.html

Standards Council of Canada
270 Albert Street, Suite 200
Ottawa, Ontario K1P 6N7
Phone: (613) 238-3222/Fax: (613) 995-4564
www.scc.ca
info@scc.ca

Government, Research, and Educational Organizations

Alliance to Save Energy
Efficient Windows Collaborative (EWC)
1850 M Street, NW, Suite 600
Washington, DC 20036
Phone: 202-857-0666/Fax: 202-331-9588
www.ase.org
www.efficientwindows.org

Building Codes Assistance Project (BCAP)
Alliance to Save Energy
1850 M Street, NW, Suite 600
Washington, DC 20036
www.bcap-energy.org
bcap@ase.org

Center for Sustainable Building Research (CSBR)
College of Design, University of Minnesota
1425 University Avenue SE, Suite 115
Minneapolis, MN 55414
Fax: 612-626-7424
www.csbr.umn.edu
csbr@umn.edu

ENERGY STAR Program
www.energystar.gov

Florida Solar Energy Center (FSEC)
1679 Clearlake Road
Cocoa, FL 32922-5703
Phone: (321) 638-1000/Fax: (321) 638-1010
www.fsec.ucf.edu
info@fsec.ucf.edu

Lawrence Berkeley National Laboratory (LBNL)
Building Technologies Department
Environmental Energy Technologies Division
MS 90-3111
Berkeley, CA 94720
Phone: (510) 486-4344/Fax: (510) 486-4089
eetd.lbl.gov/BT.html

National Renewable Energy Laboratory
Center for Buildings and Thermal Energy Systems
1617 Cole Blvd.
Golden, CO 80401
(303) 384-7520
Fax: (303) 384-7540
www.nrel.gov/buildings_thermal

National Technical Information Service (NTIS)
Springfield, Virginia 22161
Phone: (703) 605-6000
www.ntis.gov
info@ntis.gov

Oak Ridge National Laboratory (ORNL)
Building Envelope Systems and Materials
P.O. Box 2008, Mail Stop 6070
Oak Ridge, TN 37831-6070
Fax: (865) 574-9354
www.ornl.gov/sci/roofs+walls

U.S. Department of Energy's Building America Program
www.eere.energy.gov/buildings/building_america

U.S. Department of Energy's Energy Efficiency and Renewable Energy
www.eere.energy.gov

U.S. Department of Energy
www.energy.gov

U.S. Department of Housing and Urban Development (HUD)
451 7th Street SW
Washington, DC 20410
Phone: (202) 708-1112
www.hud.gov

U.S. Government's Federal Information Network
www.fedworld.gov
helpdesk@fedworld.gov

Window Installation Guidelines

AAMA 2400-02 - Standard Practice for Installation of Windows with a Mounting Flange in Stud Frame Construction
American Architectural Manufacturers Association (AAMA)
1827 Walden Office Square, Suite 550
Schaumberg, IL 60173-4268
Phone: (847) 303-5664/Fax: (847) 303-5774
www.aamanet.org

AAMA 2410-03 - Standard Practice for Installation of Windows with an Exterior Flush Fin Over an Existing Window Frame
American Architectural Manufacturers Association (AAMA)
1827 Walden Office Square, Suite 550
Schaumberg, IL 60173-4268
Phone: (847) 303-5664/Fax: (847) 303-5774
www.aamanet.org

InstallationMasters™ Training and Certification Program
Developed by American Architectural Manufacturers Association (AAMA) and administered by Architectural Testing, Inc.
www.installationmastersusa.com

Residential Window and Door Installation Guide,
Version 1.2
Association of Window and Door Installers
515 N. Flagler Drive
West Palm Beach, FL 33401
(407) 655-0696

Water Management Guide by Joseph W. Lstiburek
Energy & Environmental Building Association (EEBA)
10740 Lyndale Avenue South, Suite 10W,
Bloomington, MN 55420-5615
Phone: (952) 881.1098/Fax: (952) 881.3048
www.eeba.org

Window and Door Installation Certification Program Procedural Guide
National Certified Testing Laboratories
National Accreditation & Management Institute, Inc.
5 Leigh Drive
York, PA 17402
Phone: (717)846-1200/Fax: (717)767-4100
www.nctlinc.com

CSA A440.4 - Window and Door Installation
Canadian Standards Association
5060 Spectrum Way, Suite 100
Mississauga, Ontario L4W 5N6
http://www.csa-intl.org/onlinestore/

CEGS Section 08520 - Aluminum Window Installation Guide Specification
Department of the Army
Engineer Division, Huntsville
CEHND-ED-ES (GS Section)
PO Box 1600
Huntsville, AL 35807-4301

E2112-01 Standard Practice for Installation of Exterior Windows, Doors and Skylights
American Society for Testing and Materials (ASTM)
100 Barr Harbor Drive
West Conshohocken, PA 19428-2959
Phone: (610) 832-9585 /Fax: (610) 832-9555
www.astm.org

Window Durability

Insulating Glass Durability Knowledgebase
Aspen Research Corporation
1700 Buerkle Road
White Bear Lake, MN 55110
Phone: (651) 264-6000 /Fax: (651) 264-6270
www.igdurability.org

Insulating Glass Manufacturers Alliance (IGMA)
1500 Bank Street, Suite 300
Ottawa, Ontario K1H 1B8
Phone: (613) 233-1510/Fax: (613) 482-9436
www.igmaonline.org/technical/codes/

APPENDIX E

Codes and Standards

Air Conditioning Contractors of America (ACCA)

Manual J, "Residential Load Calculation Procedure."

American Architectural Manufacturers Association (AAMA)

AAMA 303-97, "Voluntary Specification for PVC Exterior Profile Extrusions."

AAMA 304-98, "Voluntary Specification for Acrylonitrile-Butadiene-Styrene (ABS) Exterior Profiles Capped with ASA or ASA/PVC Blends."

AAMA 305-2000, "Voluntary Specification for Fiberglass Reinforced Thermoset Profiles."

AAMA 310-99, "Voluntary Specifications for Reinforced Thermoplastic Fenestration Exterior Profile Extrusions."

AAMA 902-90, "Voluntary Specifications for Sash Balances."

AAMA 910-93, "Voluntary Life Cycle Specifications and Test Methods for Architectural Grade Windows and Sliding Glass Doors."

AAMA 1503-98, "Voluntary Test Method for Thermal Transmittance and Condensation Resistance of Windows, Doors and Glazed Wall Sections."

AAMA 2400-02, "Standard Practice for Installation of Windows with a Mounting Flange in Stud Frame Construction"

AAMA 2410-03, "Standard Practice for Installation of Windows with an Exterior Flush Fin Over an Existing Window Frame"

AAMA TIR-A10-1992, "Wind Loads on Components and Cladding for Buildings Less Than 90 Feet Tall."

AAMA CW-RS-1-96, "The Rain Screen Principle and Pressure Equalized Wall Design."

AAMA CW #11-1985, "Design Wind Loads for Buildings and Boundary Layer Wind Tunnel Testing."

AAMA/WDMA/CSA 101/I.S.2/A440-05, "Specifications for Windows, Doors & Unit Skylights."

AAMA/WDMA 1600/I.S. 7-2000, "Voluntary Specifications for Skylights."

ANSI/AAMA/NWWDA 101/I.S. 2-97, "Voluntary Specifications for Aluminum, Vinyl (PVC), and Wood Windows and Glass Doors."

ANSI/AAMA 1002.10-93, "Voluntary Specifications for Insulating Storm Products for Windows and Sliding Glass Doors."

American Society of Heating, Refrigerating and Air Conditioning Engineers, Inc. (ASHRAE)

ASHRAE 55-2004, "Thermal Environmental Conditions for Human Occupancy."

ANSI/ASHRAE Standard 74-1988, "Method of Measuring Solar-Optical Properties of Materials."

ASHRAE-2004, ASHRAE Handbook of Fundamentals-2004.

ASHRAE-2004, ASHRAE HVAC Systems and Equipment Handbook-2004.

American Society for Testing and Materials (ASTM)

ASTM C 1199-97, "Standard Test Method for Measuring the Steady State Thermal Transmittance of Fenestration Systems Using Hot Box Methods."

ASTM C1363-97, "Standard Test Method for the Thermal Performance of Building Assemblies by Means of a Hot Box Apparatus."

ASTM D 4726-96, "Standard Specification for Rigid PVC Exterior Profile Extrusions Used for Assembled Windows and Doors."

ASTM E-283-04, "Test Method for Determining the Rate of Air Leakage Through Exterior Windows, Curtain Walls and Doors Under Specified Pressure Differences Across the Specimen."

ASTM E 330, "Standard Test Method for Structural Performance of Exterior Windows, Curtain Walls and Doors by Uniform Static Air Pressure Difference."

ASTM E 331-96, "Standard Test Method for Water Penetration of Exterior Windows, Curtain Walls and Doors by Uniform Static Air Pressure Difference."

ASTM E 413-94, "Classification for Rating Sound Insulation."

ASTM E 547-96, "Standard Test Method for Water Penetration of Exterior Windows, Curtain Walls and Doors by Cyclic Static Air Pressure Differential."

ASTM E 631-93a(1998), "Standard Terminology of Building Constructions."

ASTM E 1332-90, "Classification for Determination of Outdoor-Indoor Transmission Class."

ASTM E 1423-91, "Standard Practice for Determining the Steady State Thermal Transmittance of Fenestration Systems."

ASTM E 1585-93, "Standard Test Method for Measuring and Calculating Emittance of Architectural Flat Glass Products Using Spectrometric Measurements."

ASTM E 2112, "Standard Practice for Installation of Exterior Windows, Doors and Skylights."

ASTM E 2190, "Certification and Testing for Insulating Glass Units."

Canadian Standards Association (CSA)

CAN/CSA-A440.1-M1990-M, "User Selection Guide to CSA Standard CAN/CSA-A440-M90."

CAN/CSA A440-M90/A440.1-M, "Windows: User Selection Guide to CSA Standards."

CAN/CSA A440.2-93, "Energy Performance Evaluation of Windows and Sliding Glass Doors."

AAMA/WDMA/CSA 101/I.S.2/A440-05, "Specifications for Windows, Doors & Unit Skylights."

International Code Council (ICC)

International Energy Conservation Code (IECC), 1998, 2000, 2004 Supplement and 2006 Editions.

International Residential Code, 2000, 2003 and 2006 Editions.

International Building Code, 2000, 2003 and 2006 Editions.

International Standards Organization (ISO)

ISO 7345 (1987), "Thermal Insulation: Physical Quantities and Definitions."

ISO 9050 (1988), "Glass in Building: Determination of Light Transmittance, Direct Solar Transmittance, Total Solar Energy Transmittance, and Related Glazing Factors."

ISO 10293 (1992), "Glass in Building: Determination of Steady-State U-Values (Thermal Transmittance) of Multiple Glazing: Heat Flow Meter Method."

ISO 10292 (1994), "Glass in Building: Calculation of Steady-State U Values (Thermal Transmittance) of Multiple Glazing."

ISO 10291 (1994), "Glass in Building: Determination of Steady State U-Values (Thermal Transmittance) of Multiple Glazing: Guarded Hot Plate Method."

ISO 8990 (1994), "Thermal Insulation: Determination of Steady-State Thermal Transmission Properties: Calibrated and Guarded Hot Box."

ISO 12567 (1995), "Thermal Insulation: Determination of Thermal Resistance of Components: Hot Box Method For Doors and Windows."

ISO 15099 (1999), "Thermal Performance of Windows, Doors and Shading Devices—Detailed Calculations."

National Fenestration Rating Council (NFRC)

NFRC 100-2004, "Procedure for Determining Fenestration Product U-Factors."

NFRC 101-2006, "Procedure for Determining Thermo-Physical Properties of Materials for Use in NFRC-Approved Software Programs."

NFRC 102-2004, "Procedure for Measuring the Steady-State Thermal Transmittance of Fenestration Systems."

NFRC 200-2004, "Procedure for Determining Fenestration Product Solar Heat Gain Coefficients and Visible Transmittance at Normal Incidence."

NFRC 201-2004, "Procedure for Interim Standard Test Method for Measuring the Solar Heat Gain Coeffcient of Fenestration Systems Using Calorimetry Hot Box Methods."

NFRC 300-2004, "Test Method for Determining the Solar Optical Properties of Glazing Materials and Systems."

NFRC 301-2004, "Standard Test Method for Emittance of Specular Surfaces Using Spectrometric Measurements."

NFRC 302-2004, "Verification Program for Optical Spectral Data."

NFRC 400-2004, "Procedure for Determining Fenestration Product Air Leakage."

NFRC 500-2004, "Procedure for Determining Fenestration Product Condensation Resistance Values."

Window and Door Manufacturers Association (WDMA)

Specifiers Guide to Wood Windows and Doors (a compendium of WDMA standards).

ANSI/AAMA/NWWDA 101/I.S. 2-97, "Voluntary Specifications for Aluminum, Vinyl (PVC), and Wood Windows and Glass Doors."

AAMA/WDMA/CSA 101/I.S.2/A440-05, "Specifications for Windows, Doors & Unit Skylights."

AAMA/WDMA 1600/I.S. 7-2000, "Voluntary Specifications for Skylights."

Industry Standards for Wood Window Units (I.S.–2), Wood Sliding Patio Doors (I.S.–3), and Wood Swinging Patio Doors (I.S.–8).

WDMA I.S. 4-99, Water-Repellent Preservative Non-Pressure Treatment for Millwork.

U.S. Department of Housing and Urban Development

HUD Minimum Property Standards (MPS): 24 CFR Part 200, Subpart S.

Federal Manufactured Housing Construction and Safety Standards (FMHCSS): 24 CFR Part 3280 (FYI: Thermal Protection standards are found in Subpart F).

Glossary

AAMA. American Architectural Manufacturers Association. A national trade association that establishes voluntary standards for the window, door, storefront, curtain wall, and skylight industries.

Absorptance. The ratio of radiant energy absorbed to total incident radiant energy in a glazing system.

Acrylic. A thermoplastic with good weather resistance, shatter resistance, and optical clarity, used for glazing.

Absorptance. The ratio of the absorbed radiant energy to the total incident radiant energy.

Aerogel. A microporous, transparent silicate foam used as a glazing cavity fill material, offering possible U-values below 0.10 BTU/(h-sq ft-°F) or 0.56 W/(sq m-°C).

Air-leakage (air infiltration). The amount of air leaking in and out of a building through cracks in walls, windows, and doors.

Air-leakage rating (AL). A measure of the rate of air-leakage around a window, door, or skylight in the presence of a specific pressure difference. It is expressed in units of cubic feet per minute per square foot of frame area (cfm/sq ft). Formerly expressed as cubic feet per minute per foot of window perimeter length (cfm/ft) but not now in use. The lower a window's air-leakage rating, the better its airtightness.

Ambient temperature. Temperature at a given set of environmental conditions.

Angle of incidence. The angle between the solar beam and the normal (perpendicular) to the plane on which it is incident.

Annealed glass. Standard sheet of float glass which has not been heat-treated.

Annealing. Heating above the critical or recrystallization temperature, then controlled cooling of metal, glass, or other materials to eliminate the effects of cold-working, relieve internal stresses, or improve strength, ductility, or other properties.

ANSI. American National Standards Institute. Clearing house for all types of standards and specifications.

Argon. An inert, nontoxic gas used in insulating glass units to reduce heat transfer.

ASHRAE. American Society of Heating, Refrigerating and Air Conditioning Engineers.

ASTM. American Society for Testing and Materials. Organization that develops methods for testing of materials.

Awning window. A window, with one or more sash that rotate about its top hinge and projects outward.

Balance. A mechanical device (normally spring-loaded) used in single- and double-hung windows as a means of counterbalancing the weight of the sash during opening and closing.

Bay window. An arrangement of three or more individual window units, attached so as to project from the building at various angles. In a three-unit bay, the center section is normally fixed, with the end panels operable as single-hung or casement windows.

Bead. A wood strip against which a swinging sash closes, as in a casement window. Also, a finishing trim at the sides and top of the frame to hold the sash, as in a fixed sash or a double-hung window. Also referred to as bead stop.

Blackbody. The ideal, perfect emitter and absorber of thermal radiation. It emits radiant energy at each wavelength at the maximum rate possible as a consequence of its temperature, and absorbs all incident radiance.

BOCA. Building Officials and Code Administrators.

Bottom rail. The bottom horizontal member of a window sash.

Bow window. A rounded bay window that projects from the wall in an arc shape, commonly consisting of five sashes.

Brick molding. A standard milled wood trim piece that covers the gap between the window frame and masonry.

Btu (B.T.U.). An abbreviation for British Thermal Unit—the heat required to increase the temperature of one pound of water one degree Fahrenheit.

Caming. Material that divides and holds pieces of glazing together to form a single decorative glazing panel.

Casement window. A window containing one or more sash hinged to open from the side, that project outward or inward from the plane of the window in a vertical plane: in-swinging are French in origin; out-swinging are from England.

Casing. Exposed molding or framing around a window or door, on either the inside or outside, to cover the space between the window frame or jamb and the wall.

Caulking. A mastic compound for filling joints and sealing cracks to prevent leakage of water and air, commonly made of silicone, bituminous, acrylic, or rubber-based material.

Center-of-glazing. Referring to thermal or optical properties of a glazing system in that area of the system which is not influenced by the frame, glazing bars, mullions, or other opaque or conducting members of the fenestration product.

Certified product. A fenestration product for which product certification authorization has been granted by a licensed independent agencyy, and which is properly labeled in accordance with the requirements of the certification program.

Certified products directory. A directory of authorized fenestration products in electronic form, listing fenestration products and their performance ratings, for which, product certification authorization has been granted and can be searched by the public.

CFM. Cubic Feet per Minute.

Check rail. The bottom horizontal member of the upper sash and the top horizontal member of the lower sash which meet at the middle of a double-hung window.

Chromogenic glazing. A broad class of changeable glazings, which have means to reversibly vary their optical properties, including active materials (e.g. electrochromic and suspended Particle Device/SPD) and passive materials (e.g., photochromic and thermochromic).

Cladding. An applied rigid or semi-rigid roll-formed or extruded covering that is placed over or attached to and follows the contour of the interior or exterior framing member for the primary purpose of protection from environmental elements and/or aesthetics and adds no structural integrity to the framing member.

Clerestory. A window in the upper part of a lofty room that admits light to the center of the room.

Composite frame. A frame consisting of two or more materials—for example, an interior wood element with an exterior fiberglass element.

Combination assembly. A window, door or skylight assembly formed by a combination of two or more separate units whose frames are mulled together.

Condensation. The deposit of water vapor from the air on any cold surface whose temperature is below the dew point, such as a cold window glass or frame that is exposed to humid indoor air.

Condensation resistance (CR). A relative indicator of a fenestration product's ability to resist the formation of condensation at a specific set of environmental conditions. The higher the CR value the greater the resistance to the formation of condensation.

Condensation Resistance Factor (CRF). An indication of a window's ability to resist condensation. The higher the CRF, the less likely condensation is to occur. Based on AAMA standard.

Conduction. Heat transfer through a solid material by contact of one molecule to the next. Heat flows from a higher-temperature area to a lower-temperature one.

Convection. A heat transfer process involving motion in a fluid (such as air) caused by the difference in density of the fluid and the action of gravity (natural convection). Convection affects heat transfer from the surface to air, whether it is for enclosed spaces (like insulating glazing unit cavity) or open spaces (like indoor glass surface to room air).

Degree day. A unit that represents a one-degree Fahrenheit deviation from some fixed reference point (usually 65° F) in the mean, daily outdoor temperature. See also heating degree day.

Desiccant. An extremely porous crystalline substance used to absorb moisture from within the sealed air space of an insulating glass unit.

Dewpoint. The temperature at which water vapor in air will condense at a given state of humidity and pressure.

Divided light. A window with a number of smaller panes of glass separated and held in place by muntins.

DOE-2.1E. A building-simulation computer program used to calculate total annual energy use.

Double glazing. In general, two thicknesses of glass separated by an air space within an opening to improve insulation against heat transfer and/or sound transmission. In factory-made double glazing units, the air between the glass sheets is thoroughly dried and the space is sealed airtight, eliminating possible condensation and providing superior insulating properties.

Double-hung window. A window consisting of two sashes operating in a rectangular frame, in which both the upper and lower halves can be slid up and down. A counterbalance mechanism usually holds the sash in place.

Double-strength glass. Sheet glass between 0.115" and 0.133" (3–3.38 mm) thick.

Drip. A projecting fin or a groove at the outer edge of a sill, soffit, or other projecting member in a wall designed to interrupt the flow of water downward over the wall or inward across the soffit.

Dual action window. A window that operates into two different ways. Typically, the window consists of a sash that tilts from the top and swings inward from the side.

Dynamic glazing. Any glazing system that has the fully reversible ability to change its performance properties, including U-factor, SHGC, or VT. This includes, but is not limited to, shading systems between the glazing layers and chromogenic glazing.

Edge effects. Two-dimensional heat transfer at the edge of a glazing unit due to the thermal properties of spacers and sealants.

Electrochromics. Glazing with optical properties that can be varied continuously from clear to dark with a low-voltage signal. Ions are reversibly injected or removed from an electrochromic material, causing the optical density to change.

Electromagnetic spectrum. Radiant energy over a broad range of wavelengths.

Emergency exit window. Fire escape window (egress window) large enough for a person to climb out. In U.S. building codes, each bedroom must be provided with an exit window. The exact width, area, and height from the floor are specified in the building codes.

Emissivity. The relative ability of a surface to reflect or emit heat by radiation. Emissivity ranges from 0.00 to 1.00.

Emittance. The ratio of the radiant flux emitted by a specimen to that emitted by a blackbody at the same temperature and under the same conditions.

Evacuated glazing. Insulating glazing composed of two glass layers, hermetically sealed at the edges, with a vacuum between to eliminate convection and conduction. A spacer system is needed to keep the panes from touching.

Exterior stop. The removable glazing bead that holds the glass or panel in place when it is on the exterior side of the light or panel, in contrast to an interior stop located on the interior side of the glass.

Extrusion. The process of producing vinyl or aluminum shapes by forcing heated material through an orifice in a die. Also, any item made by this process.

Eyebrow windows. Low, inward-opening windows with a bottom-hinged sash. These attic windows built into the top molding of the house are sometimes called "lie-on-your-stomach" or "slave" windows. Often found on Greek Revival and Italianate houses.

Fanlight. A half-circle window over a door or window, with radiating bars. Also called circle top transom.

Fenestration. Products that fill openings in a building envelope, such as windows, doors, skylights, curtain walls, etc., designed to permit the passage of air, light, vehicles, or people. Also, a window, door, or skylight and its associated interior or exterior elements, such as shades or blinds.

Fenestration attachment. A device (such as shades, films, or blinds) designed to be physically attached to, incorporated with or covering a fenestration product.

Fiberglass. A composite material made by embedding glass fibers in a polymer matrix. May be used as a diffusing material in sheet form, or as a standard sash and frame element.

Film. Fenestration attachment products which consist of a flexible adhesive-backed polymer film which may be applied to the interior or exterior surface of an existing glazing system.

Fixed light. A pane of glass installed directly into non-operating framing members; also, the opening or space for a pane of glass in a non-operating frame.

Fixed panel. An inoperable panel of a sliding glass door or slider window.

Fixed window. A window designed to be non-operable.

Flashing. Sheet metal or other material applied to seal and protect the joints formed by different materials or surfaces.

Float glass. Glass formed by a process of floating the material on a bed of molten metal. It produces a high-optical-quality glass with parallel surfaces, without polishing and grinding.

Fogging. A deposit of contamination left on the inside surface of a sealed insulating glass unit due to extremes of temperatures or failed seals.

Frame. The enclosing structure of a window, door or skylight which fits into the wall or roof opening and receives either, glass, sash or vents.

Fritted glass. Glass on which a pattern has been created by application of a ceramic material to the glass surface, which is subsequently fused at high temperature.

Gas fill. A gas other than air, usually argon or krypton, placed between window or skylight glazing panes to reduce the U-factor by suppressing conduction and convection.

Gasket. Pre-formed shapes, such as strips, grommets, etc., of elastomeric composition, providing continuous sealing of the glass, or frame members.

Glass. An inorganic, amorphous substance, usually transparent, composed of silica (sand), soda (sodium carbonate) and lime (calcium carbonate) with small quantities of other materials.

Glazing. The glass or plastic panes in a window, door, or skylight.

Glazing bead. A molding or stop around the inside of a window frame to hold the glass in place.

Glazing system/Glazing in-fill. A generic term used to describe an infill material, such as glass, plastic or other transparent or translucent material, or assembly of glazing material, spacer and desiccant, used to enclose openings in a building created by a specific framing system.

Greenhouse window. A three-dimensional window that projects from the exterior wall and usually has glazing on all sides except the bottom, which serves as a shelf.

Head track. The track provided at the head of a sliding glass door. Also, the head member incorporating the track.

Header. The upper horizontal member of a window frame. Also called head.

Heat-absorbing glass. Window glass containing chemicals (with gray, bronze, or blue-green tint) which absorb light and heat radiation, and reduce glare and brightness. See also Tinted glass.

Heat flux. The density of heat flow through a surface of unit area perpendicular to the direction of heat flow.

Heat gain. The transfer of heat from outside to inside by means of conduction, convection, and radiation through all surfaces of a house.

Heating degree day. Term used to relate the typical climate conditions of different areas to the amount of energy needed to heat and cool a building. The base temperature is 65 degrees Fahrenheit. A heating degree day is counted for each degree below 65 degrees reached by the average daily outside temperatures in the winter. For example, if on a given winter day, the daily average temperature outdoors is 30 degrees, then there are 35 degrees below the base temperature of 65 degrees. Thus, there are 35 heating degree days for that day.

Heat loss. The transfer of heat from inside to outside by means of conduction, convection, and radiation through all surfaces of a house.

Heat-strengthened glass. Glass that is reheated, after forming, to just below melting point, and then cooled, forming a compressed surface that increases its strength beyond that of typical annealed glass.

Hinged windows. Windows (casement, awning, and hopper) with an operating sash that has hinges on one side. See also Projected window.

Holographic glazing. Glazing with a thin-film microstructure coating which diffracts incident light.

Hopper window. Window with sash hinged at the bottom.

Horizontal slider window. A window that contains one or more manually operated sash that slide horizontally within a common frame.

ICC. International Code Council. A national organization that publishes model codes for adoption by states and other agencies. Codes include the International Building Code (IBC) and the International Energy Conservation Code (IECC).

IECC. International Energy Conservation Code published by the ICC. The successor to the Model Energy Code, which is cited in the 1992 U.S. Energy Policy Act (EPAct) as the baseline for residential Energy Codes in the United States.

Infiltration. See air leakage.

Infrared radiation. Invisible, electromagnetic radiation beyond red light on the spectrum, with wavelengths greater than 0.7 microns.

Insulated shutters. Insulating panels that cover a window opening to reduce heat loss.

Insulating glass (IG). Two or more glazing panes separated to reduce heat flow.

Insulating glass unit, sealed insulated glass unit, (IGU). A combination of two or more glazing panes separated by a spacer with a sealed gap.

Insulating value. See U-factor.

Insulation. Construction materials used for protection from noise, heat, cold or fire.

Interlocker. An upright frame member of a panel in a sliding glass door which engages with a corresponding member in an adjacent panel when the door is closed. Also called interlocking stile.

Interlayer. A layer of material acting as an adhesive between layers of glass.

Jalousie. Window made up of horizontally-mounted louvered glass slats that abut each other tightly when closed and rotate outward when cranked open.

Jamb. A vertical member at the side of a window frame, or the horizontal member at the top of the window frame, as in head jamb.

Krypton. An inert, nontoxic gas used in insulating windows to reduce heat transfer.

KWH. KiloWatt Hour. Unit of energy or work equal to one thousand watt-hours.

Label. Permanent and/or temporary marker or device applied to a fenestration product, listing rating information and indicating compliance with certification requirements.

Laminated glass. Two or more sheets of glass with an inner layer of transparent plastic to which the glass adheres if broken. Used for safety glazing and sound reduction.

Lift. Handle for raising the lower sash in a double-hung window. Also called sash lift.

Light. A window; a pane of glass within a window. Double-hung windows are designated by the number of lights in upper and lower sash, as in six-over-six. Also spelled informally lite.

Light-to-solar-gain ratio. A measure of the ability of a glazing to provide light without excessive solar heat gain. It is the ratio between the visible transmittance of a glazing and its solar heat gain coefficient. Abbreviated LSG.

Lintel. A horizontal member above a window or door opening that supports the structure above.

Liquid crystal glazing. Glass in which the optical properties of a thin layer of liquid crystals are controlled by an electrical current, changing from a clear to a diffusing state.

Lite. Another term for glazing used in a fenestration product. Frequently spelled "lite" in industry literature to avoid confusion with "light," as in "visible light".

Long-wave infrared radiation. Invisible radiation, beyond red light on the electromagnetic spectrum (above 3.5 micro meters), emitted by warm surfaces such as a body at room temperature radiating to a cold window surface.

Low-conductance spacers. An assembly of materials designed to reduce heat transfer at the edge of an insulating window. Spacers are placed between the panes of glass in a double- or triple-glazed window.

Low-emittance (low-E) coating. Microscopically thin, virtually invisible, metal or metallic oxide layers deposited on a window or skylight glazing surface primarily to reduce the U-factor by suppressing radiative heat flow. A typical type of low-E coating is transparent to the solar spectrum (visible light and short-wave infrared radiation) and reflective of long-wave infrared radiation.

Meeting rail. The part of a sliding glass door, a sliding window, or a hung window where two panels meet and create a weather barrier.

Metal-clad windows. Exterior wood parts covered with extruded aluminum or other metal, with a factory-applied finish to deter the elements.

Micron. One millionth (10^{-6}) of a metric meter.

Mil. One thousandth of an inch, or 0.0254 millimeter.

Model Energy Code (MEC). The Model Energy Code is cited in the 1992 U.S. Energy Policy Act (EPAct) as the baseline for residential Energy Codes in the United States. It has been succeeded by the International Energy Conservation Code (IECC) published by the International Code Council (ICC).

Mullion. A major structural vertical or horizontal member connecting window units or sliding glass doors.

Muntin. A secondary framing member (horizontal, vertical, or diagonal) to hold the window panes in the sash. This term is often confused with mullion.

Muntin grilles. Wood, plastic, or metal grids designed for a single-light sash to give the appearance of muntins in a multilight sash, but removable for ease in cleaning the window.

Nailing fin. An integral extension of a window or patio door frame which generally laps over the conventional stud construction and through which nails are driven to secure the frame in place.

NFRC. National Fenestration Rating Council.

Obscure glass. Glass having an image, pattern, or texture that distorts the vision through the glass.

Opaque. Not allowing visible light to pass through.

Operable window. Window that can be opened for ventilation.

Operator. Crank-operated device for opening and closing casement or jalousie windows.

Operator type. A designation used to distinguish among fenestration products based on mode of operation, and the intended use of the installed product as defined by the manufacturer.

Pane. One of the compartments of a door or window consisting of a single sheet of glass in a frame; also, a sheet of glass.

Panel. A major component of a sliding glass door, consisting of a light of glass in a frame installed within the main (or outer) frame of the door. A panel may be sliding or fixed.

Panning. In replacement window work, the outside aluminum trim that can extend around the perimeter of the window opening; used to cover up the old window material. Panning can be installed in the opening before the window, or can be attached directly to the window before installation.

Particle dispersed glazing. Glazing in which the orientation of small particles between two sheets of glass is controlled electrically, thus changing its optical properties.

Parting stop. A narrow strip, either integral or applied, that holds a sash or panel in position in a frame.

Patterned glass. Glass in which a design has been incorporated onto one or both surfaces of the glass.

Peak load. The maximum thermal load to be provided by a heating or cooling system in a house.

Permeance. A measure of the transmission of a fluid through a material.

Photochromics. Glazing with the optical properties that change in response to the amount of incident light.

Picture window. A large, fixed window framed so that it is usually, but not always, longer horizontally than vertically to provide a panoramic view.

Pivot window. A window consisting of a sash which pivots about an axis within the frame.

Plastic film. A thin plastic substrate, sometimes used as the inner layers in a triple- or quadruple-glazed window.

Plastics. Artificial substances made of organic polymers that can be extruded or molded into various shapes including window frames and sashes.

Plate glass. A rolled, ground, and polished product with true flat parallel plane surfaces affording excellent vision. It has been replaced by float glass.

Polyvinylchloride (PVC). An extruded or molded plastic material used for window framing and as a thermal barrier for aluminum windows.

Prismatic glazing. A daylighting device; a light-redirecting glazing with a fine-structure saw tooth cross-section, designed to refract incident sunlight and skylight towards the ceiling.

Profile. Referring to the cross-sectional geometry or property of a frame, sash, or its component.

Projected window. A window fitted with one or more sashes opening on pivoted arms or hinges. Refers to casements, awnings, and hoppers.

R-value. A measure of the resistance of a glazing material or fenestration assembly to heat flow. It is the inverse of the U-factor (R = 1/U) and is expressed in units of hr-sq ft-°F/Btu. A high-R-value window has a greater resistance to heat flow and a higher insulating value than one with a low R-value.

Radiation. The transfer of heat in the form of electromagnetic waves from one separate surface to another. Energy from the sun reaches the earth by radiation, and a person's body can lose heat to a cold window or skylight surface in a similar way.

Rail. A horizontal member of a fenestration product sash or panel.

Reflectance. The ratio of reflected radiant energy to incident radiant energy.

Reflective glass. Window glass coated to reflect radiation striking the surface of the glass.

Refraction. The deflection of a light ray from a straight path when it passes at an oblique angle from one medium (such as air) to another (such as glass).

Relative humidity. The ratio of the amount of water vapor in the air compared to the maximum amount of water vapor that the air could hold at a particular temperature and pressure. At 100 percent relative humidity, moisture condenses and falls as rain.

Resistance, thermal. A property of a substance or construction which retards the flow of heat.

Retrofitting. Adding or replacing items on existing buildings. Typical retrofit products are replacement doors and windows, insulation, storm windows, caulking, weatherstripping, vents, landscaping.

RESFEN. A computer program used to calculate energy use based on window selection in residential buildings.

Roof Window. See Skylight.

Rough opening. The framed opening in a wall or roof where a fenestration product is to be installed.

Safety glass. A strengthened or reinforced glass that is less subject to breakage or splintering.

Sash. The portion of a fenestration assembly that is installed in a frame and includes the glazing, stiles and rails. A sash may be operable or fixed.

Screen. Woven mesh of metal, plastic, or fiberglass stretched over a window opening to permit air to pass through, but not insects.

Sealant. A flexible material placed between two or more parts of a structure, with adhesion to the joining surfaces, to prevent the passage of certain elements such as air, moisture, water, dust and other matter.

Shade screen. A specially fabricated screen of sheet material with small narrow louvers formed in place to intercept solar radiation striking a window; the louvers are so small that only extremely small insects can pass through. Also called sun screen. Also, an awning with fixed louvers of metal or wood.

Shading coefficient (SC). A measure of the ability of a window or skylight to transmit solar heat, relative to that ability for 1/8-inch clear, double- strength, single glass. It is being phased out in favor of the solar heat gain coefficient, and is approximately equal to the SHGC multiplied by 1.15. It is expressed as a number without units between 0 and 1. The lower a window's solar heat gain coefficient or shading coefficient, the less solar heat it transmits, and the greater is its shading ability.

Sheet glass. A transparent, flat glass found in older windows, now largely replaced by float glass.

Short-wave infrared radiation. Invisible radiation, just beyond red light on the electromagnetic spectrum (between 0.7 and 2.5 microns), emitted by hot surfaces and included in solar radiation.

Sidelite. A fenestration product that is used as a companion product installed on one or both sides of a door. Sidelites may consist of a glazed frame or a non-operable sash within a frame.

Sill. The bottom horizontal member in a fenestration product frame.

Sill track. The track provided at the sill of a sliding glass door. Also, the sill member incorporating such a track.

Simulated divided lights. A window that has the appearance of a number of smaller panes of glass separated by muntins, but actually is a larger glazing unit with the muntins placed between or on the surfaces of the glass layers.

Single glazing. Single thickness of glass in a window or door.

Single-hung window. A window consisting of two sashes of glass, the top one stationary and the bottom movable.

Single-strength glass. Glass with thickness between 0.085" and 0.100" (2.16–2.57 mm).

Skylight (operable or pivot). A roof window designed for sloped or horizontal application, the primary purpose of which is to provide daylighting and/or ventilation.

Sliding glass door. A door that contains one or more manually operated panels that slide horizontally within a common frame. Moving action is usually of rolling type (rather than sliding type). Also called gliding door, rolling glass door, and patio sliding door.

Sliding window. A window fitted with one or more sashes opening by sliding horizontally or vertically in grooves provided by frame members. Vertical sliders may be single- or double-hung.

Sloped glazing. A glazed system that is mounted at a slope greater than 15° from the vertical plane.

Smart window. Generic term for windows with switchable coatings to control solar gain.

Solar control coatings. Thin film coatings on glass or plastic that absorb or reflect solar energy, thereby reducing solar gain.

Solar Heat Gain (SHG). The quantity of incident solar energy passing through a fenestration system. Included are both directly transmitted solar radiation as well as solar energy absorbed by the fenestration system and re-transmitted into the inside space.

Solar Heat Gain Coefficient (SHGC). The ratio of the solar heat gain entering the space through the fenestration product to the incident solar radiation. It is expressed as a number between 0 and 1. The lower a window's solar heat gain coefficient, the less solar heat it transmits, and the greater its shading ability. SHGC can be expressed in terms of the glass alone or can refer to the entire window assembly.

Solar radiation. The total radiant energy from the sun, including ultraviolet and infrared wave lengths as well as visible light.

Solar screen. A sun shading device, such as screens, panels, louvers, or blinds, installed to intercept solar radiation.

Solar spectrum. The intensity variation of sunlight across its spectral range.

Sound Transmission Class (STC). The sound transmission loss rating of a material over a selected range of sound frequencies. The higher the number, the less sound transmitted.

Spectrally selective glazing. A coated or tinted glazing with optical properties that are transparent to some wavelengths of energy and reflective to others. Typical spectrally selective coatings are transparent to visible light and reflect short-wave and long-wave infrared radiation.

Stile. The upright or vertical edges of a door, window, or screen.

Stool. The shelf-like board of the interior part of the window sill, against which the bottom rail of the sash closes.

Stop. The molding on the inside of a window frame against which the window sash closes; in the case of a double-hung window, the sash slides against the stop. Also called bead, side stop, window stop, and parting stop.

Storm windows. A second set of windows installed on the outside or inside of the primary windows to provide additional insulation and wind protection.

Sun control film. A tinted or reflective film applied to the glazing surface to reduce visible, ultra-violet, or total transmission of solar radiation. Reduces solar heat gain in summer and glare. Some can be removed and reapplied with changing seasons.

Sunroom/Solarium. A multi sided structure comprised of a high percentage of glazed area vs. framing area, usually attached to the exterior of a building.

Superwindow. A window with a very low U-factor, typically less than 0.15, achieved through the use of multiple glazings, low-E coatings, and gas fills.

Switchable glazings. Glazings with optical properties that can be reversibly switched from clear to dark or reflective.

Tempered glass. Treated glass that is strengthened by reheating it to just below the melting point and then suddenly cooling it. When shattered, it breaks into small pieces. Approximately five times stronger than standard annealed glass; is required as safety glazing in patio doors, entrance doors, side lights, and other hazardous locations. It cannot be recut after tempering.

Thermal break. A component made of material of relatively low thermal conductivity, which is inserted between two components having high thermal conductivity, in order to reduce heat transfer. Often used in aluminum windows.

Thermal Bridge. A path of high thermal conductance from the exterior to interior surfaces of a system which has lower thermal conductance in all other areas. An example would be metal fasteners penetrating an insulating wall or thermally broken frame.

Thermal conductivity. Heat transfer property of materials expressed in units of energy per time per length per degree temperature difference.

Thermal expansion. Change in dimension of a material as a result of temperature change.

Thermal mass. Mass in a building (furnishings or structure) that is used to absorb solar gain during the day and release the heat as the space cools in the evening.

Thermochromics. Glazing with optical properties that can change in response to temperature changes.

Thermogram. An image of an object taken with an infrared camera that shows surface temperature variations.

Threshold. See Sill.

Tilt window. A single- or double-hung window whose operable sash can be tilted into the room for interior washability.

Tinted glass. Glass colored by incorporation of mineral additives or surface coatings. Any tinting reduces both visual and radiant transmittance.

Translucent. Permitting light to pass through but with differing degrees of obscuration and diffusion. Transmittance. The percentage of radiation that can pass through glazing. Transmittance can be defined for different types of light or energy, e.g., visible light transmittance, UV transmittance, or total solar energy transmittance.

Transom. A non-operable fenestration product that is used as a companion product installed above another fenestration product. Transoms may consist of a glazed frame or a non-operable sash within a frame.

Transom window. The window sash located above a door. Also called transom light.

Transparent. Permitting light to pass through with clear vision.

Triple glazing. Three panes of glass or plastic with two air spaces between.

Tubular Daylighting Device (TDD). A non-operable device primarily designed to transmit daylight from a roof surface to an interior ceiling surface via a tubular conduit.

U-factor (U-value). A measure of the rate of non-solar heat loss or gain through a material or assembly. It is expressed in units of Btu/hr-sq ft-°F (W/sq m-°C). Values are normally given for NFRC/ASHRAE winter conditions of 0° F (18° C) outdoor temperature, 70° F (21° C) indoor temperature, 15 mph wind, and no solar load. The U-factor may be expressed for the glass alone or the entire window, which includes the effect of the frame and the spacer materials. The lower the U-factor, the greater a window's resistance to heat flow and the better its insulating value.

UBC. Uniform Building Code.

Ultraviolet light (UV). The invisible rays of the spectrum that are outside of the visible spectrum at its short-wavelength violet end. Ultraviolet rays are found in everyday sunlight and can cause fading of paint finishes, carpets, and fabrics.

Vapor retarder. A material that reduces the diffusion of water vapor across a building assembly.

Vent. The movable framework or sash in a glazed window that is hinged or pivoted to swing open.

Vertical sliding window. A window that contains at least one manually operated sash that slides vertically within a common frame.

Vinyl. Polyvinyl chloride material, which can be both rigid or flexible, used for window frames.

Vinyl-clad window. A window with exterior wood parts covered with extruded vinyl.

Visible light. The portion of the electromagnetic spectrum that produces light that can be seen. Wavelengths range from 380 to 720 nanometers.

Visible Transmittance (VT). The percentage or fraction of the visible spectrum (380 to 720 nanometers) weighted by the sensitivity of the eye, that is transmitted through the glazing.

Warm-edge technology. The use of low-conductance spacers to reduce heat transfer near the edge of insulated glazing.

WDMA. Window and Door Manufacturing Association. is a trade association representing U.S. and Canadian manufacturers and suppliers of windows and doors for the domestic and export markets.

Weather-strip. A flexible component used to reduce air leakage or water penetration or both between the sash or panels and/or sash or panels and frame.

Weep hole. A small opening in a wall or window sill member through which water may drain to the building exterior.

Window. An assembled unit consisting of a frame/sash component holding one or more pieces of glazing functioning to admit light and/or air to an enclosure.

Window hardware. Various devices and mechanisms for the window including catches, fasteners and locks, hinges, pivots, lifts and pulls, pulleys and sash weights, sash balances, and stays.

References

GENERAL REFERENCES

American Architectural Manufacturers Association. *Skylight Handbook: Design Guidelines*. Palatine, IL: Author, 1988.

———. *Industry Statistical Review and Forecast*. Palatine, IL: Author, 1995.

———. *Glass and Glazing*. Palatine, IL: Author, 1997.

American Institute of Architects. "Daylighting Design." *Architect's Handbook of Energy Practice*. Author, 1982a.

———. "Shading and Sun Controls." *Architect's Handbook of Energy Practice. Author*, 1982b.

American Society of Heating, Refrigeration, and Air Conditioning Engineers. "Fenestration." In *ASHRAE Handbook of Fundamentals*. Author, 1997.

Arasteh, D. "Advances in Window Technology: 1973–1993." In *Advances in Solar Energy, An Annual Review of Research and Development 9*. Boulder, CO: American Solar Energy Society, 1994. Lawrence Berkeley Laboratory Report 36891.

Bass, Michael, Ed. *Handbook of Optics, Vol. I—Fundamentals, Techniques, and Design*, 2nd ed. New York: McGraw-Hill, 1995.

Brown, G.Z. and Mark DeKay. *Sun, Wind & Light*: Architectural Design Strategies, 2nd ed. John Wiley & Sons, Inc., 2001.

Canada Mortgage and Housing Corporation. *Door and Window Installation*. Ottawa, Ontario: Author, 1988a.

———. *Trouble Free Windows, Doors and Skylights*. Ottawa, Ontario: Author, 1988b.

Canadian Electricity Association. *Energy-Efficient Residential and Commercial Windows Reference Guide*. Montreal, PQ: Author, 1995.

Collins, B. *Windows and People: A Literature Survey, Psychological Reaction with and without Windows*. National Bureau of Standards, Building Science Series 70, 1975.

Creative Homeowner Press. *Quick Guide: Windows & Doors*. Upper Saddle River, NJ: Author, 1994.

Fricke, J. "Aerogels." *Scientific American 258-5* (1988): 92–97.

Geller, H., and J. Thorne. *U.S. Department of Energy's Office of Building Technologies: Successful Initiatives of the 1990s*. Washington, DC: American Council for an Energy-Efficient Economy, 1999.

Gilmore, V. E. "Superwindows." *Popular Science 3* (1986): 76.

International Energy Agency Solar Heating and Cooling Programme. *Passive Solar Commercial and Institutional Buildings: A Sourcebook of Examples and Design Insights*. West Sussex, England: John Wiley & Sons, Inc., 1994.

———. *Solar Energy Houses: Strategies, Technologies, Examples*. London: James & James, 1996.

Huizenga, C., H. Zhang, P. Mattelaer, T. Yu, and E. Arens. "Window Performance for Human Thermal Comfort." *Final Report to the National Fenestration Rating Council*. Center for the Built Environment, University of California, Berkeley, 2006.

Iqbal, M. An *Introduction to Solar Radiation*. Toronto, Ontario: Academic Press, 1983.

Kaufman, J., and H. Haynes, Eds. *IES Lighting Handbook: Reference Volume*. Illuminating Engineering Society of North America, 1981.

Konzo, S. *Speaking of Windows*. Urbana, Champaign: University of Illinois Small Homes Council, 1984.

Lam, William. *Perception and Lighting as Formgivers for Architecture*. New York: McGraw-Hill, 1987.

Lstiburek, Joseph W., Ph.D.,P.Eng. *Water Management Guide*. Energy & Environmental Building Association (EEBA), Minneapolis, MN, 2006.

Mazria, E. *The Passive Solar Energy Book*. Emmaus, PA: Rodale Press, 1979.

McCluney, R. *Choosing the Best Window for Hot Climates*. Cape Canaveral, FL: Florida Solar Energy Center, 1993.

———. *Introduction to Radiometry and Photometry*. Boston, MA: Artech House, 1994.

———. *Fenestration Solar Gain Analysis*. Cape Canaveral, FL: Florida Solar Energy Center, 1996.

———. "Let there be Daylight." *Window Rehabilitation Guide for Historic Buildings*. The Window Conference and Exposition for Historic Buildings II, National Park Service, Washington, DC, February 1997.

McCluney, R., M. Huggins, and C. Emrich. *Fenestration Performance: An Annotated Bibliography*. Cape Canaveral, FL: Florida Solar Energy Center, 1990.

McGowan, A. *Energy-Efficient Residential and Commercial Windows Reference Guide*. Montreal, PQ: Canadian Electricity Association, 1995.

Mitchell, R., J. Huang, D. Arasteh, C. Huizenga, S. Glendenning, "RESFEN 5: A PC Program for Calculating the Heating and Cooling Energy Use of Windows in Residential Buildings". May 2005, *Lawrence Berkeley Laboratory Report 40682 Rev.*

National Research Council of Canada. "Window Performance and New Technology." In the proceedings of the Building Science Insight Conference. Ottawa, Ontario: Author, 1988.

Natural Resources Canada. *Consumer's Guide to Buying Energy-Efficient Windows and Doors*. Minister of Supply and Services, 1994.

Ortho Books. *Doors, Windows & Skylights: Selecting and Installing*. San Ramon, CA: Author, 1992.

Passive Solar Industries Council. *Designing Low-Energy Buildings: Passive Solar Strategies and ENERGY-10 Software*. Washington, DC: Author, 1996.

Selkowitz, S., and S. LaSourd. "Amazing Glazing." *Progressive Architecture* (June 1994).

Shurcliff, W. *Thermal Shutters and Shades: Over 100 Schemes for Reducing Heat-Loss Through Windows*. Andover, MA: Brick House Publishing, 1980.

Sunset Books. *Windows & Skylights*. Menlo Park, CA: Author, 1996.

Warner, J. L. "How to Avoid Window Condensation." *Home Energy 8* (5), (Sept/Oct. 1991): 27–29.

TECHNICAL REFERENCES

Arasteh, D. "Analysis of Frame and Edge Heat Transfer in Residential Windows." In the proceedings of Thermal Performance of the Exterior Envelopes of Buildings IV. Orlando, FL: December 1989. *Lawrence Berkeley Laboratory Report 26068.*

Arasteh, D., F. Beck, N. Stone, W. duPont, and M. Koenig. "Phase I Results of the NFRC U-Value Procedure Validation Project." *ASHRAE Transactions 100* (1), 1994. *Lawrence Berkeley Laboratory Report 34270.*

Arasteh, D., E. Finlayson, D. Curcija, J. Baker and C. Huizenga. "Guidelines for Modeling Projecting Fenestration Products." *ASHRAE Transactions 104* (1), 1998. *Lawrence Berkeley Laboratory Report 40707.*

Arasteh, D., E. Finlayson, J. Huang, C. Huizenga, R. Mitchell and M. Rubin. "State-of-the-Art Software for Window Energy-Efficiency Rating and Labeling." Proceedings of the ACEEE 1998 Summer Study on Energy Efficiency in Buildings. *Lawrence Berkeley Laboratory Report 42151.*

Arasteh, D., E. Finlayson, and C. Huizenga. "WINDOW 4.1: A PC Program for Analyzing Window Thermal Performance in Accordance with Standard NFRC Procedures." Lawrence Berkeley Laboratory, Energy & Environment Division. Berkeley, CA, 1993. *Lawrence Berkeley Laboratory Report 35298.*

Arasteh, D., H. Gowdy, J. Huang, C. Kohler, and R. Mitchell. "Performance Criteria for Residential Zero Energy Windows." Presented at the 2007 ASHRAE Winter Meeting, January 27-31, 2007, Dallas Texas and to be published in the proceedings. *Lawrence Berkeley Laboratroy Report 59190.*

Arasteh, D., B. Griffith, and P. LaBerge. "Integrated Window Systems: An Advanced Energy-Efficient Residential Fenestration Product." In the proceedings of the 19th National Passive Solar Conference. San Jose, CA: American Solar Energy Society, 1994. *Lawrence Berkeley Laboratory Report 35417.*

Arasteh, D., J. Hartman, and M. Rubin. "Experimental Verification of a Model of Heat Transfer Through Windows." In the proceedings of the ASHRAE Winter Meeting, Symposium on Fenestration Performance. New York, NY: 1987.

Arasteh, D., J. Huang, and J. Apte. "Future Advanced Windows for Zero-Energy Homes." *ASHRAE Transactions 109* (2), 2003. *Lawrence Berkeley Laboratory Report 51913.*

Arasteh, D., J. Huang, R. Mitchell, R. Clear, and C. Kohler. "A Database of Window Annual Energy Use in Typical North American Residences." Presented at the 2000 ASHRAE Winter Meeting, February 5–9, 2000, Dallas, Texas. *Lawrence Berkeley Laboratory Report 44020.*

Arasteh, D., R. Johnson, S. Selkowitz, and R. Sullivan. "Energy Performance and Savings Potentials with Skylights." *ASHRAE Transactions 91* (1), 1984:154–179. *Lawrence Berkeley Laboratory Report 17457.*

Arasteh, D., R. Mathis, and W. duPont. "The NFRC Window U-Value Rating Procedure." In the proceedings of Thermal Performance of the Exterior Envelopes of Buildings V. Clearwater Beach, Florida: 1992. *Lawrence Berkeley Laboratory Report 32442.*

Arasteh, D., S. Reilly, and M. Rubin. "A Versatile Procedure for Calculating Heat Transfer Through Windows." Paper presented at ASHRAE Meeting. Vancouver, British Columbia: June 1989. *Lawrence Berkeley Laboratory Report 27534.*

Arasteh, D., and S. Selkowitz. "A Superwindow Field Demonstration Program in Northwest Montana." In the proceedings of Thermal Performance of the Exterior Envelopes of Buildings IV. Orlando, FL: December 1989. *Lawrence Berkeley Laboratory Report 26069.*

Arasteh, D., S. Selkowitz, and J. Hartman. "Detailed Thermal Performance Data on Conventional and Highly Insulating Window Systems." In the proceedings of the BTECC Conference. Clearwater Beach, FL: 1985. *Lawrence Berkeley Laboratory Report 20348.*

Arasteh, D., S. Selkowitz, and J. Wolfe. "The Design and Testing of a Highly Insulating Glazing System for Use with Conventional Window Systems." *Journal of Solar Energy Engineering 111*, 1989:44–53. *Lawrence Berkeley Laboratory Report 24903.*

Arschehoug, O., M. Thyholt, I. Andresen, and B. Hugdal. "Frame and Edge Seal Technology: A State of the Art Survey." IEA Solar Heating and Cooling Program, Norwegian Institute of Technology. Trondheim, Norway: 1994.

Beck, F., and D. Arasteh. "Improving the Thermal Performance of Vinyl-Framed Windows." In the proceedings of Thermal Performance of the Exterior Envelopes of Buildings V. Clearwater Beach, FL: 1992. *Lawrence Berkeley Laboratory Report 32782.*

Bliss, R. W. "Atmospheric Radiation Near the Surface of the Ground." *Solar Energy 5* (3): 103, 1961.

Brambley, M., and S. Penner. "Fenestration Devices for Energy Conservation I: Energy Savings During the Cooling Season." *Energy* (February 1979).

Brandle, K., and R. Boehm. "Air-Flow Windows: Performance and Applications." In the proceedings of Exterior Envelopes of Buildings Conference II: ASHRAE, 1982.

Burkhardt, W. C. "Solar Optical Properties of Gray and Brown Solar Control Series Transparent Acrylic Sheet." *ASHRAE Transactions 81* (1), 1975: 384–97.

———. "Acrylic Plastic Glazing: Properties, Characteristics and Engineering Data." *ASHRAE Transactions 82* (1), 1976: 683.

Byars, N., and D. Arasteh. "Design Options for Low-Conductivity Window Frames." *Solar Energy Materials and Solar Cells 25*, 1992. Elsevier Science Publishers B.V. and *Lawrence Berkeley Laboratory Report 30498.*

Canadian Standards Association. *Windows.* Publication CAN/CSA-A440, 1990.

CANMET. *Long Term Performance of Operating Windows Subjected to Motion Cycling.* Ottawa, Ontario: Author, M91-7/235-1993E.

Carpenter, S., and A. Elmahdy. "Thermal Performance of Complex Fenestration Systems." *ASHRAE Transactions 100* (2), 1994.

Carpenter, S. and J. Hogan. "Recommended U-factors for Swinging, Overhead and Revolving Doors." *ASHRAE Transactions*, 1996.

Carpenter, S., and A. McGowan. "Frame and Spacer Effects on Window U-Value." *ASHRAE Transactions 95* (1), 1989.

———. "Effect of Framing Systems on the Thermal Performance of Windows." *ASHRAE Transactions 99* (1), 1993.

Collins, R., and S. Robinson. *Evacuated Glazing*. Sydney, Australia: University of Sydney Press, 1996.

Crooks, B., J. Larsen, R. Sullivan, D. Arasteh, and S. Selkowitz. "NFRC Efforts to Develop a Residential Fenestration Annual Energy Rating Methodology." In the proceedings of Window Innovations Conference. Toronto, Ontario: 1995. *Lawrence Berkeley Laboratory Report 36896.*

Curcija, D., and W. P. Goss. "Two-Dimensional Finite Element Model of Heat Transfer in Complete Fenestration Systems." *ASHRAE Transactions 100* (2), 1994.

———. "Three-Dimensional Finite Element Model of Heat Transfer in Complete Fenestration Systems." In the proceedings of Window Innovations Conference. Toronto, Ontario: 1995a.

———. "New Correlations for Convective Heat Transfer Coefficient on Indoor Fenestration Surfaces: Compilation of More Recent Work." In the proceedings of Thermal Performance of the Exterior Envelopes of Buildings VI. Clearwater Beach, Florida: 1995b.

Curcija, D., W. P. Goss, J. P. Power, and Y. Zhao. *Variable-h' Model For Improved Prediction of Surface Temperatures in Fenestration Systems*. Amherst, MA: University of Massachusetts, 1996.

de Abreu, P., R. A. Fraser, H. F. Sullivan, and J. L. Wright. "A Study of Insulated Glazing Unit Surface Temperature Profiles Using Two-Dimensional Computer Simulation." *ASHRAE Transactions 102* (2), 1996.

Duffie, J. A., and W. A. Beckman. *Solar Engineering of Thermal Processes*. New York: John Wiley, 1980.

Elmahdy, A. H. "A Universal Approach to Laboratory Assessment of the Condensation Potential of Windows." Paper presented at the 16th Annual Conference of the Solar Energy Society of Canada. Ottawa, Ontario: 1990.

Elmahdy, A. H., "Air Leakage Characteristics of Windows Subjected to Simultaneous Temperature and Pressure Differentials." In the proceedings of the Windows Innovations Conference. Toronto, Ontario: CANMET, 1995.

Elmahdy, A. H., and S. A. Yusuf. "Determination of Argon Concentration and Assessment of the Durability of High Performance Insulating Glass Units Filled with Argon Gas." *ASHRAE Transactions*, 1995.

ElSherbiny, S. M. "Heat Transfer by Natural Convection Across Vertical and Inclined Air Layers." *Journal of Heat Transfer 104*, 1982: 96–102.

Enermodal Engineering Ltd. "The Effect of Frame Design on Window Heat Loss: Phase 1." Ottawa, Ontario: 1987.

Eto, J., D. Arasteh, and S. Selkowitz. "Transforming the Market for Residential Windows: Design Considerations for DOE's Efficient Window Collaborative." Proceedings of the ACEEE 1996 Summer Study on Energy Efficiency in Buildings: Profiting from Energy Efficiency, Pacific Grove, CA: August 1996. *Lawrence Berkeley Laboratory Report 42254.*

Ewing, W. B. and J. I. Yellott. "Energy Conservation through the Use of Exterior Shading of Fenestration. *ASHRAE Transactions 82* (1), 1976: 703–33.

Finlayson E., D. Arasteh, C. Huizenga, D. Curcija, M. Beall, and R. Mitchell. "THERM 2.0: Program Description." *Lawrence Berkeley Laboratory Report 37371 Rev.*

Finlayson, E. U., D. Arasteh, C. Huizenga, M. Rubin, and M. Reilly. "Window 4.0: Documentation of Calculation Procedures." Berkeley, CA: Lawrence Berkeley Laboratory, 1993. *Lawrence Berkeley Laboratory Report 33943.*

Frost K., D. Arasteh, and J. Eto. Savings from Energy Efficient Windows: Current and Future Savings from New Fenestration Technologies in the Residential Market. Berkeley, CA: Lawrence Berkeley Laboratory, 1993. *Lawrence Berkeley Laboratory Report 33956.*

Frost K., J. Eto, D. Arasteh, and M. Yazdanian. "The National Energy Requirements of Residential Windows in the U.S.: Today and Tomorrow." ACEEE 1996 Summer Study on Energy Efficiency in Buildings: Profiting from Energy Efficiency, Pacific Grove, CA: August 1996. *Lawrence Berkeley Laboratory Report 39692.*

Galanis, N. and R. Chatiguy. "A Critical Review of the ASHRAE Solar Radiation Model." *ASHRAE Transactions 92* (1), 1986.

Gates, D. M. "Spectral Distribution of Solar Radiation at the Earth's Surface." *Science 151* (2), 1966: 3710.

Griffith, B., and D. Arasteh. "Buildings Research Using Infrared Imaging Radiometers with Laboratory Thermal Chambers." Proceedings of the SPIE, Vol. 3700, April 6–8, 1999. *Lawrence Berkeley Laboratory Report 42682.*

Griffith, B., F. Beck, D. Arasteh, and D. Turler. "Issues Associated with the Use of Infrared Thermography for Experimental Testing of Insulated Systems." In the proceedings of Thermal Performance of the Exterior Envelopes of Buildings VI. Clearwater Beach, FL: December 1995. *Lawrence Berkeley Laboratory Report 36734.*

Griffith, B., D. Curcija, D. Turler, and D. Arasteh. "Improving Computer Simulations of Heat Transfer for Projecting Fenestration Products: Using Radiation View-Factor Models." *ASHRAE Transactions 104* (1), 1998. *Lawrence Berkeley Laboratory Report 40706.*

Griffith, B., D. Turler, and D. Arasteh. "Surface Temperature of Insulated Glazing Units: Infrared Thermography Laboratory Measurements." *ASHRAE Transactions 102* (2), 1996.

Gueymard, C. A. "Development and Performance Assessment of a Clear Sky Spectral Radiation Model." In the proceedings of the 22nd Annual Solar Conference. Washington, DC: American Solar Energy Society, 1993.

———. "An Anisotropic Solar Irradiance Model for Tilted Surfaces and Its Comparison with Selected Engineering Algorithms." *Solar Energy 38*, 1987: 367–86.

———. "A Simple Model of the Atmospheric Radiative Transfer of Sunshine: Algorithms and Performance Assessment." Cape Canaveral, FL: Florida Solar Energy Center, 1995. *Florida Solar Energy Center Report FSEC-PF-270-95.*

Harrison, S., and S. van Wonderen. "A Test Method for the Determination of Window Solar Heat Gain Coefficient." *ASHRAE Transactions 100* (1), 1994.

Hartman, J., M. Rubin, and D. Arasteh. "Thermal and Solar-Optical Properties of Silica Aerogel for Use in Insulated Windows." Paper presented at the 12th Annual Passive Solar Conference. Portland, OR: July 1987. *Lawrence Berkeley Laboratory Report 23386.*

Hickey, J. R. "Observations of the Solar Constant and Its Variations: Emphasis on Nimbus 7 Results." Paper presented at the Symposium on the Solar Constant and the Special Distribution of Solar Irradiance. Hamburg, Germany: IAMAP 1981.

Hogan, J. F. "A summary of tested glazing U-values and the case for an industry wide testing program." *ASHRAE Transactions 94* (2), 1988.

Huang, Y.J., R. Mitchell, D. Arasteh and S. Selkowitz. "Residential Fenestration Performance Analysis Using RESFEN 3.1." In the proceedings of the Thermal VII: Thermal Performance of the Exterior Envelopes of Buildings, Clearwater, FL, December 7–11, 1998. *Lawrence Berkeley Laboratory Report 42871.*

Huizenga, C., D. Arasteh, E. Finlayson, R. Mitchell, B. Griffith, and D. Curcija. "Teaching Students About Two-Dimensional Heat Transfer Effects in Buildings, Building Components, Equipment, and Appliances Using THERM 2.0." *ASHRAE Transactions 105* (1), 1999a. *Lawrence Berkeley Laboratory Report 42102.*

———. "THERM 2.0: A Building Component Model For Steady-State Two-Dimensional Heat Transfer." Building Simulation September 1999b. IBSPA. *Lawrence Berkeley Laboratory Report 43991.*

Illuminating Engineering Society of North America. *Recommended Practice of Daylighting.* New York: Author, 1979.

Johnson, B. *Heat Transfer through Windows.* Stockholm, Sweden: Swedish Council for Building Research, 1985.

Keyes, M. W. "Analysis and Rating of Drapery Materials Used for Indoor Shading." *ASHRAE Transactions 73* (1), 1967.

Klems, J. H. "Methods of Estimating Air Infiltration through Windows." *Energy and Buildings 5*, 1983: 243–252. *Lawrence Berkeley Laboratory Report 12891.*

———. "Method of Measuring Nighttime U-Values Using the Mobile Window Thermal Test (MoWiTT) Facility." *ASHRAE Transactions 98* (2), 1992. *Lawrence Berkeley Laboratory Report 30032.*

———. "A New Method for Predicting the Solar Heat Gain of Complex Fenestration Systems: I. Overview and Derivation of the Matrix Layer Calculation." *ASHRAE Transactions 100* (1), 1994a: 1065–1072.

———. "A New Method for Predicting the Solar Heat Gain of Complex Fenestration Systems: II. Detailed Description of the Matrix Layer Calculation." *ASHRAE Transactions 100* (1), 1994b: 1073–1086.

———. "Greenhouse Window U-Factors Under Field Conditions." *ASHRAE Transactions 104*, 1998. *Lawrence Berkeley Laboratory Report 40448.*

Klems, J. H., and H. Keller. "Thermal Performance Measurements of Sealed Insulating Glass Units with Low-E Coatings Using the MoWitt Field Test Facility." Paper presented at the ASHRAE Winter Meeting, Symposium on Fenestration Performance. New York: January 1987. *Lawrence Berkeley Laboratory Report 21583.*

Klems, J. H., and G. O. Kelley. "Calorimetric Measurements of Inward-Flowing Fraction for Complex Glazing and Shading Systems." *ASHRAE Transactions*, 1995.

Klems, J. H., and J. L. Warner. "Measurement of Bidirectional Optical Properties of Complex Shading Devices." *ASHRAE Transactions 101* (1), 1995: 791–801.

———. "Solar Heat Gain Coefficient of Complex Fenestrations with a Venetian Blind for Differing Slat Tilt Angles." *ASHRAE Transactions 103* (1), 1997. *Lawrence Berkeley Laboratory Report 39248.*

Klems, J. H., J. Warner and G. Kelley. "A comparison between calculated and measured SHGC for complex glazing systems." *ASHRAE Transactions 102* (1), 1996. *Lawrence Berkeley Laboratory Report 37037.*

Klems, J. H., M. Yazdanian, and G. Kelley. "Measured Performance of Selective Glazings." In the proceedings of Thermal Performance of the Exterior Envelopes of Buildings VI. Clearwater Beach, FL: 1995. *Lawrence Berkeley Laboratory Report 37747.*

Krochmann, J. "Zur frage der beleuchtung von museen." *Lichttechnik* (I)2 (1978a): 66–70.

———. *Lichttechnik* (II)3 (1978b): 275–288.

Lampert, C. "Chromogenic Switchable Glazing: Towards the Development of the Smart Window." In the proceedings of Window Innovations Conference. Toronto, Canada: CANMET, 1995. *Lawrence Berkeley Laboratory Report 37766.*

Lee E., L. Beltran, and S. Selkowitz. "Demonstration of a Light-Redirecting Skylight System at the Palm Springs Chamber of Commerce." ACEEE 1996 Summer Study on Energy Efficiency in Buildings: "Profiting from Energy Efficiency," August 2–31, 1996. Asilomar, Pacific Grove, CA. *Lawrence Berkeley Laboratory Report 38131.*

Lee, E., D. Hopkins, M. Rubin, D. Arasteh, and S. Selkowitz. "Spectrally Selective Glazings for Residential Retrofits in Cooling-Dominated Climates." *ASHRAE Transactions 100* (1), 1994. *Lawrence Berkeley Laboratory Report 34455.*

Lyons, P., D. Arasteh, and C. Huizenga. "Window Performance for Human Comfort." *ASHRAE*, February 2000. *Lawrence Berkeley Laboratory Report 44032.*

Mathis, R. C., and R. Garries. "Instant, Annual Life: A Discussion on the Current Practice and Evolution of Fenestration Energy Performance Rating." In the proceedings of Window Innovations Conference. Toronto, Canada: CANMET, 1995.

McCluney, R. "Determining Solar Radiant Heat Gain of Fenestration Systems." *Passive Solar Journal 4* (4), 1987: 439–87.

———. "The Death of the Shading Coefficient?" *ASHRAE Journal*, March 1991: 36–45.

———. "Sensitivity of Optical Properties and Solar Gain of Spectrally Selective Glazing Systems to Changes in Solar Spectrum" In the proceedings of the 22nd Annual Solar Conference. Washington, DC: American Solar Energy Society, 1993.

———. "Angle of Incidence and Diffuse Radiation Influences on Glazing System Solar Gain," In the proceedings of the Annual Solar Conference. San Jose, CA: American Solar Energy Society, 1994.

———. "Sensitivity of Fenestration Solar Gain to Source Spectrum and Angle of Incidence." *ASHRAE Transactions 102*, June 1996.

McCluney, R., and L. Mills. "Effect of Interior Shade on Window Solar Gain." *ASHRAE Transactions 99* (2), 1993.

Moore, G. L., and C. W. Pennington. "Measurement and Application of Solar Properties of Drapery Shading Materials." *ASHRAE Transactions 73* (1), 1967.

Ozisik, N., and L. F. Schutrum. "Solar Heat Gain Factors for Windows with Drapes." *ASHRAE Transactions*, 1960.

Papamichael, K. "New Tools for the Analysis and Design of Building Envelopes." In the proceedings of Thermal Performance of the Exterior Envelopes of Buildings VI. Clearwater Beach, FL: 1995. *Lawrence Berkeley Laboratory Report 36281.*

Parmelee, G. V., and R. G. Huebscher. "Forced Convection Heat Transfer from Flat Surfaces." *ASHRAE Transactions*, 1947: 245–84.

Parmelee, G. V., and W. W. Aubele. "Radiant Energy Emission of Atmosphere and Ground." *ASHRAE Transactions*, 1952.

Patenaude, A. "Air Infiltration Rate of Windows Under Temperature and Pressure Differentials." In the proceedings of Window Innovation Conference. Toronto, Ontario: CANMET, 1995.

Pennington, C. W. "How Louvered Sun Screens Cut Cooling, Heating Loads." *Heating, Piping, and Air Conditioning*, December 1968.

———. "Experimental Analysis of Solar Heat Gain through Insulating Glass with Indoor Shading." *ASHRAE Journal 2*, 1964.

Pennington, C. W., and G. L. Moore. "Measurement and Application of Solar Properties of Drapery Shading Materials." *ASHRAE Transactions 73* (1), 1967.

Pennington, C. W., C. Morrison, and R. Pena. "Effect of Inner Surface Air Velocity and Temperatures Upon Heat Loss and Gain through Insulating Glass." *ASHRAE Transactions 79* (2), 1973.

Perez, R. "An Anisotropic Hourly Diffuse Radiation Model for Sloping Surfaces—Description, Performance Validation, and Site Dependency Evaluation." *Solar Energy 36*, 1986: 481–98.

Reilly, M. S. "Spacer Effects on Edge-of-Glass and Frame Heat Transfer." *ASHRAE Transactions*, 1994.

Reilly, M. S., D. Arasteh, and S. Selkowitz. "Thermal and Optical Analysis of Switchable Window Glazings." *Solar Energy Materials 22*, 1991. Elsevier Science Publishers B.V. *Lawrence Berkeley Laboratory Report 29629.*

Reilly S., F. Winkelmann, D. Arasteh, and W. Carroll. "Modeling Windows in DOE-2.1E." Thermal Performance of the Exterior Envelopes of Buildings V Conference Proceedings, December 7–10, 1992. Clearwater Beach, Florida. *Lawrence Berkeley Laboratory Report 33192.*

Rubin, M. "Solar Optical Properties of Windows." *International Journal of Energy Research 6*, 1982: 123–133. *Lawrence Berkeley Laboratory Report 12246.*

———. "Optical Properties of Soda Lime Silica Glasses." *Solar Energy Materials 12*, 1985.

Rudoy, W., and F. Duran. "Effect of Building Envelope Parameters on Annual Heating/Cooling Load." *ASHRAE Journal 7*, 1975.

Selkowitz, S. "Thermal Performance of Insulating Window Systems." *ASHRAE Transactions 85* (2), 1981. *Lawrence Berkeley Laboratory Report 08835.*

———. "Influence of Windows on Building Energy Use." Paper presented at the Windows in Building Design and Maintenance. Gothenburg, Sweden: June 1984.

———. "High-Performance Glazing Systems: Architectural Opportunities for the 21st Century." Presented at the Glass Processing Days (GPD). Tampere, Finland: June 1999. *Lawrence Berkeley Laboratory Report 42724.*

Simko T., R. Collins, F. Beck, and D. Arasteh. "Edge Conduction in Vacuum Glazing. Thermal Performance of the Exterior Envelopes of Buildings." VI Conference Proceedings, December 4–8, 1995. Clearwater Beach, Florida. *Lawrence Berkeley Laboratory Report 36958.*

Smith, W. A., and C. W. Pennington. "Shading Coefficients for Glass Block Panels." *ASHRAE Journal 5*, December 1964.

Sodergren, D., and T. Bostrom. "Ventilating with the Exhaust Air Window." *ASHRAE Journal 13* (4), 1971.

Sterling, E. M., A., Arundel, and T. D. Sterling. "Criteria for Human Exposure in Occupied Buildings." *ASHRAE Transactions 91* (1), 1985.

"Study of the U.S. Market for Windows, Doors and Skylights." A Ducker Research Company, Inc. executive report prepared for the American Architectural Manufacturers Association (AAMA) and the Window and Door Manufacturers Association (WDMA), 2006.

Sullivan, H. F., J. L. Wright, and R. A. Fraser. "Overview of a Project to Determine the Surface Temperatures of Insulated Glazing Units: Thermographic Measurement and 2-D Simulation." *ASHRAE Transactions 102* (2), 1996.

Sullivan, R., F. Beck, D. Arasteh, and S. Selkowitz. "Energy Performance of Evacuated Glazings in Residential Buildings." Paper presented at ASHRAE Conference. San Antonio, TX: June 1996. *Lawrence Berkeley Laboratory Report 37130.*

Sullivan, R., L. Beltran, M. Rubin, and S. Selkowitz. "Energy and Daylight Performance of Angular Selective Glazings." Proceedings of the ASHRAE/DOE/BTECC Conference, Thermal Performance of the Exterior Envelopes of Buildings VII, Clearwater Beach, Florida, December 7–11, 1998. *Lawrence Berkeley Laboratory Report 41694*.

Sullivan, R., K. Frost, D. Arasteh, and S. Selkowitz. "Window U-Value Effects on Residential Cooling Load." Berkeley, CA: Lawrence Berkeley National Laboratory, 1993. *Lawrence Berkeley Laboratory Report 34648*.

Sullivan, R., E. Lee, K. Papamichael, M. Rubin, and S. Selkowitz. "Effect of Switching Control Strategies on the Energy Performance of Electrochromic Windows." In the proceedings of SPIE International Symposium on Optical Materials Technology for Energy Efficiency and Solar Energy Conversion XIII. Friedrichsbau, Freiburg, Germany: April 1994. *Lawrence Berkeley Laboratory Report 35453*.

Sullivan, R., M. Rubin, and S. Selkowitz. "Reducing Residential Cooling Requirements Through the Use of Electrochromic Windows." In the proceedings of Thermal Performance of the Exterior Envelopes of Buildings VI. Clearwater Beach, FL: December 1995. *Lawrence Berkeley Laboratory Report 37211*.

Sullivan, R and S. Selkowitz. "Energy Performance Analysis of Fenestration in a Single-Family Residence." *ASHRAE Transactions 91* (2), 1984. *Lawrence Berkeley Laboratory Report 18561*.

———. "Residential Window Performance Analysis Using Regression Procedures." In the proceedings of CLIMA 2000 World Conference on Heating, Ventilation, and Air-Conditioning. Copenhagen, Denmark: August 1985. *Lawrence Berkeley Laboratory Report 19245*.

———. "Window Performance Analysis in a Single-Family Residence." In the proceedings of the BTECC Conference. Clearwater Beach, FL: 1985. *Lawrence Berkeley Laboratory Report 20079*.

———. "Residential Heating and Cooling Energy Cost Implications Associated with Window Types." *ASHRAE Transactions 93* (1), 1986: 1525–1539. *Lawrence Berkeley Laboratory Report 21578*.

———. "Fenestration Performance Analysis Using an Interactive Graphics-Based Methodology on a Microcomputer." *ASHRAE Transactions 95* (1), 1989. *Lawrence Berkeley Laboratory Report 26070*.

Sullivan, R., and F. Winklemann. "Validation Studies of the DOE-2 Building Energy Simulation Program." August 1998. *Lawrence Berkeley Laboratory Report 42241*.

Sweitzer, G., D. Arasteh, and S. Selkowitz. "Effects of Low-E Glazing on Energy Use Patterns in Nonresidential Daylighting Buildings." *ASHRAE Transactions 93* (1), 1986: 1553–1566. *Lawrence Berkeley Laboratory Report 21577*.

Tait Solar Company. "WinSARC: Solar Angles and Radiation Calculation for MS Windows." *User's Manual*. Tempe, AZ: Author, 1996.

Terman, M., S. Fairhurst, B. Perlman, J. Levitt, and R. McCluney. "Daylight Deprivation and Replenishment: A Psychobiological Problem with a Naturalistic Solution." In the proceedings of International Daylighting Conference. Long Beach, CA: 1986.

Turler D., B. Griffith, and D. Arasteh. "Laboratory Procedures for Using Infrared Thermography to Validate Heat Transfer Models." ASTM Third Symposium on "Insulation Materials: Testing and Applications: Third Volume," *ASTM STP 1320*, R.S. Graves and R.R. Zarr, Eds., American Society for Testing and Materials, Quebec City, Quebec: 1997. *Lawrence Berkeley Laboratory Report 38925*.

Van Dyke, R. L., and T. P. Konen. "Energy Conservation through Interior Shading of Windows: An Analysis, Test and Evaluation of Reflective Venetian Blinds." Lawrence Berkeley Laboratory, March 1982. *Lawrence Berkeley Laboratory Report 14369*.

Vild, D. J. "Solar Heat Gain Factors and Shading Coefficients." *ASHRAE Journal 10*, 1964: 47.

Warner, J., S. Reilly, S. Selkowitz, and D. Arasteh. "Utility and Economic Benefits of Electrochromic Smart Windows." In the proceedings of the ACEEE 1992 Summer Study on Energy Efficiency. Pacific Grove, CA: ACEEE, June 1992. *Lawrence Berkeley Laboratory Report 32638*.

Weidt, J., and S. Selkowitz. "Field Air Leakage of Newly Installed Residential Windows." *ASHRAE Transactions 85* (1), 1981: 149–159. *Lawrence Berkeley Laboratory Report 09937*.

Wright, J. L. "Summary and Comparison of Methods to Calculate Solar Heat Gain." *ASHRAE Transactions 101* (1), 1995a.

———. "VISION4 Glazing System Thermal Analysis: User Manual." Advanced Glazing System Laboratory. University of Waterloo: 1995b.

———. "VISION4 Glazing System Thermal Analysis: Reference Manual." Advanced Glazing System Laboratory. University of Waterloo: 1995c.

———. "A Correlation to Quantify Convective Heat Transfer between Window Glazings." *ASHRAE Transactions*, 1996.

Wright, J. L., R. Fraser, P. de Abreu, and H. F. Sullivan. "Heat Transfer in Glazing System Edge-Seals: Calculations Regarding Various Design Options." *ASHRAE Transactions 100* (1), 1994.

Wright, J. L., and H. F. Sullivan. "A 2-D numerical model for glazing system thermal analysis." *ASHRAE Transactions 100* (1), 1995a.

———. "A 2-D numerical model for natural convection in a vertical, rectangular window cavity." *ASHRAE Transactions 100* (2), 1995b.

———. "A Simplified Method for the Numerical Condensation Resistance Analysis of Windows." In the proceedings of Window Innovations Conference. Toronto, Ontario: 1995c.

Yazdanian, M., and J. Klems. "Measurement of the Exterior Convective Film Coefficient for Windows in Low-Rise Buildings." *ASHRAE Transactions 100* (1), 1994. *Lawrence Berkeley Laboratory Report 34717.*

Yellott, J. I. "Selective Reflectance: A New Approach to Solar Heat Control." *ASHRAE Transactions 69*, 1963: 418.

———. "Drapery Fabrics and Their Effectiveness in Sun Control." *ASHRAE Transactions 71* (1), 1965: 260–72.

———. "Shading Coefficients and Sun-Control Capability of Single Glazing." *ASHRAE Transactions 72* (2), 1966: 72.

———. "Effect of Louvered Sun Screens upon Fenestration Heat Loss." *ASHRAE Transactions 78* (1), 1972: 199–204.

Zhao, Y., Curcija, D., and Goss, W.P. "Condensation resistance validation project." *ASHRAE Transactions 102* (Pt. 2), 1996.

Index

Due to an error, the index on pages 243–47 is incorrect. This error will be corrected in the next printing.

Index

13—16; impact of improving, 17—20; installation of, see window installation; location/placement of, 122, 123, 129; as net energy provider, 74; new technologies for, 7—8, 9, 11—13, 16—20, 81—88; orientation, 7, 121, 132, 141, 143—45; peak loads affected by type of, 188—190; rating system for, 23, 174, 199—200; replacement, 115—16, 191—92, 198; roof, 10, 27, 76, 92, 128, 131; sash, see separate entry; selection considerations, 21, 22—23, 172; shading to reduce summer heat gain, 135—39; sliding, 91, 95, 131, 168; solar heat gain in, see solar-heat-gain coefficient; storm, 57, 99; types of, 90—98, 133; U-factor effects and, see separate entry; views provided by, 121—23. See also glass; glazing

Window and Door Manufacturers Association (WDMA), 170

window installation: altitude affecting, 117—18, 125; guidelines for, 114; insulating around unit, 114; overview of, 110—11; of replacement windows and sashes, 115—16, 191—92; of skylights, 116—17; water-tight, 111—13

Windows and Glazing Research Program, 5

winds: minimizing winter effects, 142—43; structural resistance to, 170